T0247748

Common Sense Economics

Common Sense Economics

What Everyone Should Know
About Wealth and Prosperity

Fourth Edition

JAMES D. GWARTNEY
FLORIDA STATE UNIVERSITY

DWIGHT R. LEE
UNIVERSITY OF GEORGIA

TAWNI HUNT FERRARINI
LINDENWOOD UNIVERSITY

JOSEPH P. CALHOUN
FLORIDA STATE UNIVERSITY

JANE SHAW STROUP
JAMES G. MARTIN CENTER FOR ACADEMIC RENEWAL

ST. MARTIN'S PRESS
NEW YORK

First published in the United States by St. Martin's Press, an imprint of St. Martin's Publishing Group

COMMON SENSE ECONOMICS: FOURTH EDITION. Copyright © 2005, 2010, 2016, 2024 by James D. Gwartney, Dwight R. Lee, Tawni Hunt Ferrarini, Joseph P. Calhoun, and Jane Shaw Stroup. All rights reserved. Printed in the United States of America. For information, address St. Martin's Publishing Group, 120 Broadway, New York, NY 10271.

www.stmartins.com

Library of Congress Cataloging-in-Publication Data

Names: Gwartney, James D., author. | Lee, Dwight R., author. | Ferrarini, Tawni Hunt, author. | Calhoun, Joseph P., author. | Shaw, Jane S., 1944– author.
Title: Common sense economics : what everyone should know about wealth and prosperity / James D. Gwartney, Florida State University, Dwight R. Lee, University Of Georgia, Tawni Hunt Ferrarini, Lindenwood University, Joseph P. Calhoun, Florida State University, Jane Shaw Stroup, James G. Martin Center for Academic Renewal.
Description: Fourth edition. | New York: St. Martin's Press, 2024. | Includes bibliographical references and index.
Identifiers: LCCN 2024003513 | ISBN 9781250292629 (hardcover) | ISBN 9781250292612 (ebook)
Subjects: LCSH: Free enterprise. | Wealth. | Economics. | Finance, Personal. | Saving and investment.
Classification: LCC HB95 .G9 2024 | DDC 339.2—dc23/eng/20240323
LC record available at https://lccn.loc.gov/2024003513

Our books may be purchased in bulk for promotional, educational, or business use. Please contact your local bookseller or the Macmillan Corporate and Premium Sales Department at 1-800-221-7945, extension 5442, or by email at MacmillanSpecialMarkets@macmillan.com.

Fourth Edition: 2024

10 9 8 7 6 5 4 3 2 1

In 1993, James Gwartney and Richard Stroup wrote *What Everyone Should Know About Economics and Prosperity*. After thirty years of teaching college economics, their goals were simple: present the insights of economics that really matter and write in a manner that is concise and organized. This first edition laid the foundation for those that followed.

Dwight Lee joined the authoring team in 2005. The title was changed to *Common Sense Economics: What Everyone Should Know About Wealth and Prosperity*, and the book was expanded to include "Part 4: Twelve Key Elements of Practical Personal Finance." Later editions added coauthors Tawni Hunt Ferrarini, Joseph Calhoun, and Jane Shaw Stroup.

We lost Rick in November 2021 and Jim in January 2024. These two esteemed individuals left an indelible mark through their contributions. They taught thousands of undergraduates and impacted hundreds of thousands more through their textbooks. Their other scholarly works and op-eds have influenced countless individuals. They provided invaluable guidance to graduate students, their colleagues, and policymakers.

The remaining coauthors are forever grateful for the impact Rick and Jim had on our lives. They were faithful husbands, cherished friends, and beloved colleagues. Though they may not be here with us physically, this edition of *Common Sense Economics* will keep their spirit and memory alive.

Thank you, Rick and Jim. You made our lives and the world better. This book is dedicated to you and your legacies.

Contents

Preface

The authors of this book want you to live a successful and fulfilling life. We also want to enhance your understanding of our fast-changing world. Because your time is valuable, we have crafted this publication in a way that minimizes the time spent learning new terms, memorizing formulas, or mastering intricate details important only to professional economists. Rather, we focus on the general insights of economics that really matter—those that will help you make better choices, improve your understanding of our increasingly complex world, and live a more satisfying life.

Regardless of your current knowledge of economics, this book will provide you with important insights. It is concise, thoughtfully organized, and reader-friendly. Part 1 introduces the basic principles of economics, which primarily reflect common sense. Parts 2, 3, and 4 then put the principles to work, demonstrating their power to explain real-world events and improve our personal decision-making. A glossary of key terms is included, and these terms are highlighted in bold in the text.

Even advanced students of economics and business will find this book valuable because it pulls together the "big picture." The book explains why some nations prosper and others do not. It sheds light on the remarkable economic progress of the Industrial Revolution around 1800 and the equally remarkable progress of the half century following 1970. The political process is examined, and differences between government and market allocation are investigated. The source of the bias of even democratic political decision-making toward both special-interest spending and debt financing is explained, the implications examined, and the potential structural changes to minimize the adverse consequences are considered.

In recent years, many economies have been shaken by a worldwide pandemic, a huge increase in government spending, surging inflation, and unprecedented government mandates and regulations. Central planners from China to Russia to the World Economic Forum have sought to use these events to enhance their political power. How did the mandated shutdowns accompanying the COVID pandemic impact the economy? What caused the surge in inflation? How has the increased central planning of recent years influenced Western economies? The basic principles, analysis, and historical evidence of this book will enhance your understanding of these questions and related issues.

You will be introduced to a variety of easy-to-use online calculators, spreadsheets, and websites, which will help you take important steps toward financial security. (See the digital assets listed at the end of the book.) You will be challenged to think about your preferences, choices, and goals. You will also be provided with tools to improve the quality of your life and the value of the services you provide to others.

The authors—the *Common Sense Economics* (*CSE*) team—are all economics educators. If you are an economics instructor, we want to help you become a great teacher. To that end, we have developed a multimedia course package to accompany the book. The package takes into account the revealed learning preferences of today's "multimedia" students. It includes short video clips, classic readings, podcasts, innovative assignments, and interactive classroom activities. For details, visit CommonSenseEconomics.com.

The supplementary package accompanying the book is the result of a long-term collaboration with a team of master economics educators dedicated to compiling everything an instructor needs for an exciting introductory course. It incorporates the "read, watch, listen, and do" approach that will help you engage your students and get them excited about economics and personal finance. The book and package meet voluntary K–12 standards and benchmarks. The materials are designed to provide a strong foundation, especially for students who may not go on to take another economics course.

PART 1

Twelve Key Elements of Economics

TWELVE KEY ELEMENTS OF ECONOMICS

1. Incentives matter: Changes in benefits and costs will influence choices in predictable ways.

2. All choices involve costs.

3. Decisions are made at the margin.

4. Voluntary trade promotes economic progress.

5. Transaction costs are obstacles to trade.

6. Prices bring the choices of buyers and sellers into balance.

7. Profits direct businesses toward productive activities that increase the value of resources, while losses direct them away from wasteful activities.

8. The "invisible hand" of market prices guides buyers and sellers toward activities promoting the general welfare.

9. Mistakes and misconceptions in economic analysis often occur because of failure to consider long-term consequences and secondary effects.

10. People earn income by providing others with what they value.

11. Production of goods and services that people value, not just jobs, provides the source of high living standards.

12. Economic progress comes primarily through voluntary trade, investment, stable capital markets, better ways of doing things, and sound economic institutions.

Introduction

Life is about choices, and economics is about how incentives affect those choices and shape our lives. Choices about our education, how we spend and invest, what we do in the workplace, and many other personal decisions will influence our well-being and quality of life. Moreover, the choices we make as voters and citizens affect the laws or "rules of the game," and these rules exert an enormous impact on our freedom and prosperity. To choose intelligently, both for ourselves and for society, we must understand some basic principles about how people choose, what motivates their actions, and how their actions influence their personal welfare and that of others. Thus, economics is about human decision-making, the analysis of the forces underlying choice, and the implications for how societies work.

The economic way of thinking involves integrating key concepts into your thought processes. This section presents twelve concepts that are crucial for the understanding of economics and will help you understand why some countries grow and achieve high income levels while others stagnate and remain poor. You will learn such things as the true meaning of costs, why prices matter, how trade enhances prosperity, and why production of things people value underpins our standard of living. In the subsequent parts of the book, these concepts will be used to address other vitally important topics.

1. Incentives matter: Changes in benefits and costs will influence choices in predictable ways.

All of economics rests on one simple principle: Changes in **incentives** influence human behavior in predictable ways. Both monetary and nonmonetary factors influence incentives. If something becomes more costly, people will be less likely to choose it. Correspondingly, when the benefits of an option increase, people will be more likely to choose it. This simple idea, sometimes called the basic postulate of economics, is a powerful tool because it applies to almost everything we do.

People will be less likely to choose an option as it becomes more costly. Think about the implications of this proposition. When late for an appointment, a person will be less likely to take time to stop and visit with a friend. Fewer people will go picnicking on a cold and rainy day. Higher gas prices will reduce the number of gallons sold. Attendance in college classes will be below normal the day before spring break. In each case, the explanation is the same: As the option becomes more costly, less is chosen.

Similarly, when the payoff derived from a choice increases, people will be more likely to choose it. A person will be more likely to bend over and pick up a quarter than a penny. Students will attend and pay more attention in class when they know the material will be on the exam. Customers will buy more from stores that offer low prices, high-quality service, and a convenient location. Employees will work harder and more efficiently when they are rewarded for doing so. All of these outcomes are highly predictable, and they merely reflect the "incentives matter" postulate of economics.

This basic postulate explains how changes in **market** prices change incentives in ways that work to coordinate the actions of buyers and sellers. If buyers want to purchase more of an item than producers are willing (or able) to sell, its price will soon rise. As the price increases, sellers will be more willing to provide the item, while buyers will want to purchase less, until the higher price brings the amount demanded and the amount supplied into balance. At that point the price stabilizes.

What happens if it starts out the other way: if sellers want to supply more than buyers are willing to purchase? If sellers cannot sell all of a good at the current price, they will cut the price. In turn, the lower price will encourage people to buy more—but it will also discourage producers from producing as much, since it is less attractive to them to supply the product at the new, lower price. Again, the price change works to bring the amount demanded by consumers into balance with the amount produced by suppliers.

Consider what happens when strong demand pushes a price up. Take gasoline, for example. The higher price will make it more costly to purchase gasoline. Consumers will respond by driving less, combining trips, and carpooling more often. In time, consumers will also shift to electric-powered and smaller, more fuel-efficient vehicles to reduce expenditures on gasoline. At the same time, the higher price will entice sellers to produce more. If not restricted, producers of gasoline will increase their drilling, develop new techniques such as fracking to recover more oil from existing wells, and intensify their search for new oil fields. This combination of forces will bring the amount demanded by consumers into balance with the amount supplied by producers. Over time, the larger supply will reverse the price increases. Price signals provide both buyers and sellers with incentives to make adjustments and bring their choices into harmony.

Just as incentives influence choices in the marketplace, they also influence political choices. Voters will be more likely to support those candidates and policies they think will provide them with the most personal benefits, net of their costs. Voters will tend to oppose policies when the personal costs are high relative to the expected benefits. For example, senior citizens consistently vote against candidates and proposals that would reduce their Social Security or Medicare benefits. Similarly, polls indicate that students disproportionally support candidates promising loan forgiveness and "free" education. Producers in businesses ranging from sugarcane and beet farming to steel and lumber tend to support candidates that favor trade restrictions, pushing up the prices of the goods they sell and reducing foreign **competition**. As discussed later, social programs and trade policies can often be counterproductive once costs are compared to the benefits.

There's no way to get around the importance of incentives. They are a part of human nature. Incentives matter just as much under **socialism** as under capitalism. In the former Soviet Union, managers and employees of glass plants were at one time paid according to the tons of sheet glass produced. Because their revenues depended on the weight of the glass, sheet glass at some factories was so thick that you could hardly see through it. In response, the rules were changed so that compensation was based on the number of square meters of glass produced. Under these new rules, Soviet firms made glass so thin that it broke easily.[1]

Some people think that incentives matter only when people are greedy and selfish. This is untrue. People act for a variety of reasons, some selfish and some charitable. But the choices of both the self-centered and the altruistic will be influenced by changes in personal costs and benefits. For example, both the selfish and the altruistic person will be more likely to attempt to rescue a child in a shallow swimming pool than in the rapid currents approaching Niagara Falls. And

1. P. C. Roberts and K. L. Follette, *Meltdown: Inside the Soviet Economy* (Washington, DC: Cato Institute, 1990).

both are more likely to give a needy person their gently used clothes rather than their best ones.

Even though no one would have accused the late Mother Teresa of greediness, her self-interest caused her to respond to incentives, too. Consider Mother Teresa's organization, the Missionaries of Charity. It attempted to open a shelter for the homeless in New York City, but the city government required expensive (and, in Mother Teresa's view, unneeded) alterations to its building. The organization abandoned the project. This decision did not reflect any change in Mother Teresa's commitment to the poor. Instead, it reflected a change in incentives. When the cost of helping the poor in New York increased, Mother Teresa searched for alternative locations where her **resources** could do more good compared to costs.[2] Changes in incentives influence everyone's choices and drive decisions, regardless of the mix of greedy, materialistic goals on the one hand and compassionate, altruistic goals on the other.

2. All choices involve costs.

The reality of life on our planet is that **productive resources** are limited, while the human desire for goods and services is virtually unlimited. Would you like to have some new clothes, a luxury boat, or a new smartphone? How about more time for leisure, recreation, and travel? Do you dream of driving your brand-new electric sports car into the driveway of your home? Most of us would like to have all of these things and many others! However, we are constrained by the **scarcity** of resources, including a limited availability of time.

In the late nineteenth century, many taverns offered a "free lunch"

2. Philip K. Howard, *The Death of Common Sense* (New York: Random House, 1994), 3–5.

to anyone who bought a drink. Of course, since you had to buy a drink, the lunch wasn't actually free—in addition (the story goes), the lunch had salty foods like ham, cheese, and peanuts, causing customers to buy more drinks. Thus, they paid in full for their "free lunches."

This led to a phrase popular among economists: "There is no such thing as a free lunch." We cannot have as much of everything as we would like. So we choose among alternatives. The choice to do one thing requires sacrificing the opportunity to do something else. This is why all costs are **opportunity costs**, and all choices involve forgoing other opportunities.

Many costs are measured in terms of money, but these, too, are opportunity costs. The money you spend one way is not available to spend in other ways or for savings. The opportunity cost of your purchase reflects the value you place on the options you have given up because of your initial purchase. Even when you don't have to spend money to do something, the action is not costless. You don't spend money to take a walk and enjoy a beautiful sunset, but there is an opportunity cost to taking the walk. The time you spend walking could be used to do something else you value, like visiting a friend, working out, or reading.

Everyone has heard people claim that some things are so important that costs do not matter. Making such a statement may sound reasonable at first and may be an effective way to encourage people to spend more money on things that we value (and for which we would like others to help pay). But the unreasonableness of ignoring cost becomes obvious once the costs of the forgone alternatives are considered. Saying that something should be done without considering the costs is really saying that we should do it without considering the value of the alternatives. When we choose between mutually exclusive alternatives, the least-cost alternative is the most valuable one.

The choices of both consumers and producers involve costs. As consumers, the cost of a good, as reflected in its price, helps us compare our desire for a product against our desire for alternative products. If we do not consider the costs, we will probably end up using our income to purchase the "wrong" things. You know—buyer's remorse. You bought something without seriously considering the more valuable alternatives.

Producers face costs, too—the costs of the resources used to make a product or to provide a service. For example, using resources such as labor, lumber, steel, and Sheetrock to build new houses takes resources away from the production of other goods, such as hospitals and schools. High costs signal that the resources have other highly valued uses, as judged by buyers and sellers in other markets. Profit-seeking firms will heed those signals and act accordingly, such as seeking out less costly substitutes.

Government policies can distort and override these signals; they can introduce taxes or subsidies that help those interest groups inconvenienced by the competitive prices that emerge in free and **open markets**. But such policies reduce the ability of market incentives to guide resources to where consumers ultimately, on balance, value them most highly.

Politicians, government officials, and lobbyists often speak of "free education," "free medical care," or "free housing." This terminology is deceptive. These things are not free. Production of each requires the use of scarce resources that could have been used to produce other things. For example, the buildings, labor, and other resources used to produce schooling could have been used to produce more food or recreation, protect the environment, or provide health care. The cost of the schooling is the value of those goods that must be sacrificed. Governments may be able to shift costs, but they cannot eliminate them.

Opportunity cost is an important concept. Everything in life is about opportunity cost. Everyone lives in a world of scarcity and, therefore, must make choices. By looking at opportunity costs, we can better understand the world in which we live. Let us consider the impact of opportunity cost on workforce participation, the birth rate, and population growth, topics many would consider outside the realm of opportunity-cost application.

Have you ever thought about why women with more education are more likely to work outside the home than their less-educated counterparts? Opportunity cost provides the answer. The more highly educated women will have better earning opportunities in the workforce, and therefore it will be more costly for them to stay at home. The data are consistent with this view. In 2019, 81 percent of women aged twenty-five to sixty-four with a college education (or more) were in the labor force, compared to only 64 percent of their counterparts with only a high school education and 47 percent of the women with less than twelve years of schooling.[3] Just as economic theory predicts, when being out of the labor force is more costly, fewer women (and men) will choose this option.

What do you think happens to the birth rate as an economy grows and earnings rise? Time spent on household responsibilities reduces the time available for market work. As earnings rise, the opportunity cost of having children and raising a large family increases. Therefore, the predicted result is a reduction in the birth rate and slower population growth. During the past two centuries, as the per capita income of a country increased, a reduction in the birth rate and a slowdown in population growth soon followed. Moreover, this pattern has occurred in every country. Even though there are widespread cultural, religious, ethnic, and political differences among countries, nonetheless the higher opportunity cost of having children exerted the same impact on the birth rate in all cases.

3. "Women in the Labor Force: A Databook," *BLS Reports,* Report 1092, Table 8, U.S. Bureau of Labor Statistics (April 2021), https://www.bls.gov/opub/reports/womens-databook/2020/home.htm.

Opportunity cost is a powerful tool. It will be applied again and again throughout this book. If you integrate this tool into your thought process, it will greatly enhance your ability to understand the real-world behavior of consumers, producers, business owners, political figures, and other decision-makers. Even more important, the concept will also help you make better personal choices.

3. Decisions are made at the margin.

To get the most value from our scarce resources, economics provides a simple rule: Pursue those actions that generate more benefits than costs; avoid those actions that generate more costs than benefits. This principle of sound decision-making applies to individuals, businesses, government officials, and society as a whole.

Nearly all choices are made at the margin. That means that they almost always involve additions to (or subtractions from) current conditions, rather than "all-or-nothing" decisions. The word "additional" is a substitute for "**marginal**." We might ask, "What is the marginal cost of producing or consuming one more unit?" Marginal decisions may involve large or small changes. The "one more unit" could be a new shirt, a new house, a new factory, an additional investment, or even an expenditure of time, as in the case of a student choosing how to spend some more time among competing activities after pulling back from others. All these decisions are marginal because they involve consideration of additional costs and benefits.

People do not make "all-or-nothing" decisions, such as choosing between eating or wearing clothes. Instead they compare the marginal benefits (a little more food) with the marginal costs (a little less clothing or doing without as much of something else). In making decisions individuals don't compare the total value of food and the total value of clothing and choose one or the other. Rather, they compare their marginal values—a little more of one item and a little less of others. Incentives guide us to choose options only when their marginal benefits exceed the marginal costs.

Similarly, a business executive planning to build a new factory will consider whether the **marginal benefits** of the new factory (for example, additional sales revenues) are greater than the **marginal costs** (the expenses of constructing the new building and sacrifice of other things). If not, the executive and the company are better off without the new factory.

Effective political actions also require marginal decision-making. Consider the policy decision of how much effort and resources to put into cleaning up pollution. If asked how much pollution is acceptable, many people would respond "none." In other words, pollution levels need to move to zero. In the voting booth they might vote that way. But marginal thinking reveals that this would be extraordinarily wasteful.

When there is a lot of pollution—so much, say, that we are choking on the air we breathe—the marginal benefit of reducing pollution is quite likely to exceed the marginal cost of the reduction. But as the amount of pollution goes down, so does the marginal benefit—the value of the additional improvement in the air. There is still a benefit to an even cleaner atmosphere (for example, we would be able to see distant mountains), but this benefit is not nearly as valuable as protecting our lungs. Before the pollution disappears 100 percent, the additional benefit of pollution reduction approaches zero.

As the marginal benefit of reducing pollution by an additional unit goes down, the marginal cost rises. As more and more resources are diverted away from other viable uses, the cost of cleaner air becomes higher. The marginal cost is the value of things that are sacrificed to reduce pollution a little bit more. Spending in health care, education, improved infrastructure, and other expenditures are but a few examples. They must be considered when evaluating the wisdom of reducing pollution to still lower levels. Once the marginal cost of a cleaner atmosphere exceeds the marginal benefit, additional pollution reduction is wasteful and counterproductive. It would simply not be worth the cost.

To continue with the pollution example, consider the following hypothetical situation: Assume that pollution is doing $100 million worth of damage, and only $1 million is being spent to reduce pollution. Given this information, are we doing too little or too much to reduce pollution? Most people would say that we are spending too little. This may be correct, but we need more information before drawing a conclusion.

The $100 million in damage is total damage, and the $1 million in cost is the total cost of cleanup. To make an informed decision about next steps, we need to know the marginal benefit of cleanup and the marginal cost of doing so. If spending another $10 on pollution reduction would reduce damage by more than $10, then we should spend more. The marginal benefit exceeds the marginal cost. But if an additional $10 spent on antipollution efforts would reduce damages by only a dollar, additional spending would be unwise.

People commonly ignore the implications of marginalism in their comments and votes but seldom in their personal actions. Consider food versus recreation. When viewed as a whole, food is far more valuable than recreation because it allows people to survive. When people are poor and living in impoverished countries, they devote most of their income to securing an adequate diet. They devote little time, if any, to playing golf, waterskiing, or other recreational activities.

But as people become wealthier, the opportunity cost of acquiring food declines. Although food remains vital to life, continuing to spend most of their money on more food would be foolish. At higher levels of affluence, people find that at the margin—as they make decisions about how to spend each additional dollar—food is often worth less than recreation. So as Americans and others become wealthier, they spend a smaller portion of their income on food and a larger portion of their income on recreation.[4]

The concept of marginalism reveals that marginal costs and marginal benefits are relevant to sound decision-making. If we want to get the most value out of our resources, only actions for which the marginal benefits are greater than marginal costs must be undertaken. Both individuals and nations are more prosperous when personal and policy choices reflect the implications of marginalism.

4. Voluntary trade promotes economic progress.

The foundation of voluntary trade is mutual gain. People agree to an exchange because they expect it to improve their well-being. Voluntary trade is a win-win transaction. Both parties gain more than they give up; if they did not, they would not agree to the exchange. This positive-sum activity permits each of the trading partners to get more of what they value at a relatively low cost. There are three major sources of gains from trade.

First, trade moves goods from people who value them less to people who value them more. Thus, trade can increase the value of goods even when nothing new is produced. For example, when used goods are bought and sold, the exchanges do not increase the quantity of goods available (as new products do). But the trades do create value by moving products toward the buyers who value them more than the sellers. Both gain. Otherwise, the voluntary exchange would not occur.

People's preferences, knowledge, and goals vary widely. A product that is virtually worthless to one person may be a precious gem to another. A highly technical book on artificial intelligence may be worth

---

4. See the chapter "Time for Symphonies and Softball" in W. Michael Cox and Richard Alm, *Myths of Rich and Poor* (New York: Basic Books, 1999).

nothing to an art collector but valued at hundreds of dollars by an engineer. Similarly, a painting that an engineer cares little for may be cherished by an art collector. Voluntary exchange that moves the AI book to the engineer and the painting to the art collector will increase the net benefit derived from both goods. The trade will increase the wealth of both people and also of their nation. It is not just the amount of goods and services produced in a nation that determines the nation's wealth, but how those goods and services are allocated to create value.

Second, trade expands production and consumption possibilities. Trading partners will be able to produce a larger output when each specializes in production of items they can produce at a low opportunity cost and acquires everything else through trade. When people specialize, they can then sell these products to others. Revenues received can be used to purchase items that would be costly to produce themselves. This specialization and voluntary exchange makes it possible for people to produce larger quantities of goods and services than would be otherwise possible. Economists refer to this principle as the **law of comparative advantage**. This law applies to trade among individuals, businesses, regions, and nations.

The law of comparative advantage is just common sense. If someone can provide you with a product at a lower cost (remember, all costs are opportunity costs) than you can supply it yourself, voluntary trade makes sense. You can then use your time and resources to produce more of the things for which you are a low-cost provider. In other words, produce what you produce best, and trade for the rest. The result is that you and your trading partners will mutually gain from specialization and trade, leading to greater total production, higher incomes, and elevated standards of living. In contrast, trying to produce everything yourself and being self-sufficient requires using your time, talents, and treasures to produce many things for which you are a high-cost provider. This would result in lower production and income while sacrificing the items and benefits others can offer.

For example, even though most doctors might be good at record-keeping and arranging appointments, hiring someone to perform these services is generally in everyone's best interest. The time doctors use to keep records is time they could spend caring for patients. Because the time with patients is worth a lot, the opportunity cost of doctors keeping records will be high. Thus, doctors will almost always find that hiring specialists to manage their records is advantageous for themselves, their office staff, and, most important, their patients. Moreover, when doctors specialize in the provision of physician services and hire others with comparative advantages in recordkeeping and office management, costs will be lower, services will be better, and combined output in health care will be larger.

Third, voluntary exchange allows businesses to achieve lower per-unit costs by adopting large-scale production methods. Trade allows businesses to expand their market areas so they can plan for larger outputs and adopt processes that take advantage of **economies of scale**. Such processes often lead to substantially lower per-unit costs and enormous increases in output per worker. Without trade, these gains could not be achieved. **Market forces** are continuously reallocating production toward low-cost producers (and away from high-cost ones). As a result, open markets tend to allocate products and resources in ways that maximize the value, amount, and variety of the goods and services channeled to paying consumers.

The importance of trade in our modern world can hardly be exaggerated. In fact, the World Bank credits global trade and lowering trade barriers for helping eradicate extreme poverty.[5] Trade grants people living in extreme poverty access to products and resources far beyond what is available within their borders. The net benefits of trade move across nations, income groups, races, genders, and people

5. World Bank Group and World Trade Organization, "The Role of Trade in Ending Poverty" (Geneva: World Trade Organization, 2015).

of differing political views and cultural values. Can you imagine the difficulty involved in and costs associated with producing your own housing, clothing, and food, to say nothing of computers, smart devices, dishwashers, automobiles, and vaccines without trade? People who acquire these things have them largely because their economies are organized in ways that motivate individuals to cooperate, specialize, and trade. Countries that impose obstacles to exchange—either domestic or international—reduce the ability of their citizens to achieve gains from trade and to enjoy more prosperous lives.

5. Transaction costs are obstacles to trade.

Voluntary exchange promotes cooperation and helps us get more of what we need, want, and value. However, trade itself is costly. It takes time, effort, and other resources to search out potential trading partners, negotiate terms, determine risks, and complete exchanges. Resources spent in these ways are called **transaction costs**, and they are obstacles to the creation of wealth. They limit both our productive capacity and the realization of gains from mutually advantageous trades.

Transaction costs are sometimes high because of physical obstacles, such as oceans, rivers, and mountains, which make getting products to customers difficult. Investment in roads, transportation, and communication improvements can reduce these transaction costs. In other instances, transaction costs may be high because of the lack of information. For example, you may want to buy a used car, but you don't know someone willing to sell a reliable car at an attractive price. The time and energy spent searching for a car, assessing trustworthiness, and negotiating a price are part of your transaction costs. In still other cases, transaction costs are high because of political obstacles, such as taxes, licensing requirements, **price controls**, and **tariffs**. Regardless of whether the roadblocks are physical, informational, or political, high transaction costs reduce the potential gains from trade.

People who help others arrange trades and make better choices reduce transaction costs. They help promote economic progress. Such specialists are sometimes called **middlemen**. They include campus bookstores, real estate agents, stockbrokers, automobile dealers, and a wide variety of merchants. Many people claim that middlemen merely increase the price of goods and services without providing benefits. If this were the case, people would not continue to use their services. Transaction costs are obstacles to trade, and middlemen reduce these costs and benefit others through their services. This is why people value their services and are willing to pay for them.

The grocer, for example, is a middleman. (Of course, today's giant supermarkets reflect the actions of many people, but together their services are those of a middleman.) Without the grocer, think of the time and effort involved in preparing even a single meal. You would have to deal directly with farmers when purchasing vegetables, citrus growers when buying fruit, dairy operators if you want milk or cheese, and ranchers or fishermen if you want to serve beef or fish. Grocers make these contacts for you and other consumers, place the items in convenient selling locations, and maintain reliable inventories. The services of grocers and other middlemen reduce transaction costs significantly, helping potential buyers and sellers realize gains from trade. These services increase the volume of trade, promote economic progress, and release resources for other uses.

The amazing growth of Amazon illustrates the importance of reductions in transaction costs. In just two decades, Amazon grew from a small online bookstore to the world's largest retailer. How did they do it? Lower transaction costs provide the answer. Amazon grew in leaps and bounds by reducing the cost of exchange. Rather than trudging from store to store searching for desired items, buyers can view products and prices on the Amazon website, including reviews by previous purchasers. After placing their orders with a few clicks, the items appear like magic at their front doors the next day or soon thereafter.

In recent years, technology has reduced the transaction costs of numerous exchanges. In a few swipes on a device, buyers can now acquire information about potential sellers of almost every product. Apps are routinely used to shop for groceries, clothing, household items, and homes. They locate hotel rooms and flights, obtain tickets for major events, and even share rides.

Similarly, technological improvements and discovery of better ways of doing things have vastly reduced the cost of shipping goods in recent decades. Adjusted for inflation, the cost of shipping per ton via both ocean and air is now more than 50 percent lower than in the early 1970s. These reductions in transaction costs, including transport costs, have increased the volume of trade, expanded our production, and enhanced our living standards. They have played a central role in the worldwide rapid growth of per-person income and huge reductions in poverty.

6. Prices bring the choices of buyers and sellers into balance.

Market prices influence the choices of both buyers and sellers. When the price of a product rises, purchasing the item is more expensive and consumers normally choose to buy less. Thus, there is a negative relationship between the price of a good or service and the quantity demanded. This negative relation is known as the **law of demand.**

For sellers, the rise in the price of a product brings extra revenue that makes them willing to supply more. Thus, there is a positive relationship between the price of a good and the quantity producers will supply. This positive relationship is known as the **law of supply.**

Economists often use graphics to illustrate the relationships among price, quantity demanded, and quantity supplied. When

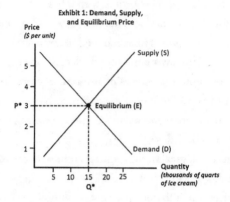

Exhibit 1: Demand, Supply, and Equilibrium Price

doing so, the price of a good is placed on the vertical y-axis and the quantity per unit of time (for example, a week, month, or year) on the horizontal x-axis. Using ice cream as an example, Exhibit 1 illustrates the classic demand-and-supply graphic. The demand curve indicates the various quantities of ice cream that consumers will purchase at alternative prices. Note how the demand curve slopes downward to the right, indicating that consumers will purchase more ice cream as its price declines. This is merely a graphic representation of the law of demand.

The supply curve indicates the various quantities of ice cream that producers are willing to supply at alternative prices. As Exhibit 1 illustrates, the curve slopes upward to the right, indicating that producers will be inclined to supply larger quantities at higher prices. The supply curve provides a graphic representation of the law of supply.

Now for a really important point: The price will tend to move toward a level—$3 per quart of ice cream in our example—that will bring the quantity demanded into equality with the quantity supplied. At the **equilibrium** price of $3, consumers will want to purchase fifteen thousand quarts of ice cream per day. This is the same quantity that ice cream producers are willing to supply. Price coordinates the choices of both consumers and producers of ice cream and brings them into balance.

If the price is higher than $3, for example $4, producers will want to supply more ice cream than consumers will want to purchase. This means that at $4, producers will be unable to sell as much as they would like. Inventories will rise, and this excess supply will lead some producers to cut their price to reduce their inventories. The price will tend to decline until the $3 equilibrium price is reached. As long as the price is above equilibrium, market forces will push the price downward.

Correspondingly, if the price of ice cream is less than $3, for example $2, consumers will want to purchase more than producers are willing to supply. This $2 price generates excess demand, leaving producers without adequate inventories. Upward pressure on price will move it back toward the equilibrium of $3. The choices of buyers and sellers will be consistent with each other only at the equilibrium price, and the market price will gravitate toward this level.

The auction system on eBay illustrates the operation of demand and supply in a setting that is familiar to many. On eBay, sellers enter their reserve prices—the minimum prices they will accept for goods. Buyers enter their maximum bids—the maximum prices they are willing to pay. The auction management system will bid on behalf of the buyers in predetermined monetary increments. Bidding ensues until the trading period expires or a person agrees to pay the stated "Buy It Now" price. Exchange occurs only when buyers bid a price greater than the seller's minimum asking price. But when this happens, an exchange will occur, and both the buyer and seller will gain. Remember, voluntary trade is mutually beneficial.

Though somewhat less visible than the eBay electronic market, the forces of demand and supply in other markets work similarly. The height of the demand curve indicates the maximum amount the consumers are willing to pay for another unit of the good, while the height of the supply curve shows the minimum price at which producers are willing to supply another unit. When the price is between the maximum the consumer is willing to pay and the minimum offer price of a seller, potential gains from trade are present. Moreover, when the equilibrium price is present, all potential gains from exchange will be realized by both consumers and producers.

Marginal thinking explains why, when the equilibrium price is present, buyers and sellers will have an incentive to make mutually advantageous exchanges and the outcome will be efficient. Consumers purchase only those units that bring them more value than the actual price. Similarly, producers supply only those units that can be sold at a price that covers cost. When the equilibrium price is present, units will be produced and purchased as long as the value of the good to consumers exceeds the cost of the resources required for their production. The implication: Market prices not only bring the quantity demanded and quantity supplied into balance, but they also direct producers to supply those goods that consumers value more than their cost of production. This holds true in any market.

Of course, we live in a dynamic world. Through time, changes will occur. They will alter the demand and supply of goods and services. Factors such as consumer income, prices of related products, expectations about future prices, government policy changes, and the number of consumers in the market area will influence the demand for a good. Changes in any of these factors will change the amount of a good consumers will want to purchase at the various possible prices. Put another way, changes in these factors will cause a change in demand, a shift in the entire demand curve.

It is important to distinguish between a change in demand—a shift in the entire demand curve—and a change in quantity demanded, a movement along a demand curve as the result of a change in the price of the good. (Important note to students: Failure to distinguish between a change in demand and a change in quantity demanded is one of the greatest challenges students face in their courses. Questions on this topic are favorites of many economics instructors. So, make sure you understand this difference.)

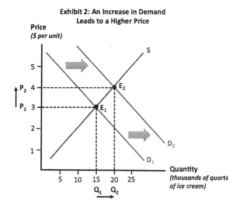

Exhibit 2: An Increase in Demand Leads to a Higher Price

Exhibit 2 illustrates the impact of an increase in demand on the market price of a good. Suppose there is an increase in consumers' incomes or a rise in the price of frozen yogurt, a common substitute for ice cream. These changes will increase the demand for ice cream, causing the demand curve to shift to the right, from D_1 to D_2. In turn, the stronger demand will push the equilibrium price of ice cream upward from $3 to $4. At the new higher equilibrium price, the quantity demanded by consumers will once again be brought into balance with the quantity supplied by producers. Note: The increase in demand (the shift in the entire demand curve) will result in an increase in the quantity supplied from fifteen thousand to twenty thousand, a movement along the existing supply curve).

A reduction in consumers' incomes or lower frozen-yogurt prices would exert the opposite impact. These changes would reduce the demand for ice cream (shift the demand curve to the left), lower the price, and reduce the equilibrium quantity exchanged.

Now let's turn to the supply side of a market. Changes that alter the per-unit cost of supplying a good will cause the entire supply curve to shift. For example, an improvement in technology, lower prices for the resources used in production, or subsidies to the producers will increase supply, causing the entire supply curve to shift to the right. In contrast, changes that make it more expensive to produce the good—such as higher prices for the materials used to produce the good or higher taxes imposed on the producers—will reduce supply, causing the supply curve to shift to the left.

Suppose there is a reduction in the prices of cream and milk, ingredients used to produce ice cream. What impact will these resource price reductions have on the supply and market price of ice cream? If your answer is that supply will increase and the market price will decline, you are correct. Exhibit 3 illustrates this point within the demand-and-supply framework. The lower prices of cream and milk will reduce the per-unit cost of producing ice cream, causing the supply curve to shift to the right (from S_1 to S_2). As a result, the equilibrium price of ice cream will decline from \$3 to \$2. At the new lower price, the quantity demanded will increase and once again equal the quantity supplied at twenty thousand quarts per day. Note: The increase in the supply (the shift of the entire curve) lowered the price of ice cream and increased the quantity demanded—a movement along the existing demand curve. If changes had occurred that increased the cost of producing ice cream (for example, higher prices for the ingredients), the results would be just the opposite: a decrease in supply (a shift to the left), an increase in the price of ice cream, and a reduction in the quantity exchanged.

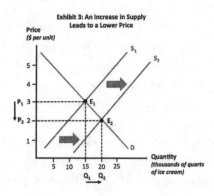

Exhibit 3: An Increase in Supply Leads to a Lower Price

Market adjustments like the ones outlined here do not take place instantaneously. It takes time for both consumers and producers to adjust fully to new conditions. In fact, the adjustment process we are describing is constantly changing in a dynamic world.

The impact of changes in demand and supply and factors that underlie shifts in these curves are central to the understanding of the market process. Demand-and-supply analysis will be utilized again and again throughout this book. The website accompanying this text—CommonSenseEconomics.com—contains a supplementary reading, "Demand, Supply, and Adjustments to Dynamic Change." It provides additional analyses of shifts in demand and supply and the impact of various types of dynamic changes on the market price.

7. *Profits direct businesses toward productive activities that increase the value of resources, while losses direct them away from wasteful activities.*

Businesses purchase natural resources, labor, capital (machines, tools, and other productive assets), and entrepreneurial talent. These productive resources are then transformed into goods and services that are sold to consumers. In a market economy, producers must bid resources away from their alternative uses because the owners of the resources will supply them only at prices at least equal to what they could earn elsewhere. The payments required to bid the resources away from their other potential uses are a producer's opportunity cost of supplying a good or service.

There is an important difference between the opportunity cost of production and standard accounting measures of cost of the business firm. Accountants focus on the calculation of the firm's net income, which is slightly different from economic **profit** because it omits the opportunity cost of assets owned by the firm. While accountants omit this opportunity cost, economists do not.[6] As a result, the firm's net income will overstate profit, as measured by the economist. Economists consider the fact that the assets can be used in alternative ways. Unless these opportunity costs are covered, profits will eventually diminish and resources will be shifted to other productive activities.

A firm's profit can be calculated in the following manner:

Profit = Total Revenue – Total Cost

The firm's total revenue is simply the sales price of all goods sold (P) times the quantity (Q) of all goods sold. In order to earn a profit, a firm must generate more revenue from the sale of its product than the opportunity cost of the resources required to make it. Thus, a firm will earn a profit only if it is able to produce a good or service that consumers value more than the cost of the resources required for its production.

Consumers will not purchase a good unless they value it as much as, or more than, the price. If consumers are willing to pay more than the production costs, then the decision by the producer to bid the resources away from alternative uses is a profitable one. Profit is a reward for transforming resources into something of greater value than costs.

Business decision-makers will seek to undertake production of goods and services that will generate profit. However, things do not always turn out as expected. Sometimes business firms are unable to sell their products at prices that cover costs. **Losses** occur when

6. For example, if a corporation invests $100 million in buildings and equipment to produce a product, it is forgoing the earnings these funds could have earned if invested in other ways. The corporation could have simply put the $100 million in the bank and let it draw interest at, say, a 5 percent rate. In a year's time, the interest earnings would sum to $5 million. This $5 million in forgone interest is an opportunity cost of the activities of the corporation, but it will not be reflected on the firm's accounting statement. Because of this omission, accounting costs understate the opportunity costs of the resources utilized. Therefore, net income overstates profit.

the total revenue from sales is less than the opportunity cost of the resources used to produce a good or service. Losses impose a penalty on firms when they produce goods and services that consumers value less than the resources required for their production. The losses indicate that the resources would have been better used producing other things.

Suppose a business firm producing shirts pays $20,000 per month to lease a building, rent the required machines, and purchase the labor, cloth, buttons, and other materials necessary to produce and market one thousand shirts per month. If the firm sells the one thousand shirts for $22 each, monthly revenue is $22,000. Profit is $2,000. The firm has created wealth. By their willingness to pay more than the costs of production, consumers reveal they value the shirts more than the resources required for their production. The firm's profit is a reward for increasing the value of resources by converting them into the more highly valued product.

On the other hand, if the demand for shirts declines and they can be sold only for $17 each, then the firm will earn $17,000, losing $3,000 a month. This loss occurs because the firm's actions reduced the value of the resources used. The shirts—the final product—were worth less to consumers than the value of other things that could have been produced with the resources. We are not saying that consumers consciously know that the resources used to make the shirts would have been more valuable if converted into some other product. But their combined choices and the prices they are willing to pay provide valuable information to the firm, along with creating an incentive to take steps to reduce the loss.

In a market economy, losses and business failures work constantly to bring inefficient activities—such as producing shirts that sell for less than their cost—to a halt. Losses and business failures will redirect the resources toward the production of other goods that are valued more highly. Thus, even though business failures are often painful for the owners, investors, and employees involved, there is a positive side: They release resources that can be directed toward wealth-creating activities.

The people of a nation will be better off if resources—available land, buildings, labor, and entrepreneurial talent—produce valuable goods and services. At any given time, an endless array of investment activities can be undertaken. Some of these investments will increase the value of resources by transforming them into goods and services that consumers value more highly than cost. These will promote economic progress. Other investments will reduce the value of resources and slow economic progress. If we are going to be wise stewards of available resources, activities that increase value must be encouraged, while those that use resources counterproductively must be discouraged. This is precisely what profits and losses do.

We live in a world of changing tastes and technology, changing government policies, imperfect knowledge, and uncertainty. Business owners cannot know with certainty the future of market prices or production costs. Their decisions are based on expectations. But the reward-penalty structure of a market economy is clear. **Entrepreneurs** who produce efficiently and correctly anticipate the goods and services that attract consumers at prices above production costs will prosper. In contrast, business owners who allocate resources inefficiently, into areas where demand is such that the firm is unable to cover its costs, will face losses and financial difficulties.

There is an inclination to think that entrepreneurs are also the owners of a firm, but this is not necessarily the case. Owners of business firms, particularly large corporate firms with many shareholders, often retain entrepreneurs who provide the strategy and direction of the firm. Similarly, entrepreneurs often seek investors willing to provide financial capital in the form of ownership shares even though the direction of the business will be determined by the entrepreneur. Thus, entrepreneurship and business ownership are not synonymous.

Some criticize the fact that business failures accompany the market process. Interestingly, many entrepreneurs who initially fail eventually succeed in a big way. Steve Jobs provides an example. After leaving Apple in 1985, Jobs founded neXT, a firm that he thought would produce the next generation of personal computers. The company struggled. But Jobs learned from the experience. He returned to Apple in 1997 and soon introduced the iPhone, the iPad, and other innovative products that succeeded spectacularly in the marketplace.

The bottom line is straightforward: Profits direct business investment toward productive projects that promote economic progress, while losses channel resources away from projects that are counterproductive. This is a vitally important function. Economies that fail to perform this function well will almost surely stagnate or even regress.

8. The "invisible hand" of market prices guides buyers and sellers toward activities promoting the general welfare.

> *Every individual is continually exerting himself to find out the most advantageous employment for whatever capital he can command. It is his own advantage, indeed, and not that of the society, which he has in view. But the study of his own advantage naturally, or rather necessarily, leads him to prefer that employment which is most advantageous to society. . . . He intends only his own gain, and he is in this, as in many other cases, led by an invisible hand to promote an end which was not part of his intention.* [7]
>
> —ADAM SMITH (1776)

7. Adam Smith, *An Inquiry into the Nature and Causes of the Wealth of Nations*, vol. II, Glasgow Edition (Indianapolis: Liberty Fund [1776] 1981), 660. Also available at www.econlib.org/library/Smith/smWN.html.

Self-interest is a powerful motivator. As Adam Smith noted long ago, as if directed by an **invisible hand**, self-interested individuals have a strong incentive to undertake actions that promote the general prosperity of a community or nation. The "invisible hand" to which Smith refers is the price system. The individual "intends only his own gain" but is directed by the invisible hand of market prices to promote the goals of others, contributing to greater prosperity.

The principle of the "invisible hand" can be difficult to grasp. There is a natural tendency to perceive that orderly outcomes can only be achieved when someone is in charge or through directions from a centralized authority. Yet Adam Smith contended that pursuing one's own advantage creates an orderly society in which demands are routinely satisfied without centralized planning. This order occurs because when private property and freedom of exchange are present, market prices will direct self-interested individuals toward actions that promote the general welfare. One statistic—the current market price of a particular good or service—provides buyers and sellers with what they need to bring their actions into harmony with the preferences and choices of others. Market prices register the choices of millions of consumers, producers, and resource suppliers. They reflect information about consumer preferences, costs, and matters related to timing, location, and circumstances—information that in any large market is well beyond the comprehension of any individual or central-planning authority.

Have you ever thought about why your local grocery stores have approximately the right amount of milk, bread, vegetables, and other goods—quantities large enough that the goods are nearly always available but not so large that it results in a lot of spoilage and waste? How is it that refrigerators, automobiles, and touch-screen tablets, produced at diverse places around the world, are available in your local market in about the quantities that consumers desire? Where is the technical manual for businesses to follow to get this done? Of course, there is no manual. The invisible hand of market prices performs the task. It directs self-interested individuals into cooperative action and brings their choices into line with each other through price signaling, as described in Element 1.6.

The 1974 Nobel laureate F. A. Hayek called the market system a "marvel." A single indicator, the market price, spontaneously carries so much information that it guides buyers and sellers to make decisions that help both obtain what they want.[8] The market price of a product reflects thousands, even millions, of decisions made around the world by people who don't know what the others are doing. For each product or service, the market acts like a cloud-based network grinding out an indicator that gives all participants both the information they need and the incentive to act on it.

Throughout human history, no individual or central-planning authority has been able to obtain or consider all the information needed for millions of consumers and producers to coordinate their actions the way markets do. Moreover, market prices contain this information in a distilled form. They direct producers and resource suppliers toward production of those things that consumers value most (relative to their costs). No one has to force a farmer to raise apples or tell a construction firm to build houses or convince a furniture manufacturer to produce chairs. When the prices of these and other products indicate that consumers value them as much as or more than their production costs, producers seeking personal gain will supply them.

Nor is it necessary for anyone to remind producers to search for and use low-cost methods of production. Self-interest directed by market prices provides suppliers with the incentive to seek out the best combination of resources and the most cost-effective production methods. Because lower costs mean higher profits, each producer strives to

---

8. F. A. Hayek, "The Use of Knowledge in Society," *American Economic Review* 35 (September 1945): 519–30.

keep costs down and quality up. In fact, competition virtually forces them to do so.

In a modern economy, the cooperation that comes from self-interest directed by the invisible hand of market prices is truly amazing. The next time you prepare a nice dinner, think about all the people who helped you make it possible. It is unlikely that any of them, from the farmer to the truck driver to the grocer, was motivated by concern that you have an enjoyable meal at the lowest possible cost. Market prices, however, brought their interests into harmony with yours. Farmers who raise the best beef or turkey receive higher prices; truck drivers and grocers earn more money if their products are delivered fresh and in good condition to the consumer; and so on, always using the low-cost means to do so. Literally tens of thousands of people, most of whom we will never meet, make contributions that help each of us consume a bundle of goods that is far greater than what we could produce for ourselves.

Further, the invisible hand works so quietly and automatically that the order, cooperation, and vast array of goods available are largely taken for granted. Even though underappreciated, the combination of self-interest and the invisible hand is nonetheless a powerful force for economic progress.

9. Mistakes and misconceptions in economic analysis often occur because of failure to consider long-term consequences and secondary effects.

In 1946, Henry Hazlitt, a famous economic journalist, wrote a book titled *Economics in One Lesson.* This economics primer, which builds on an 1850 essay by Frédéric Bastiat, a French economist and member of the French parliament, is perhaps the all-time best-selling treatise on economics.

The book starts with the story of a young boy whose thrown ball breaks the window of a shopkeeper. As a result, the shopkeeper hires a glazier to fix it. Some observers, noting the highly visible employment of the glazier, argue that the broken window is a good thing. It created a job for the glazier. However, as Hazlitt stresses, this is shortsighted. It ignores the **secondary effects**.

If the shopkeeper had not spent the funds fixing the window, he would have spent them on other things, perhaps a pair of shoes, new clothes, or similar items. If the window had not been broken, employment in these other areas of production would have been larger. The community would have had both the window and the items purchased by the shopkeeper. Once the secondary effects are considered, it is clear that destructive actions, such as the broken window or those resulting from floods, hurricanes, and counterproductive policies, harm a society. They reduce the availability of goods and fail to expand net employment: Jobs gained in one place are lost in other areas. The view that destructive acts create employment and are good for the economy is now known as the "broken-window fallacy."

Hazlitt's one lesson was that when analyzing an economic proposal, a person

> . . . *must trace not merely the immediate results but the results in the long run, not merely the primary consequences but the secondary consequences, and not merely the effects on some special group but the effects on everyone.*[9]

Hazlitt contended that failure to consider the future effects of today's policies is the most common error in public economic decision-making. He wrote extensively on the economy during the Great Depression of the 1930s. He highlighted, especially in politics, the

---

9. Henry Hazlitt, *Economics in One Lesson* (New Rochelle: Arlington House, 1979), 103.

tendency to stress the short-term benefits of a policy while ignoring the longer-term, often unintended consequences.

Let's consider a couple of examples that illustrate the potential importance of secondary effects. In an effort to reduce gasoline consumption, the federal government mandates that automobiles be more fuel-efficient. Is this regulation a sound policy? It may be, but the secondary effects must be considered when evaluating the overall impact of the policy.

In order to achieve the mandated fuel efficiency, auto manufacturers reduced the size and weight of cars, making them less crash-worthy. As a result, there are more highway deaths than would otherwise have occurred. Furthermore, because the higher mileage standards for cars and light trucks make driving cheaper, people tend to drive more than they otherwise would. This increases congestion and results in a smaller reduction in gasoline consumption than initially projected. Once you consider the secondary effects, the fuel efficiency regulations are less beneficial than the projections of their proponents. They may even be counterproductive.

Proponents of trade restrictions, such as tariffs and **import quotas**, often argue that they increase employment. This may be true in the industries protected from international competition. But consideration of the secondary effects on consumer behavior and other industries should cause one to seriously question the view that the restrictions increase overall employment.

Consider the secondary effects of import quotas that limit sales of foreign-produced sugar in the United States. The quotas reduce supply and result in higher domestic sugar prices. The price of sugar in the United States has been approximately twice the level of the rest of the world for many years. The higher sugar prices increase the costs of U.S. producers of candy and other products using a lot of sugar. As a result of this increased expense, many candy producers, including the makers of Life Savers, Jawbreakers, Red Hots, Fannie May chocolates, and Oreo cookies, have moved to countries like Canada and Mexico, where sugar can be purchased at its true market price. Thus, employment among sugar-using firms in the United States is lower than it otherwise would be. Further, because foreigners sell less sugar in the United States, they have less purchasing power with which to buy products we export to them. This, too, reduces U.S. employment. Moreover, consumers are among the casualties of tariffs. They pay higher prices for sugar, leaving them to purchase less or search for substitutes like corn syrup.

Once the secondary effects of trade restrictions, like the sugar quota program, are taken into consideration, there is no reason to expect net U.S. employment to increase. There may be more jobs in favored industries, but there will be less employment in others. Trade restrictions reshuffle employment rather than increase it. Clearly, when evaluating policies, informed consideration of secondary effects is an important ingredient of the economic way of thinking.

Secondary effects are not just a problem with political decision-making. They can also lead to unanticipated outcomes for individuals. The experience of a first-grade teacher in West Virginia illustrates this point. Her students constantly lost their pencils, so she reasoned that paying them 10 cents per stub would incentivize them to hang on to their pencils until all was used up. To her dismay, the students soon formed long lines at the pencil sharpener, creating stubs just as fast as she could pay for them. It makes sense to be alert for unintended consequences!

10. People earn income by providing others with what they value.

People differ in many ways—in their productive abilities, specialized skills, career preferences, work attitudes, and willingness to take risks. These differences influence people's incomes because they affect the value of the goods and services they are willing and able to provide to others at attractive prices and wages.

In a market economy, it is advantageous to produce goods, develop skills, and take actions others value highly. There is a moral here: If you want to earn a lot of income, figure out how to provide others with goods and services they value highly relative to their cost. Even if you don't strive to earn a lot of income and, instead, want to help the world, use the economic way of thinking to choose which charitable works, social endeavors, and nonprofit activities make the most sense among the various alternatives. In all scenarios, gather information about available resources and consider opportunity costs to make those choices that help you gain the most by supplying what is valued at the least cost. If you are unable or unwilling to help others in ways they value, your income will be low.

This direct link between helping others and receiving income gives each of us a strong incentive to acquire skills, develop talents, and cultivate habits that help us provide others with valuable goods and services. College students study for long hours, endure stress, and incur the financial costs in order to become doctors, teachers, accountants, and engineers. Other people acquire training, certification, and experience that will help them become electricians, maintenance workers, or website designers. Still others invest and start businesses. Why do people do these things? How do they survive and thrive?

Some people think that high-income individuals must be exploiting others. But people who earn high incomes in the marketplace generally do so by providing consumers with what they value and at attractive prices. Consider billionaire David Steward, the chair of World Wide Technology. Steward was born in a segregated town in Missouri as part of a family of ten. His father worked in a variety of jobs in the service sector, including as a mechanic, janitor, and trash collector. These beginnings influenced Steward in many ways. After earning a college degree, he worked many jobs before launching World Wide

Technology in 1990. Through various trials and tribulations, Steward customized existing computer technologies and improved information systems to help for-profit businesses and nonprofit organizations lower their production costs, improve overall efficiency, reach new markets, and enhance customer experiences at lower prices.

Billionaire and millionaire athletes and entertainers have done the same for their fans and customers. They have earned income and accumulated wealth by specializing, entertaining, and selling their talents and merchandise to others.

Business entrepreneurs who succeed in big ways do so by bringing products to millions of consumers at attractive and acceptable prices. The late Sam Walton, who founded Walmart, became one of the richest individuals in the United States by figuring out how to manage large inventories effectively and selling brand-name merchandise at discount prices to small-town America. Bill Gates and Paul Allen, cofounders of Microsoft, earned their billions by developing a set of products that dramatically improved the efficiency and compatibility of desktop computers. Billions of consumers who have never heard of Steward, Walton, Gates, or Allen have benefited from their entrepreneurial talents and products. These individuals made a lot of money because they helped a lot of people by providing them with things they valued at attractive prices.

Many people are hostile toward entrepreneurs and the profits they earn. When considering this view, it is important to recognize that the actions of entrepreneurs are a driving force of economic progress. Our living standards today are vastly higher than those of our ancestors fifty or one hundred years ago primarily because entrepreneurs have discovered and developed new products and lower-cost production methods that have improved the quality of our lives. Further, their compensation—profit derived from successful innovative actions—is only a small fraction of the gains they generate for consumers. William Nordhaus, longtime professor of economics at Yale University, estimates that the compensation of entrepreneurs was only 2.2 percent of the total gains their innovative actions generated for consumers during 1948–2001.[10] Wow, what a deal: For every $2.20 earned by entrepreneurs, they generate an estimated gain of $97.80 for others. Given these figures, it is not surprising that Steward, Walton, Gates, Allen, and millions of other entrepreneurs have exerted such a strong impact on our living standards.

11. Production of goods and services that people value, not just jobs, provides the source of high living standards.

> *Consumption is the sole end and purpose of all production; and the interest of the producer ought to be attended to only so far as it may be necessary for promoting that of the consumer.*[11]
>
> —ADAM SMITH

As Adam Smith noted nearly 250 years ago, consumption is the objective of all production. But consumption comes before production only in the dictionary. Income and living standards cannot increase without an increase in the production of goods and services people value.

Elon Musk, Tesla founder and aerospace innovator, recently highlighted this point artfully when he stated, "If you don't make stuff, there's no stuff." Musk was criticizing the view that government checks could replace lost production during the COVID-19 pandemic. As Musk put it, "This notion that you can just sort of send checks out

10. William Nordhaus, "Schumpeterian Profits in the American Economy: Theory and Measurement" (National Bureau of Economic Research Working Paper 10433, April 2004), http://www.nber.org/papers/w10433.

11. Smith, *Wealth of Nations,* 454.

to everybody and things will be fine is not true." His point is right on target. The government checks will not buy more if there are not more goods and services available. Instead, they will merely lead to higher prices, which is what happened in 2021 and 2022.

The linkage between more goods and services valued by people and higher living standards is straightforward. Similarly, destruction of goods and services people value will make a society worse off. These propositions are so intuitively obvious, it would seem unnecessary to highlight them. But policies based on the fallacious idea that destroying goods will benefit society have sometimes been adopted. In 1933, Congress passed the Agricultural Adjustment Act (AAA) in an effort to reduce the supply of agricultural products and thus prevent their prices from falling. Under this New Deal legislation, the federal government paid farmers to plow under portions of their cotton, corn, wheat, and other crops. Potato farmers were paid to spray their potatoes with dye to make them unfit for human consumption. Healthy cattle, sheep, and pigs were slaughtered and buried in mass graves to keep them off the market. Six million baby pigs were killed under the AAA in 1933 alone. The Supreme Court declared the act unconstitutional in 1936, but not before it had kept millions of valuable agricultural products from American consumers. Moreover, under modified forms of the act, even today the government continues to pay various farmers to limit their production, increasing the prices to consumers. While the political demands of those benefiting from the policies are understandable, such programs destroy valuable resources and create artificially high prices. These types of policies make the nation poorer and increase the burden on at-risk communities and low-income households.

The 2009 "Cash for Clunkers" program provides another example of politicians attempting to promote prosperity by destroying productive assets—used cars, in this case. Under the Cash for Clunkers program, car dealers were paid between $3,500 and $4,500 to destroy older cars traded in for new vehicles. Dealers were required to ruin the car engines with a sodium silicate solution, then smash the cars and send them to the junkyard, assuring that not even the parts could be used in the future. Proponents argued that this policy would stimulate recovery by inducing people to buy new cars. But the new cars cost more than used ones. Plus, the price of used vehicles increased because of the decline in supply. As a result, consumers spent more on automobiles (both new and used), and therefore less money was available for saving or spending elsewhere. Thus, the Cash for Clunkers program failed to stimulate total demand. In essence, taxpayers provided $3 billion in subsidies for new-car purchases, while destroying approximately seven hundred thousand used cars valued at about $2 billion. Those who could afford new cars were subsidized, while low- and middle-income people who depend on used cars were punished. And new car sales plunged when the program expired.[12]

If destroying automobiles is a good idea, why not require everyone to destroy their automobiles every year? Think of all the new-car sales this would generate. All of this is unsound economics. You may be able to help specific producers by increasing the scarcity of their products, but you cannot make the general populace better off by destroying marketable goods with consumption value. Policies of this type are counterproductive and harmful to society.

A more subtle form of destruction involves government policies that increase the opportunity cost of obtaining various goods. For example, the federal government has subsidized the production of ethanol even though it costs more per gallon than a gallon of gasoline that produces the same amount of energy. These subsidies increase our cost of obtaining energy. Experts also find that these subsidies push up food prices

12. T. Gayer and E. Parker, *Cash for Clunkers: An Evaluation* (Washington, DC: Brookings Institution, March 9, 2022), https://www.brookings.edu/interactives/cash -for-clunkers-an-evaluation/.

and exert an adverse impact on the environment. But the subsidies provide highly visible benefits to corn farmers in the important presidential primary state of Iowa, making the subsidies difficult to repeal.[13]

Politicians and proponents of government spending programs generally exaggerate their benefits and boast about the jobs created. This makes economic literacy particularly important. While employment is often described as a means to create wealth, we must remember that it is not simply more jobs that improve our economic well-being, but rather jobs that produce goods and services that people value. When that elementary fact is forgotten, people are often misled into acceptance of programs that reduce wealth rather than create it.

The focus on creating jobs can be extremely misleading, as an apocryphal story about an engineer visiting China illustrates. He came across a large crew of men building a dam with picks and shovels. When the engineer pointed out to the supervisor that the project could be completed in a few days, rather than many months, if the men were given motorized earthmoving equipment, the supervisor said that such equipment would destroy many jobs. "Oh," the engineer responded, "I thought you were interested in building a dam. If it's more jobs you want, why don't you have your men use spoons instead of shovels?"

12. *Economic progress comes primarily through voluntary trade, investment, stable capital markets, better ways of doing things, and sound economic institutions.*

On the first day of an introductory economics class, the authors of this book often inform students that Americans produce and earn approximately thirty times as much per person today as in 1750. Then we so-

13. See Wallace E. Tyner, "U.S. Ethanol Policy: Possibilities for the Future," Purdue Extension BioEnergy Series, ID-342-W (West Lafayette, IN: Purdue University Extension, January 2007), https://www.extension.purdue.edu/extmedia/id/id-342-w.pdf.

licit student views on the following question: "Why are Americans so much more productive and, consequently, earn more today than nearly three centuries ago?" Think for a moment how you would respond to this question.

Invariably, our students mention three things: First, today's scientific knowledge and technological abilities are far beyond anything imagined in 1750. Second, complex machines and factories, far better roads, and extensive systems of communications make work both easier and more productive. Finally, students mention that in 1750 individuals and families directly produced most of the items that they consumed, whereas today we typically purchase them from others through markets.

Basically, the students provide the correct explanation for human progress even though they have little or no prior knowledge of economics. They recognize the importance of technology, capital (productive assets), trade, and sound **institutions**. Their responses reinforce our view that economics is the "science of common sense."

We have already highlighted gains from trade and the reduction of transaction costs as sources of economic progress. Economic analysis pinpoints three other sources of higher income levels and living standards: **investments** in people and productive assets, advancements in technology, and improvements in economic organizations. Let's consider each of these sources of economic progress.

First, investments in **physical capital** (such as tools, machines, and buildings) and **human capital** (education, skills, training, and experience of workers) enhance our ability to produce goods and services. Workers can produce more if they use better machines and technology. A logger can produce more when working with a chain saw rather than a hand-operated, crosscut blade. Similarly, a transport worker can haul more with a truck than with a mule and wagon. Likewise, an experienced, highly trained mechanic can fix your automobile more quickly and at a lower cost than an unskilled person can.

Second, advances in technology (the use of brainpower to discover new products and less costly methods of production) spur economic progress. Since 1750, the steam engine, followed by the internal combustion engine, electricity, and nuclear power, replaced human and animal power as the major sources of energy. Automobiles, buses, trains, and airplanes replaced horse and buggies (and walking) as popular methods of transportation. Technological improvements continue to change our lifestyles. Consider the impact of personal computers, microwave ovens, smart devices, streaming services available anywhere and anytime, heart bypass surgery, hip replacements, air conditioners, and even voice-controlled personal assistants. The introduction and development of these products during the last sixty years have vastly changed the way that we work, play, and entertain ourselves. They have improved our well-being.

Investment and improvements in technology do not just happen. They reflect the actions of entrepreneurs, people who face risks in hope of profits. No one knows what the next innovative breakthrough will be or just which production techniques will reduce costs. Furthermore, entrepreneurs are often found in unexpected places. Thus, economic progress depends on a system that allows a very diverse set of people from all walks of life to test their ideas to see if they are profitable, and it simultaneously discourages the squandering of resources and the pursuit of counterproductive projects.

For this progress to occur, markets must be open so that individuals are free to test their innovative ideas. An entrepreneur with a new product, process, or technology needs to attract the support of enough investors to finance and sustain the project. But innovative new products must also face the "reality check" of consumers. Do consumers value what an entrepreneur is bringing to the market enough to pay a price sufficient to cover the cost of production? In a competitive market setting, consumers ultimately become judges and jury. If they do not value an innovative product enough to cover its costs, the entrepreneur-producer had best terminate production and move on to other activities. Failure to do so will lead to sustained losses and eventual bankruptcy.

Third, improvements in economic organization promote growth. By "economic organization" we mean the systems that organize human activities and the rules under which people operate—factors often taken for granted or overlooked. How easily can people engage in trade or organize businesses? The legal institutions of a country to a large extent determine the level of trade, investment, and economic cooperation undertaken by its residents. A just and objective legal system protects individuals and their property, enforces contracts fairly, and settles disputes efficiently. It is an essential ingredient for economic progress. In countries and communities without such a legal system, investment will be lacking, trade will be stifled, and the spread of innovative ideas will likely be absent. Part 2 of this book will examine in more detail the importance of the legal structure, economic institutions, and the primary sources of human progress and living standards.

PART 2

*Seven Major Sources of
Economic Progress*

SEVEN MAJOR SOURCES
OF ECONOMIC PROGRESS

1. Legal system: The foundation for economic progress is a legal system that protects privately owned property and enforces contracts in an evenhanded manner.

2. Competitive markets: Competition promotes the efficient use of resources and provides the incentive for innovative improvements.

3. Minimal regulation: Regulations that increase market competitiveness or support voluntary exchange spur progress.

4. Efficient capital markets: To realize its potential, a nation must have a mechanism that channels capital into wealth-creating projects.

5. Monetary stability: A monetary policy that ensures money of stable and predictable value will promote the efficient use of resources.

6. Low tax rates: People produce more when they can keep more of what they earn.

7. Free trade: People achieve higher incomes when they are free to trade with individuals in other countries.

Economic Growth and Development: The Historical Record

Robert Lucas, the 1995 Nobel laureate, stated, "Once you start thinking about economic growth, it is hard to think about anything else."[14] Why do Lucas and many other economists place so much emphasis on economic growth? Because the growth of real output is the only way for a nation to achieve higher income levels and living standards.

Throughout most of human history, economic growth has been extremely rare. The late Angus Maddison, an economist for the Organisation for Economic Co-operation and Development (OECD), is widely recognized as the leading authority on historical income figures. Exhibit 4 presents his estimates of per-person income during the past thousand years. (Income is expressed in 2011 dollars.) Data are presented for the West—twenty-one high-income countries of Western Europe, North America, Oceania, and Japan—along with the parallel figures for developing countries.[15]

14. See Robert E. Lucas Jr., "On the Mechanics of Economic Development," *Journal of Monetary Economics* 22, no. 1 (1988): 3–42.

15. The twenty-one high-income countries are Australia, Austria, Belgium, Canada, Switzerland, Germany, Denmark, Spain, Finland, France, United Kingdom, Ireland, Iceland, Italy, Japan, Luxembourg, Netherlands, Norway, New Zealand, Sweden, and the United States. They are commonly lumped together as "the West."

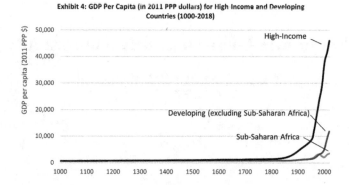

Exhibit 4: GDP Per Capita (in 2011 PPP dollars) for High Income and Developing Countries (1000-2018)

Sources: J. Bolt and J. van Zanden, "Maddison Style Estimates of the Evolution of the World Economy: A New 2020 Update," Groningen Growth and Development Center, October 2020, https://www.rug.nl/ggdc/historicaldevelopment/maddison/publications/wp15.pdf?lang=en; J. Bolt, R. Inklaar; H. de Jong, and J. van Zanden, "Rebasing 'Maddison': New Income Comparisons and the Shape of Long-Run Economic Development" (Maddison Project Working Paper No. 10, 2018), https://www.rug.nl/ggdc/html_publications/memorandum/gd174.pdf; and Angus Maddison, *Contours of the World Economy, 1–2030 AD: Essays in Macro-Economic History* (Oxford: Oxford University Press, 2007).

Look at the income figures of Exhibit 4 prior to 1800. There was virtually no change in income per person in either the West or the rest of the world during the eight hundred years before 1800. During this time, people throughout the world worked hard for fifty, sixty, and seventy hours per week to obtain enough food and shelter for subsistence. They had a constant struggle for survival, and many lost the battle. Even in 1800, living standards were not much different from those a thousand years earlier, or even two thousand years earlier during the time of ancient Rome.

In the West, this bleak economic story began to change around 1800. In your history and civics classes, you were probably told how the Industrial Revolution changed the world. Newly developed machines, technological improvements, and capital investment resulted in higher income levels and living standards. This Industrial Revolution certainly made a difference in the West. As Exhibit 4 shows, per-person income in Western Europe, North America, and other parts of the West rose dramatically, from $1,460 in 1820 to $2,506 in 1870 and $5,413 in 1913. By 1950 the per capita income in these regions had soared to $8,464. Thus, in the West, income rose from $4 per day in 1820 to $23 per day in 1950, an increase of nearly 500 percent in 130 years.

But only about 15 percent of the world's population live in developed countries, and the change was much less transformative in other regions. From 1820 to 1950, the **gross domestic product (GDP)** per person in the developing countries outside of sub-Saharan Africa rose from $816 (a little more than $2 per day) to $1,426 (approximately $4 per day).[16] This is an average growth rate of only half of a percent per year. Moreover, the $4 per day income level of the developing countries in 1950 was near the subsistence level and approximately the same as that of the high-income countries in 1820. These figures show that while the Industrial Revolution generated growth in Western Europe, North America, Oceania, and Japan, its impact on the 85 percent of the population living elsewhere was minimal. People in these countries did a little better during this period than prior to 1800, but not much.

Now look at what has happened during the past half century. Since 1970, something like a second economic revolution has occurred, and it has moved through the entire world. Per-person real-income levels in the high-income countries of the West have continued to rise, but for the first time in history, the rest of the world has also achieved sustained economic growth and income levels well above subsistence. The rising per-person real-income levels occurred first in developing countries outside of sub-Saharan Africa, but more recently, sustained growth has also occurred in the latter region. As Exhibit 4 shows, the

16. The most widely used measure of total output and income is gross domestic product (GDP). Changes in GDP are also widely used to measure the growth of an economy. For more information on GDP, see supplementary reading "Gross Domestic Product (GDP): What Is It and How Is It Measured?" at the website accompanying this book: https://commonsenseeconomics.com/supplementals/supplementals-gdp/.

real per capita GDP (adjusted for inflation) of the developing countries outside of sub-Saharan Africa rose from $1,698 in 1960 to $11,820 in 2018, a whopping increase of 596 percent. This increase in just 58 years was even larger than the growth of per capita GDP in the West during the 130 years following 1820. Moreover, during 2000–2018, the per capita GDP of sub-Saharan African countries has risen by 67 percent in just 18 years.

As history illustrates, economic growth does not happen automatically. What are the key sources of economic growth and human progress? Why do some countries grow and achieve high levels of income while others stagnate? How can the pattern of economic growth shown in Exhibit 4 be explained?

The modern view of development recognizes that institutions and policies exert a major impact on growth. By institutions we mean the rules, laws, and customs that guide behavior. This section will analyze the key institutional and policy factors underlying the growth process and how they lead to differences among nations.

1. Legal system: The foundation for economic progress is a legal system that protects privately owned property and enforces contracts in an evenhanded manner.

> *[A] private property regime makes people responsible for their own actions in the realm of material goods. Such a system therefore ensures that people experience the consequences of their own acts. Property sets up fences, but it also surrounds us with mirrors, reflecting back upon us the consequences of our own behavior.*[17]
>
> —TOM BETHELL, ECONOMIC JOURNALIST

17. Tom Bethell, *The Noblest Triumph* (New York: St. Martin's Press, 1998), 10.

The legal system provides the foundation for the protection of property rights and enforcement of contracts. "Property" is a broad term that includes ownership of oneself, one's ideas, and one's labor services, as well as physical assets such as buildings and land. The legal system protects owners against violence, theft, or fraud. Private ownership is an institution that involves three things: (1) the right to exclusive use; (2) legal protection against invaders—those who would seek to use or abuse the property without the owner's permission; and (3) the right to transfer (sell or give) property to others.

Private owners can decide how they will use their property, but they are held accountable and responsible for their actions. People who invade or infringe on the property rights of another will be subject to the same legal forces that protect their own property. For example, **private property rights** prohibit me from using my hammer to break your windshield, because doing so would be violating your property right to your car. Your property right restricts me and everyone else from using (or abusing) your car without your permission. Similarly, my ownership of my hammer and other possessions restricts you and everyone else from using them without my permission.

The important thing about private ownership is the incentives that flow from it. There are four major reasons why the incentives accompanying clearly defined and enforced private ownership rights propel economic growth and progress.

First, private ownership provides strong incentives to maintain and take good care of property. If private owners fail to maintain their property or allow it to be abused or damaged, they will bear the consequences. Their property's value will decline. For example, if you own an automobile, you have a strong incentive to change the oil, service it regularly, and maintain its interior. Why? If you do not, the car's value to both you and future owners will decline. If kept in good running order, it will be of greater value to you and others potentially interested in buying it. The market price will reflect that stewardship. Good stewardship is rewarded, but bad stewardship is penalized by a reduction in the value of the asset.

In contrast, when property is owned by the government or owned in common by a large group of people, each user's incentive to care for it weakens. For example, when the government owns housing, no individual or small group of owners has a strong financial incentive to maintain the property. Why? Because no individual or small group will pay the costs of a decline in the value of the property or benefit from its improvement. That is why government-owned housing, compared to privately owned housing, is more often run down and poorly maintained. This is true in both capitalist and socialist countries. Laxity in care, maintenance, and repair reflects the weak incentives that accompany government ownership of property, even in the midst of working markets for privately owned assets.

Second, private ownership encourages people to use their property productively and to develop it in ways others value highly. While private owners can legally do what they want with their property, they can gain from actions that enhance its value to others. If they employ and develop their property in ways attractive to others, its market value will increase. In contrast, changes that others dislike—particularly if they are customers or potential buyers—will reduce the value of one's property.

Private ownership also affects personal development. When people can keep the fruits of their labor, they have a powerful incentive to improve their skills, work harder, and work smarter. Such actions will increase their income and satisfaction. Why are college students willing to endure long hours of study and incur the cost of a college education? Private ownership of labor services provides the answer. Because they have an ownership right to their labor services, their future earnings will be higher if they acquire knowledge and develop skills valued highly by others.

Similarly, private ownership provides the owners of land, buildings, and other physical assets with motivation to use, protect, and develop them in beneficial ways. Further, those failing to do so will bear the costs in terms of lower-valued assets.

Consider the owner of an apartment complex who has no interest in providing attractive landscaping, convenient parking, on-site laundry facilities, a workout room, or a swimming pool complex. Finding renters will be difficult if potential tenants value these things highly, that is, more than the costs of providing them. If so, the apartment owner has a strong incentive to provide them. Apartment owners will be able to increase their net incomes (and the market value of their complexes) by providing consumers with what they value highly relative to cost. In contrast, owners who do not will find that their earnings and the value of their capital (their apartments) will decline. (However, if renters aren't willing to pay the cost of an amenity—such as an indoor swimming pool—the apartment owner would be making a mistake in providing it.)

Private ownership even influences the productivity of resources in socialist countries. Farming in the former Soviet Union illustrates this point. Under the Communist regime, families on small private plots, which ranged up to an acre in size, were permitted to keep or sell the goods they produced. These private plots made up only about 2 percent of the total land under cultivation; the other 98 percent consisted of huge, collectively owned farms where the land and the output belonged to the state. As reported by the Soviet press, approximately 25 percent of the total value of Soviet agricultural output was raised on that tiny fraction of privately farmed land. This indicates that the output per acre on the private plots was about sixteen times that of the state-owned farms.[18]

---

18. To learn more about the private sector's impressive contribution to total agricultural production in the Soviet Union, see J. W. Pauw, "The Private Sector in Soviet Agriculture," *Slavic Review* 28, no. 1 (1969): 63–71, at https://doi.org/10.2307 /2493038.

Third, private ownership makes owners legally responsible for damages they impose on others. Courts of law recognize and enforce the authority granted by ownership, but they also enforce the responsibility that goes with that authority. Private ownership links control with responsibility. This link provides owners with a strong incentive to use their property responsibly and to take steps to reduce the likelihood of harming others and their property.

Consider the following examples: The owner of a dying tree has an incentive to cut it down before it falls and damages a neighbor's house. Dog owners have an incentive to leash or restrain their dogs if they are likely to bite. Car owners will be held accountable if, say, poorly maintained brakes cause damage to someone else's person or property. A chemical company is legally liable for damages if chemicals are mishandled and harm others.

Fourth, private ownership promotes resource conservation as well as wise development. Using a resource may generate revenue, which reflects the desires of present consumers who want what the resources can provide. But future consumers, too, have a voice, thanks to property rights.

An owner of a resource, say a woodlot or small forest whose trees could be harvested now or later, faces a decision. Will the timber be more valuable today or in the future? In other words, will the expected value of the trees be greater when mature or if logged today? And will that future value exceed their present value now by more than the cost of holding and protecting them for future use? If so, the owner has an incentive to conserve—that is, hold back on current use—to make sure that the resource will be available when it is more valuable.

Private owners will gain by conservation whenever the future value of a resource is expected to exceed its current value. This is true even if the current owner does not expect to be around when the benefits accrue. Suppose a sixty-five-year-old tree farmer plants a crop of Douglas fir trees that typically take fifty years to grow to their optimal harvesting level. Does this elderly tree farmer have an incentive to conserve the trees for future use? With private ownership rights, the answer is "yes." With private ownership, the market value of the farmer's land will increase as the trees mature and the expected day of harvest moves closer. So even though actual logging may not take place until well after the farmer's death, the owner will be able to sell the trees (or the land including the trees) at any time, capturing their increasing value. As long as the growth of the mature trees is expected to increase future revenue as much as alternative investments would, the farmer will gain by conserving the trees for the future.

For centuries pessimists have argued that we are about to run out of trees, critical minerals, and various sources of energy. Again and again, they have been wrong. Why? They fail to recognize the role of private property.

It is instructive to reflect on these doomsday forecasts. In sixteenth-century England fear arose that the supply of wood—widely used as heating fuel—would soon be exhausted. Higher wood prices, however, encouraged conservation and led to the development of coal. The wood crisis soon dissipated.

Even when a specific resource is not owned, the market for other resources that are privately owned can often solve problems. In the middle of the nineteenth century, dire predictions arose that the world was about to run out of whale oil, at the time the primary fuel for artificial lighting. Because there was no private ownership of whales, there was no incentive to conserve them for future use. As the whale population dwindled, the price of whale oil soared. But the higher whale oil prices increased the incentive for entrepreneurs to find and develop substitutes. With time, this led to the discovery of commercially profitable sources of petroleum, the private development of relatively cheaper kerosene, and the end of the whale oil crisis.

Later, as people switched to petroleum, predictions emerged that this resource, too, would be exhausted. In 1891, the U.S. Geological

COMMON SENSE ECONOMICS

Survey concluded that finding oil in Texas was unlikely. In 1926 the Federal Oil Conservation Board estimated that the U.S. supply of oil would last only for another seven years.[19] More recently, a study sponsored by the highly influential Club of Rome warned that the world would run out of oil prior to the end of the twentieth century.[20]

All of these doomsday forecasts and many others have proven to be not only wrong but spectacularly wrong. Why? Private ownership provides the answer. When the scarcity of a privately owned resource increases, the price will rise. The increase in price provides consumers, producers, innovators, and engineers with incentives to (1) conserve on the direct use of the resource; (2) search more diligently for **substitutes**; and (3) develop new methods of discovering and recovering larger amounts of the resource. To date these forces have pushed doomsday ever farther into the future, and there is every reason to believe that they will continue to do so for resources that are privately owned.

Well-defined and enforced property rights are also crucially important for the realization of gains from trade. As discussed in Element 1.4, trade moves goods toward people who value them more and makes greater production possible as the result of gains from specialization and large-scale production methods. A legal system that provides evenhanded enforcement of contracts and protection of property rights reduces the uncertainties accompanying trade. In turn, this results in more trade, thereby expanding both the gains from trade and economic progress.

A legal system that protects property rights and enforces contracts in an evenhanded manner provides the foundation for the mainsprings

19. Predictions cited in Charles Maurice and Charles W. Smithson, *The Doomsday Myth: 10,000 Years of Economic Crises* (Stanford, CA: Hoover Institution Press, 1984), 12.

20. Donella H. Meadows. Dennis L. Meadows, and William W. Behrens, *The Limits to Growth: A Report for the Club of Rome on the Predicament of Mankind* (New York: Universe Books, 1972).

of economic growth: gains from trade, **capital formation**, and re-source development. In contrast, insecure property rights, uncertain enforcement of agreements, and legal favoritism undermine trade, investment, and the productive use of resources. Throughout history people have tried other forms of ownership, such as large-scale cooperatives and government ownership, under both socialism and communism. On any scale beyond the small village with a strong cultural harmony, these experiments have ranged from unsuccessful to disastrous. To date, no institutional arrangement other than private ownership within the framework of the **rule of law** has provided individuals with as much personal freedom and as strong an incentive to serve others by using resources productively and efficiently.

2. Competitive markets: Competition promotes the efficient use of resources and provides the incentive for innovative improvements.

Competition is conducive to the continuous improvements of industrial efficiency. It leads producers to eliminate wastes and cut costs so that they may undersell others. It weeds out those whose costs remain high and thus operates to concentrate production in the hands of those whose costs are low.[21]

—CLAIR WILCOX, FORMER PROFESSOR OF ECONOMICS,
SWARTHMORE COLLEGE

Competition is the lifeblood of a market economy. Competition is present when the market is open and alternative sellers are free to enter.

21. Clair Wilcox, *Competition and Monopoly in American Industry,* monograph no. 21, Temporary National Economic Committee, Investigation of Concentration of Economic Power, 76th Cong., 3d sess. (Washington, DC: U.S. Government Printing Office, 1940).

Rival firms may operate in local, regional, national, or even global markets. The competitive process places pressure on each to operate efficiently and cater to consumer preferences. Competition weeds out inefficient producers. Firms failing to provide consumers with quality goods at attractive prices will experience losses and eventually be driven out of business.

Successful competitors outperform rival firms. They may do so through a variety of methods, including quality of product, style, service, convenience of location, advertising, and price, but they must consistently offer consumers at least as much value relative to the cost of producing that value as is available from rivals.

What keeps McDonald's, Walmart, Amazon, General Motors, or any other business firm from raising prices, selling shoddy products, and providing lousy services? Competition is the answer. If McDonald's fails to provide a tasty sandwich at an attractive price delivered with a smile, people will turn to KFC, Chick-fil-A, Subway, and/or other rivals.

Even the largest firms will lose business to small upstarts that find ways to offer better products at lower prices. For example, when Walmart was nothing more than a few small stores in Arkansas, Sears was a retailing giant. By 2000, Walmart was one of the world's largest retailers, with sales that dwarfed those of Sears. During the last two decades, Amazon has gone from an online bookstore to a giant retailer undercutting Walmart just as Walmart did Sears. Moreover, Amazon cannot rest on its laurels, as there are numerous other retailers seeking to attract its customers. Automobile manufacturing is dominated by large firms, but competition is still intense. Firms as large as Toyota, General Motors, and Ford will lose customers to Tesla, Honda, Hyundai, and other automobile manufacturers if they fall even a step behind in providing the types of vehicles people want at competitive prices.

Competition gives firms a strong incentive to develop better products and discover lower-cost methods of production. No one knows precisely what products consumers will want next or which production techniques will minimize costs per unit. The discovery process of markets provides the answer. Is the online marketplace the greatest retail idea since the shopping mall? Or is it merely another idea that will soon be replaced by something even better? Profits and losses in open, competitive markets will constantly reveal the answer, which will change through time with changing consumer preferences, new technology, and discovery of better ways of doing things.

In a market economy, entrepreneurs are free to innovate. They need only the support of investors (often including themselves) willing to put up the necessary funds. The approval of central planners, a legislative majority, or business rivals is not required. Nonetheless, competition holds entrepreneurs and the investors who support them accountable because their ideas must face a "reality check" imposed by consumers. If consumers value an innovative new product enough to cover its costs, the new business will profit and prosper. But if consumers find that the new product is worth less than its per-unit costs, the business will suffer losses and fail. Consumers become the ultimate judges and jury of business innovation and performance.

When new products are introduced, they generally follow a predictable price-quality pattern. Typically, new products are initially very expensive and purchased by relatively few consumers, mostly those with high incomes. These consumers will pay dearly for the early availability, because during this initial phase, product quality will be low and the price high. These initial purchasers play a vital role: They provide the revenue to cover the product's start-up costs and allow entrepreneurs to acquire experience, improve quality, and reduce per-unit cost in the future. With time, entrepreneurs will figure out how to make the product more affordable and expand its availability to more and more consumers.

Smartphones illustrate this price-quality pattern. When cell phones were initially introduced in the 1980s, they sold for around $4,000, were about the size of a brick, and could not do much of anything other than make calls. With time, their size shrank, their information processing power and functions exploded, and their prices fell. Today, they are available at a fraction of the initial price, and they are viewed as a necessity by many consumers in all income brackets.

Numerous goods, including automobiles, televisions, air conditioners, dishwashers, microwave ovens, and personal computers have gone through this same pattern. All were highly expensive when initially introduced, but entrepreneurs figured out how to produce them more economically and improve their quality, making them more affordable to the overwhelming bulk of consumers. As we reflect on the role of both entrepreneurs and the competitive process, it is important to recognize this pattern of price and quality through time.

Producers who wish to survive in a competitive environment cannot be complacent. Today's successful product may not pass tomorrow's competitive test. In order to succeed in a competitive market, entrepreneurs must be good at anticipating, identifying, and quickly adopting improved ideas.

Competition reveals the business structure and size of the firm that can best keep the per-unit cost of a product low. Unlike other economic systems, a market economy does not mandate the types of firms that are permitted to compete. Any form of business organization is permissible. An owner-operated firm, partnership, corporation, employee-owned firm, consumer cooperative, commune, or any other form of business is free to enter the market. To succeed it must pass only one test: cost-effectiveness. It must produce quality products at attractive prices if it is to profit and succeed. But if its structure results in higher costs than those of other forms of business organization, competition will drive it from the market.

The competitive process will also determine the size of firms in various sectors of the economy. In some sectors—airplane and automobile manufacturing, for example—firms will need to be quite large to take full advantage of economies of scale. A firm producing a few dozen automobiles would have an extremely high per-unit cost; in contrast, when the fixed costs are spread over many thousands of units, the cost of producing each car can plummet. Naturally, consumers will tend to buy from the firms that can produce goods economically and sell them at lower prices. In such industries, small firms will be unable to compete effectively and only large firms will survive.

In other sectors, however, small firms, often organized as individual proprietorships or partnerships, will be more cost-effective. When consumers place a high value on personalized service and individualized products, small firms tend to dominate while large firms struggle. This is generally the case in the markets for legal and medical services, gourmet restaurants, personal services, and specialized printing. Thus, these markets are usually dominated by small firms.

Paradoxical as it may seem, self-interest directed by competition is a powerful force for economic progress. Dynamic competition among products, technologies, organizational methods, and business firms will weed out the inefficient and consistently lead to the discovery and introduction of preferred products and superior technologies. When the new methods improve quality and/or reduce costs, they will grow rapidly, often replacing the old ways of doing things.

History abounds with examples. The automobile replaced the horse and buggy. The supermarket replaced the mom-and-pop grocery store. Fast-food chains like McDonald's and Wendy's largely replaced the local diner. Walmart, Target, and Amazon have grown rapidly while other retailers contracted and firms like Montgomery Ward and Kmart were driven from the market. Personal computers replaced typewriters, and smartphones took the place of less mobile computer devices. Netflix pushed Blockbuster out of business, but its success is now threatened by competitors such as Max and Apple TV+. One could go on and on with similar examples. The great economist Joseph Schumpeter referred to this dynamic competition as "**creative**

destruction," and he argued that it formed the very core of economic progress.

Competition harnesses personal self-interest and puts it to work elevating our society's standard of living. As Adam Smith noted in *The Wealth of Nations*:

> *It is not from the benevolence of the butcher, the brewer, or the baker, that we expect our dinner, but from their regard to their own interest. We address ourselves, not to their humanity but to their self-love, and never talk to them of our own necessities but of their advantages.*[22]

Taken together, private ownership and competitive markets provide the foundation for cooperative behavior and efficient use of resources. When private property rights are clearly defined and enforced, producers face the opportunity cost of their resource use. That is, as we discussed in Part 1, they must provide more value from the resources used or else more cost-effective producers will overwhelm them. The prices in open and competitive markets provide them with a strong incentive to keep costs low, cater to the desires of consumers, and discover superior products and better ways of doing things.

Competition is "pro-consumer"; consumers are the big winners. Competitive markets are not "pro-business." In fact, businesses do not like to face competition, and, instead, they commonly lobby for government policies to protect themselves from it. They will often seek to erect barriers limiting the market entry of potential rivals. As we move on to the analysis of regulation in the next element and the political process in Part 3, examples of businesses' efforts to reduce the competitiveness of markets will arise again and again.

22. Adam Smith, *An Inquiry into the Nature and Causes of the Wealth of Nations,* vol. I, Glasgow Edition (Indianapolis: Liberty Fund, Inc., [1776] 1981): 18. Also available at https://www.adamsmithworks.org/documents/cannan-edition.

3. Minimal regulation: Regulations that increase market competitiveness or support voluntary exchange spur progress.

Government regulation looks like an easy way to achieve various goals, such as lower unemployment, higher wages for low-skilled workers, or removal of low-quality products from a market. However, when we think about what can be achieved with regulation, it is important to keep three points in mind.

First, competition is a great regulator. Open, competitive markets provide individuals and businesses with a strong incentive to supply others with goods and services they value because this is the source of higher income levels. Under these conditions, it is unlikely that regulation will improve the situation.

Second, regulation generates secondary effects that are often wasteful and conflict with intended objectives. In many cases, the secondary effects are directly opposite of the objectives stated by proponents.

Third, regulation reflects the political process, a process that generally favors business and other interest groups that are much better organized than consumers, taxpayers, and the general public. While proponents of regulation often argue they are seeking to achieve some noble objective, the truth is they are almost always seeking to use the political process to gain at the expense of others.

Consider the impact of regulations that restrict entry into markets. Many countries impose regulations that make it difficult to enter and compete in various businesses and occupations. In those countries, if you want to start a business or provide a service, you must acquire a license, fill out forms, get permission from different bureaus, show that you are qualified, indicate that you have sufficient financing, and meet various other regulatory tests. Some officials may refuse your application unless you are willing to provide them with political contributions or pay them a bribe. Often, well-established and politically influential businesses that you would be competing against can successfully oppose your application.

Hernando de Soto, in his revealing book *The Mystery of Capital,* reports that in Lima, Peru, it took 289 days for a team of people working 6 hours a day to meet the regulations required to legally open a small business to produce garments. In an earlier book, *The Other Path,* he revealed that along the way, ten bribes were solicited, and it was necessary to pay two of the requested bribes to get permission to operate legally.[23] The World Bank reports that given the regulations in place in 2019, legally opening a business would take 97 days in Haiti, 99 days in Cambodia, and 230 days in Venezuela. By way of comparison, opening the same business would take only 1 day in New Zealand, 2 days in Hong Kong and Singapore, and 4 days in the United States.[24]

Moreover, when governments impose regulations that restrict market entry, existing businesses will push for additional regulations that will make it more difficult for potential rivals to enter the market. In turn, this reduction in competition will lead to higher prices and larger profits for the favored firms. It will also reduce productivity as businesses spend more time seeking government favors (for example, lobbying political decision-makers) and less time producing goods and services that people value. As a result, consumers are harmed and total output falls below its potential.

Regulations that interfere with voluntary exchange generally reduce the gains from trade, entrepreneurial discovery, and social cooperation. Price controls, mandated activities, and tariffs are examples.

Consider how price controls affect the gains from trade. When the

23. Hernando de Soto, *The Mystery of Capital: Why Capitalism Triumphs in the West and Fails Everywhere Else* (New York: Basic Books, 2006); Hernando de Soto, *The Other Path: The Economic Answer to Terrorism* (New York: Basic Books, 2002).

24. World Bank, *Doing Business Project,* 2015. Available at: https://www.worldbank .org/en/businessready. The World Bank Group ended the *Doing Business Project* in 2020, with the latest report covering 2019 data.

price of a good or service is set above the normal market level, buyers will purchase fewer units than they otherwise would. This reduces the volume of mutually advantageous exchanges, reducing trade. Alternatively, when prices are set below the market level, sellers will cut back on the quantity they are willing to supply, also causing the number of exchanges and the gains from trade to decline. Regardless of whether set above or below the market level, price controls will reduce the volume of trade and the gains from production and exchange.

Minimum wage rates are perhaps the most imposed price control throughout the world. A minimum wage rate establishes a **price floor** that pushes the hourly wage of some workers (and jobs) above the market level. Minimum wages are a hot issue in the United States and, in addition to the federal minimum wage, many cities and states have adopted minimums above the federal level.

Mandating higher wages looks like an easy way to help low-skilled workers, but there are secondary effects. As the basic postulate of economics indicates, a higher minimum wage will mean less employment for low-skilled workers. There is some controversy about the size of the employment reduction, but the weight of the empirical evidence indicates that each 10 percent increase in the minimum wage will reduce the employment of affected workers by between 1 and 3 percent.[25]

There will also be other unintended secondary effects. Employers will take steps to control or compensate for their higher wage costs. These will include fewer training opportunities for low-skilled workers, less convenient work schedules, and smaller fringe benefits. Moreover, the higher minimum wage will increase the earnings of some workers to levels where they lose their eligibility for food, health care, and other transfer benefits, which means their incomes after taxes and transfers

---

25. See David Neumark and William Wascher, *Minimum Wages* (Cambridge, MA: MIT Press, 2008). Also, see David Neumark, "The Econometrics and Economics of the Employment Effects of Minimum Wages: Getting from Known Unknowns to Known Knowns," *German Economic Review* 20 (August 2019): 293–329.

will increase less, and sometimes substantially less, than the increase in the minimum wage.[26]

In essence, a minimum wage prohibits the employment of persons whose **productivity** is less than the minimum—that is, whose output does not justify the payment of the minimum wage. Is this a sound idea? Do we really want to deny persons with productivity less than the minimum wage the opportunity to work at all? This is precisely what minimum wages do.

Supporters of a higher minimum wage in the United States often argue that it will reduce the poverty rate by increasing the income of poor workers. At first glance, this appears to be true, but examination of the data indicates it is highly questionable. There are three major reasons why this is the case.

First, the bulk of minimum wage employees—about 80 percent—are members of households with incomes above the poverty level; one-third live in households with above-average incomes. Half of the minimum wage workers are between the ages of sixteen and twenty-four years and most of them work part-time. Only one out of every seven minimum wage workers (about 15 percent) is the primary earner for a family with at least one child. Thus, the typical minimum wage worker is a single, youthful, part-time secondary worker in a household with an income above the poverty level.

Second, many of the minimum wage workers are also consumers of products impacted by the higher minimum wage. A higher minimum wage will likely raise the prices of goods such as groceries and fast-food meals. These higher prices will, at least partially, offset workers' gains from the higher minimum wage.

Third, more than half of the poor families in the United States do

26. Richard B. McKenzie, "On the Minimum Wage, Both Sides Have Their Economics Wrong," *Regulation,* Summer 2021, https://www.cato.org/regulation/summer -2021/minimum-wage-both-sides-have-their-economics-wrong.

not have anyone in the labor force, and therefore a higher minimum wage will not help them. The data presented here are from government sources and are widely accepted by professional economists.

When we think about the effects of the minimum wage on youthful low-skilled workers, it is important to consider the impact in both the short and long runs. Work experience provides youths with opportunities to develop self-confidence, good work habits, valuable skills, and positive attitudes, making them more valuable to future employers. Unless young people can prove their value to employers and develop on-the-job skills, it is unlikely that they will be able to move up the job ladder and realize higher earnings in the future.

The value of work experience and skill development is widely recognized in the case of college students. Members of Congress provide college students with low-wage employment and even unpaid internships, recognizing this experience helps them develop skills and generate higher future earnings. Ironically, however, these same politicians support minimum wage levels that reduce the on-the-job training opportunities available to less-educated youths. The adverse impact of minimum wages on apprenticeships and other training opportunities for youths with less education is almost always ignored by minimum wage proponents, including the members of Congress who institute them. Nonetheless, this is an important adverse secondary effect of minimum wages.

Many countries also impose other labor market regulations that undermine economic growth. Dismissal regulations are an example. In a number of European countries, employers who want to reduce the size of their workforce must (1) obtain permission from political authorities; (2) notify the dismissed employees months in advance; and (3) continue paying the dismissed employees for several months after they leave.

Such regulations may appear to be in the interests of workers, but the secondary effects must be considered. Regulations that make it costly to dismiss workers also make it costly to hire them; employers will be reluctant to take on additional workers because of the high costs if they turn out to be unsatisfactory or unnecessary workers. As a result, jobseekers, especially entry-level workers, will find it difficult to find jobs, and the overall growth of employment will be slowed. In European countries, where restrictive labor market regulations are more pronounced than in the United States, the unemployment rates of Western European countries such as Italy, Spain, and France have been, on average, 4 or 5 percentage points higher than in the United States during the past couple of decades.[27]

While hiring and dismissal regulations are generally less restrictive in the United States than in Europe, **occupational licensing** is a major labor market restriction in the United States. Most of the occupational licensing occurs at the state level. To obtain licenses, people pay fees ranging from modest to exorbitant, complete training courses for six to twelve months, and pass examinations. As recently as 1970, fewer than 15 percent of Americans worked in jobs that required a license. Today, the figure is nearly 30 percent, and it is continuing to grow. In the mid-1980s, eight hundred occupations were licensed in at least one state; now, according to the Council on Licensure, Enforcement and Regulation, more than eleven hundred occupations are licensed.

The supporters of licensing argue that it is necessary to protect consumers from shoddy and potentially unsafe and unhealthy products. But licenses are required in numerous occupations that have little to do with public safety or protection of the consumer.[28] For example,

---

27. For evidence on this point, see Edward Bierhanzl and James Gwartney, "Regulation, Unions, and Labor Markets," *Regulation,* Summer 1998, 40–53. To compare unemployment rates across countries, see https://data.worldbank.org/indicator/SL .UEM.TOTL.ZS?locations=US-FR-IT-ES.

28. See the Department of Treasury, Office of Economic Policy, *Occupational Licensing: A Framework for Policymakers,* Washington, DC: 2015; Morris M. Kleiner, "Why License a Florist?" *New York Times,* May 28, 2014; Jacob Goldstein, "So You Think You Can Be a Hair Braider?" *New York Times,* June 12, 2012; and Knepper, L., Deyo, D. Sweetland, K. Tiezzi, J. and Mena A., *License to Work 3: A National Study of* "License

one or more states require licenses to work in the following occupations: interior designer, makeup artist, florist, barber, hair braider,
shampoo specialist, dietician, athletic trainer, tour guide, hearing-aid
fitter, casket seller, ferret breeder, and palm reader. The pressure for
licensing seldom originates from consumer groups. Instead, it nearly
always arises from those business owners already in the occupation
who are trying to protect themselves from new competition.

In many of these licensed occupations, individuals could acquire
the skills necessary for high-level performance through on-the-job experience and working with others skilled in the trade. The licensing
requirements prohibit persons from developing their skills via these
methods and pursuing their desired career. Licensing, particularly
when it mandates lengthy formal training and levies expensive fees,
reduces supply and drives up the price of the goods and services provided by the licensed practitioners. Those currently in the occupation
gain at the expense of consumers and unlicensed potential producers.

An alternative to licensing is **certification**. With certification, the government can require suppliers to provide information about their education, training, and other qualifications to consumers without prohibiting
anyone from working in his or her chosen field. In essence, certification
makes information about the suppliers' qualifications readily available to
consumers but does not restrict their choices. Further, it allows practitioners to develop and demonstrate their competence, while still providing information consumers can use to make informed choices.

Regulation is a breeding ground for cronyism, political favoritism,
and even corruption. Proponents of regulations restricting competition often use health and safety protection to obfuscate their real mo-
tivations. For example, thirty-five states and Washington, D.C., have
Certificate of Need regulations. These rules require those who want to

to Work: A National Study of Burdens from Occupational Licensing," ([Arlington, VA]:
Institute for Justice, Nov 2022). Available at: https://ij.org/report/license-to-work-3/.

start new hospitals, clinics, and other health-care facilities to convince state boards or commissions that current providers cannot supply the quantity of health services demanded. Existing firms are permitted to argue that this is not the case. Similarly, regulations prohibit American consumers from purchasing prescription drugs from Canadian sellers even if the same drug is priced lower in Canada. Regulations of this type undermine both market competition and the confidence of citizens in the political process.

To the uninformed, regulation often looks like an easy way to solve problems. Want higher wages? Increase the minimum wage. Want a lower unemployment rate? Pass laws making it harder to fire workers. Want higher earnings in an occupation? Restrict the entry of those job seekers willing to work for lower wages. But these simplistic policies do not enhance production and they ignore the secondary effects. As we have pointed out, mutually advantageous trade and competitive markets encourage low-cost production and discovery of better ways of doing things. They encourage us to obtain more value from our resources. Thus, regulatory policies that impose roadblocks against trade and entry into markets will almost always be counterproductive. If a country is going to grow and prosper, it should minimize regulations of this type.

4. Efficient capital markets: To realize its potential, a nation must have a mechanism that channels capital into wealth-creating projects.

While consumption is the goal of all production, providing consumer goods may require using resources to build machines, heavy equipment, and buildings, which are then used to produce the desired consumer goods. Productive investment increases future consumption. Thus, **capital investment**—the construction and development of long-lasting resources designed to help produce more in the future—is an important source of economic growth. For example, the purchase of an oven by a local pizzeria will help enlarge its future output. Similarly, the purchase of additional trucks helps firms like Amazon deliver more goods more rapidly.

Resources (such as labor, land, and entrepreneurship) used to produce these **investment goods** will be unavailable to produce consumer goods. If we consume all that we produce, no resources are available for investment. Therefore, investment requires **saving**—a reduction in current consumption to make the funds available for alternative uses. Someone, either the investor or someone willing to supply funds to the investor, must save to finance investment. Saving is an integral part of the investment process.

Not all investment activities, however, are productive. An investment will enhance the wealth of a nation only if the value of the additional output from the investment exceeds the cost. When it does not, the project is counterproductive and reduces wealth. Investments can never be made with perfect foresight, so even the most promising investment projects will sometimes fail to enhance wealth.

To make the most of its potential for economic progress, a nation must have mechanisms that attract savings and channel them into investments that create wealth. In a market economy, the **capital market** performs this function. The capital market, when defined broadly, includes the markets for stocks, bonds, and real estate. Financial institutions such as stock exchanges, banks, insurance companies, mutual funds, and investment firms play important roles in the operation of the wealth-enhancing capital market.

Private investors, such as small business owners, corporate stockholders, and **venture capitalists** place their own funds at risk in the capital market. Investors will sometimes make mistakes; sometimes they will undertake projects that prove to be unprofitable. If investors were unwilling to take such chances, many new ideas would go untested and many worthwhile but risky projects would not be undertaken.

Consider the roles of entrepreneurship, risk-taking, and the capital market in the development of internet services. In the mid-1990s, Sergey Brin and Larry Page were graduate students at Stanford University, working on a research project designed to make finding things on the internet easier. They might have seemed unlikely candidates for entrepreneurial success. But in 1998, Brin and Page founded Google, a business that provides free internet services while generating revenues through advertising. Their powerful internet search engine increases the productivity of millions of individuals and businesses each second. Consequently, they have earned a fortune by making Google a household name and by employing about 180,000 full-time individuals worldwide in 2023. Other internet-based companies, such as eBay and Amazon, were entrepreneurial ventures that also earned profits and achieved growth and success.

But the experience of numerous other firms was quite different. Many "dot-coms," like Broadband Sports and eVineyard, went bust because their revenues did not sufficiently cover costs. The high hopes of these firms did not materialize. They failed.

In a world of uncertainty, mistaken investments are a necessary price that must be paid for fruitful innovations in new technologies and products. Such counterproductive projects, however, must be recognized and brought to a halt. In a market economy, the capital market performs this function. If a business continuously experiences losses, eventually investors will terminate the project, stop wasting their money, and turn elsewhere.

Given the pace of change and the diversity of entrepreneurial talent, the knowledge required for sound decision-making about the allocation of capital is far beyond the scope of any single individual. More important, it is beyond the ability of any government agency. Without a private capital market, there is no mechanism that can consistently channel investment funds into wealth-creating projects and out of counterproductive ones. Why?

When investment funds are allocated by the government, rather than by the market, an entirely different set of factors comes into play. Political influence rather than potential market returns determine which projects are undertaken. Investment projects that reduce rather than create wealth become far more likely.

The experiences of the centrally planned socialist economies during the Soviet era illustrate this point. For four decades (1950–1990), the investment rates in these countries were among the highest in the world. Central planners channeled approximately one-third of the national output into capital investment. These high rates of investment, however, did little to improve living standards, because political rather than economic considerations determined which projects were funded. Resources were often wasted on projects with high costs or favored by leaders who wanted high-visibility and prestigious investments. Misdirection of investment and failure to keep up with dynamic change eventually led to the demise of socialism in most of the Soviet countries.

The U.S. experience with political allocation of capital is similar. The housing market illustrates this point. The Federal National Mortgage Association and Federal Home Loan Mortgage Corporation, commonly known as Fannie Mae and Freddie Mac, were chartered by Congress as government-sponsored corporations in 1938 and 1970, respectively. Because of their government sponsorship, Fannie Mae and Freddie Mac borrowed funds at about half of a percentage point less than private firms. This gave them a huge advantage. By the mid-1990s, Fannie Mae and Freddie Mac held approximately 40 percent of all home mortgages. Moreover, during 1998–2008, these government-sponsored enterprises purchased more than 80 percent of the mortgages sold by banks and other mortgage originators.

Beginning in the 1990s, Congress forced Fannie Mae and Freddie Mac to extend a larger and larger share of their loans to low- and middle-income borrowers. How did this political allocation of capital work out? To meet the congressional mandates, Fannie Mae and Freddie

Mac loosened lending standards. They began extending loans with little or no down payment, lending funds to borrowers with poor credit records, and permitting people to borrow larger amounts relative to their income and the price of the house purchased.

As the mortgage lending standards eroded and loose credit became more readily available, the initial effects were positive. The demand for housing increased, housing prices soared during 2001–2005, and the construction industry boomed. By midyear 2006, however, housing prices leveled off and soon many who borrowed beyond their means stopped making payments. Mortgage defaults soared, foreclosures expanded, and the financial turmoil led to the severe **recession** of 2008–2009. By the summer of 2008, Fannie Mae and Freddie Mac were insolvent, and the American taxpayer was left with approximately $400 billion of bad debt.

When governments are heavily involved, allocation of investment is inevitably characterized by favoritism, conflict of interest, inappropriate financial relations, and various forms of corruption. When actions of this type occur in other countries, they are often referred to as **crony capitalism**. Historically, the government has played a larger role in the allocation of investment in other countries than in the United States, but the American experience with government allocation of investment funds for housing illustrates that crony capitalism occurs in the United States as well. Regardless of the label, political allocation of capital imposes a heavy cost on citizens.

5. *Monetary stability: A monetary policy that ensures money of stable and predictable value will promote the efficient use of resources.*

Money emerged as a human invention to facilitate trades and reduce transaction costs. Modern money is merely paper or electronic digits indicating funds in a financial account. While neither paper nor digital money has any intrinsic value, almost everyone wants more of it. Have you ever wondered why?

Money performs three important functions that make it valuable. First, money is a medium of exchange. It provides a common denominator that makes it easier for people to exchange goods, services, and resources. Second, money serves as a store of value. It makes it possible for people to shift purchasing power to the future and conduct exchanges across time periods. Third, it provides a unit of account that makes it possible for people to keep track of benefits and costs. By performing these three functions, money increases the gains from trade and facilitates investments that make larger outputs possible.

Money's contribution to the economy is directly related to the stability of its value. In this respect, money is to an economy what language is to communication. Without words understood clearly by both speaker and listener, communication is difficult. So it is with money. If money does not have a stable and predictable value through time, borrowers and lenders find it difficult to arrive at mutually agreeable terms for loans, saving and investing involve additional risks, and uncertainty escalates. All of this makes transactions that extend over time less likely. When the value of money is unstable, many potentially beneficial exchanges do not occur, reducing output, income, and investment.

When the money supply is constant or increases at a slow, steady rate (similar to the growth of output), the purchasing power of money will be relatively stable. In contrast, when the supply of money expands rapidly compared to the output of goods and services, the general level of prices will rise.

An increase in the general level of prices is known as **inflation**. It is important to note that inflation is not merely an increase in the price of a few items such as gasoline, meat, and air travel. It is a general increase in prices across a large bundle of goods and services.

How is inflation measured? The **consumer price index** (CPI) is the most widely used measure of inflation. The CPI reflects the cost of purchasing the bundle of goods and services consumed by the typical household. When, on average, prices rise, the cost of purchasing this bundle increases, pushing the CPI upward by a proportional amount. The CPI is reported monthly, and the annual inflation rate is merely the percent increase in the index during the past twelve months. Of course, as prices rise, the purchasing power of money declines, reducing the quantity of goods and services households can buy with their income. Thus, inflation can also be thought of as a decline in the purchasing power of money.

The primary cause of inflation is rapid growth in the supply of money. The **money supply**, narrowly defined, is the total of the nation's currency plus checking deposits held by individuals and businesses. A broader definition of money would include savings deposits held at financial institutions, in addition to currency and checking deposits.[29]

When the supply of money expands more rapidly than the output of goods and services, prices rise and the purchasing power of each unit of money declines. Countries that persistently expand the supply of money more rapidly than the growth of output experience inflation. Historically, this linkage between rapid growth of the money supply and inflation has been one of the most consistent relationships in all of economics.

Inflation adversely affects income levels and living standards. As noted above, money is to an economy what language is to communication. Prices convey important information. They help a consumer decide whether to purchase a product, and they tell producers whether consumers' purchases are worth what they cost to make. In this way, prices direct decision-makers to produce goods and services people

29. Since credit cards are a popular means to make payments, students often wonder why credit-card balances are not included in the money supply. The outstanding balance on your credit card is a liability that must be repaid. In contrast, money is an asset. Thus, credit-card balances are not money.

value highly relative to cost. During inflationary periods the prices of some goods will change more rapidly than others. Thus, inflation distorts the information provided by prices.

Moreover, high rates of inflation are nearly always accompanied by large and erratic fluctuations in the inflation rate. When prices increase 10 percent one year, 5 percent the next year, 15 percent the year after that, and so on, activities that depend on accurate identification of the value of money over time, such as investing, involve greater risk. Unexpected changes in the inflation rate can generate misleading information and quickly turn apparently productive projects into counterproductive investments and personal economic disasters. Rather than dealing with these additional risks, many entrepreneurs and investors will simply forgo capital investments and other transactions involving long-term commitments. As a result, gains from investment and other business activities will be undermined and output will fall short of its potential.

The central bank controls the money supply. The central bank of the United States is the Federal Reserve Bank, often referred to as the Fed. The Fed is responsible for the control of the money supply of the United States. The Fed is legally required to pursue the twin goals of price stability and full employment. When Fed policies achieve price stability, they reduce uncertainty and provide the foundation for full employment.

How can Fed policy best achieve price stability? In recent years, the Fed has generally adopted an inflation target, promising to keep the inflation rate in the range between 0 and 2 percent. The inflation target provides the Fed with clear signals for the conduct of **monetary policy**. If the rate of inflation rises above the 2 percent upper limit, this is a signal for the Fed to shift to a more restrictive monetary policy. Correspondingly, if the inflation rate falls below the 0 limit, this signals the need to shift to a more expansionary policy.

However, inflation targeting is tricky. It requires knowledge of inflation, actual output, and potential output. Some economists believe that rather than targeting the inflation rate, it would be better for the

Fed to target **nominal GDP growth**—the sum of **real GDP** growth and inflation. Suppose the Fed adopted a 5 percent target for nominal GDP growth. If nominal GDP growth was greater than 5 percent, the Fed would shift toward a more restrictive policy. In contrast, if nominal GDP growth fell below the 5 percent target, the Fed would be more expansionary. The long-term annual real growth of the U.S. economy has averaged approximately 3 percent. Thus, 5 percent growth of nominal GDP would keep the inflation rate low—in the 2 percent range.

Exhibit 5 shows the relationship between the growth rate of the money supply (using the broad definition, called M2) and the inflation rate during 2000–2022. Both are measured as a twelve-month moving average, which is merely the percent change during the past twelve months. Because a few quarters generally elapse before a shift in monetary policy affects prices, the inflation rate data are lagged by twelve months. During the period 2000–2019, the growth rate of the money supply grew at an average of 6 percent and remained between 3 percent and 10 percent throughout this period. This growth rate of the money supply was accompanied by an average inflation rate of 2 percent.[30] Except for the period just prior to and during the Great

30. During 2010–2019, interest rates were exceedingly low. As a result, the monetary authorities were able to expand the money supply a little more rapidly than the growth of output without causing inflation. Low interest rates reduce the opportunity cost of holding money, and therefore people are willing to hold larger money balances and the turnover rate of money is lower. The turnover rate (economists call this velocity) is the number of times a unit of money is used to purchase goods and services. During the past fifteen years, demographic factors have pushed interest rates downward. In high-income countries, the share of population in the younger age categories (for example, less than age forty), in which people are generally net borrowers, has declined, while the share in older age categories, where people are generally net lenders (for example, ages fifty to seventy-five), has increased. This change has reduced the demand and increased the supply of money, pushing interest rates downward throughout the world. In turn, the lower interest rates have caused the turnover rate of money to decline, making it possible for the monetary authorities to expand the money supply a little more rapidly without causing inflation. This factor contributed to the low inflation rates during 2010–2019, as shown in Exhibit 5.

Recession (2008–09), the inflation rate generally ranged between 0 and 3 percent. Thus, when the growth of the money supply was in the single digits, the inflation rate was low, near the Fed's 2 percent target.

Exhibit 5: Money Growth and the Inflation Rate:
Twelve-Month Percentage Change in M2 and Lagged CPI

Money growth and the inflation rate: twelve-month percentage change in M2 and lagged CPI
Sources: Federal Reserve Bank of St. Louis, *M2 [M2SL]*, retrieved from FRED, Federal Reserve Bank of St. Louis; https://fred.stlouisfed.org/series/M2SL; and Federal Reserve Bank of St. Louis, *Consumer Price Index for All Urban Consumers: All Items in U.S. City Average [CPIAUCSL]*, retrieved from FRED, Federal Reserve Bank of St. Louis, https://fred.stlouisfed.org/series/CPIAUCSL; both retrieved July 5, 2022.

During 2020–2022, however, the money growth rate soared. In 2020 it was 25 percent and it continued to grow in the 12 percent range during 2021. These money growth rates were far greater than the growth of real output (nominal GDP adjusted for inflation). Just as theory predicts, soon after the surge in money growth, the inflation rate soared, reaching 9 percent during the first half of 2022. Seeking to combat the high inflation, the Fed shifted to a more restrictive policy in 2022. The Fed is trying to bring the inflation under control without causing a recession, but historically, shifts to monetary restriction to combat inflation have often led to recessions. Would this be the case in 2022–2023? By the time you read this passage, the answer to this question will have been observable.

The inflationary monetary expansion of 2020–2022 is not the only time Fed policy has caused inflation. During World War II, the Fed expanded the supply of money rapidly to finance the war effort. This led to inflation both during and immediately after the war. Similarly, during the 1970s, the Fed ratcheted the money supply upward to higher and higher rates. By the end of the decade, inflation was rising at a double-digit rate.

While excessive monetary expansion is the primary cause of inflation, monetary contraction often leads to economic instability in the form of deflation and recessions. For example, the Fed permitted the money supply to fall by 30 percent during 1929–1933. In 1937, the Fed again contracted the money supply, leading to the recession of 1938. Many economists believe that the huge 1929–1933 contraction in the money supply was the primary cause of the Great Depression.[31] There were other contributing factors, including the large tariff increases of 1930 and the huge 1932 increase in income tax rates. However, even if perverse monetary policy was not the primary cause, it was certainly a major contributor to the severity and length of the Great Depression. More recently, the Fed reduced the growth rate of the money supply during 1980–1982 to bring the double-digit inflation of the 1970s under control. This reduction in the growth rate of the money supply led to the severe recession of 1982.

Historically, monetary instability has been a major cause of economic disturbances. Why has this been the case? At various times, several different factors have played a role, but two deserve special mention. First, monetary policymakers often confront strong political pressures to finance government spending with money creation. Politicians do not like to levy taxes, because this imposes a visible cost

31. For additional details on the role of monetary policy during the Great Depression, see Milton Friedman, *Capitalism and Freedom* (Chicago: University of Chicago Press, 1962), chap. 3, "The Control of Money."

on voters. Thus, politicians will often pressure monetary policymakers to finance spending increases by expanding the money supply so they will not have to raise taxes. Second, as previously mentioned, there is a time lag of six to eighteen months between a shift in monetary policy and the time when the change exerts an impact on output and employment. Sometimes the time lag will be even longer. Therefore, when policymakers constantly shift policies in an effort to minimize economic instability, the lengthy and unpredictable time lags will result in monetary policy errors that increase rather than reduce economic instability.

It is difficult to overstate the importance of monetary and price stability. While monetary stability does not guarantee growth and prosperity, without it, strong growth and economic stability will be impossible. If investors and other business decision-makers can count on monetary policymakers to maintain price stability, a potential source of uncertainty is eliminated. When monetary policymakers follow policies that keep the inflation rate low and relatively steady, they have done their part to establish the monetary framework for economic growth and prosperity.

6. Low tax rates: People produce more when they can keep more of what they earn.

> *Taxes are paid in the sweat of every man who labors. . . . If those taxes are excessive, they are reflected in idle factories, in tax-sold farms, and in hordes of hungry people tramping the streets and seeking jobs in vain.*[32]
>
> —FRANKLIN D. ROOSEVELT

When high tax rates take a large share of income, the incentive to work and use resources productively declines. The **marginal tax rate** is

32. Franklin D. Roosevelt, *Campaign Address on the Federal Budget at Pittsburgh, Pennsylvania, October 19, 1932.* The American Presidency Project, managed by Gerhard Peters and John T. Woolley, https://www.presidency.ucsb.edu/node/289322.

particularly important. The marginal tax rate is the share of additional income that is taxed away at any given income level. For example, if your marginal tax rate is 25 percent, taxes take 25 percent of any additional funds you earn. You can keep only $75 if you earn an additional $100. If the marginal tax rate rises to 40 percent, you can keep only $60 out of a $100 increase in earnings. As marginal tax rates increase, the share of additional earnings that people take home declines.

There are three reasons why high marginal tax rates reduce output and income. First, they discourage work effort. When marginal tax rates soar to 55 or 60 percent, individuals take home less than half of their additional earnings. Some people will respond by working fewer hours, retiring earlier, or taking jobs in places with lower tax rates or with longer vacations. Some, perhaps people with working spouses, will respond by leaving the labor force. Still others will be more particular about accepting jobs when unemployed, refuse to move to take a job or to gain a pay raise, or forget about pursuing that promising but risky business venture; given the high tax rate, it just may not be worth the trouble. High tax rates can even drive a nation's most productive citizens to other countries with lower tax rates. Such responses reduce the size and productivity of the workforce, causing output to decline.

Of course, most people will not immediately quit work or even work less diligently if their marginal tax rate rises. A person with years of training for a particular occupation will probably continue working—and working hard—especially if that person is in the peak earning years of life. But many younger people who have not already made costly investments in specialized training will be discouraged from doing so because they will get less and less advantage from more income. Thus, some of the negative effects of high tax rates on work effort will be felt in the future, because as young people get older, they will not be as productive as they otherwise would be.

High tax rates will also cause some people to shift to activities in which they are less productive. For example, high taxes drive up the costs of skilled painters, because they want to make up for the diminishing value of extra pay. Some people will respond by painting their own houses even though they lack the skill to do so efficiently. Without high tax rates, the professional painter would do the job at an affordable cost, allowing homeowner painters to focus their time on work for which they are better suited. Waste and economic inefficiency result from these tax-distorted incentives.

Second, high marginal tax rates reduce both the level and efficiency of capital formation. High tax rates repel foreign investment and cause domestic investors to search for investment projects abroad in countries where both taxes and production costs are lower. This reduces investment and the availability of productive equipment, which provide the fuel for economic growth. As a result, the growth of workers' productivity and earnings in the future will be lower.

Third, high marginal tax rates encourage individuals to consume tax-deductible goods in place of nondeductible goods, even though the nondeductible goods may be more desirable. Often they do this by purchasing items for their business, because business expenses are generally tax-deductible. Individuals who purchase them do not bear their full cost, because the expenditure reduces the taxes they would otherwise pay. Taxpayers confronting high marginal tax rates will spend more money on such tax-deductible items as plush offices, extravagant conferences, business entertainment, and company-provided automobiles. Because such tax-deductible expenditures reduce their taxes, people will often buy goods they would not buy if they were paying the full cost. Waste and inefficiency are by-products of high marginal tax rates and the perverse incentives they generate.

The sales of the British-made luxury car Rolls-Royce in the 1970s provide a vivid illustration of this point. During this era, the marginal income tax rates imposed on those with the highest incomes in the United Kingdom soared to 98 percent. A business owner paying that tax rate could buy a car as a tax-deductible business expense, so why not buy an exotic, more expensive car? The purchase would reduce the owner's profit by the car's price—say £100,000. However, given the 98 percent marginal tax rate, the £100,000 tax deduction would reduce the owner's tax liability by £98,000. Thus, the owner's net cost of the luxury automobile was only £2,000. In effect, the government was paying 98 percent of the car's costs (through lost tax revenue). When the UK cut the top marginal tax rate to 70 percent, the sales of Rolls-Royces plummeted. After the rate reduction, the £100,000 car now cost the business owner not £2,000 but £30,000. The lower marginal rates made it much more expensive for wealthy Brits to purchase Rolls-Royces, and they responded by purchasing fewer of them.

Reductions in tax rates, particularly high rates, can increase the incentive to earn and improve the efficiency of resource use. The United States has had three major reductions in tax rates: the rate reductions during the 1920s in the aftermath of World War I, the Kennedy tax cuts of the 1960s, and the Reagan tax cuts of the 1980s. All were followed by strong and lengthy expansions in real GDP (output adjusted for inflation).

In contrast, large tax increases can exert a disastrous impact on the economy. The tax policy during the Great Depression illustrates this point. Seeking to reduce the federal **budget deficit** in 1932, the Republican Hoover administration and the Democratic Congress passed the largest peacetime tax rate increase in the history of the United States. The lowest marginal tax rate on **personal income** was raised from 1.5 percent to 4 percent. At the top of the income scale, the highest marginal tax rate was raised from 25 percent to 63 percent. Essentially, personal income tax rates were more than doubled in one year! This huge tax increase reduced the after-tax income of households and the incentive to earn, consume, save, and invest. The results were catastrophic. In 1932, real output fell by 13 percent, the largest single-year decline during the Great Depression era. Unemployment rose from 15.9 percent in 1931 to 23.6 percent in 1932.

Just four years later, the Roosevelt administration increased taxes again, pushing the top marginal rate to 79 percent in 1936. Thus, during the latter half of the 1930s, high earners were permitted to keep only 21 cents of each additional dollar earned. (Note: It is interesting to contrast the words of candidate Roosevelt presented at the top of this element with the tax policy followed during his presidency.) Several other factors, including a huge contraction in the money supply and a large increase in tariff rates, contributed to both the severity and length of the Great Depression. But it is also clear that the tax increases of both the Hoover and Roosevelt administrations played a major role in this tragic chapter of American history.[33]

The disincentive effects of high marginal tax rates are not just an issue for those with high earnings. Many people with relatively low incomes also face high implicit marginal tax rates. We call them "implicit" because they include both additional taxes and the loss of transfer benefits as income increases. For example, suppose that an individual's income increases from $20,000 to $30,000 and, as a result, income and payroll taxes take 30 percent of the additional earnings. Further, because of this increase in income, the individual loses $5,000 in benefits from food supplements, Medicaid, and other transfer programs. As a result, the individual confronts an implicit marginal tax rate of 80 percent! Thirty percent comes in the form of a higher tax bill, and an additional 50 percent comes from lost transfer benefits.

People in this position who earn an additional $10,000 get to keep only 20 percent of it. Obviously, this will substantially reduce their incentive to earn and make it more difficult to move up the income ladder. We will return to this issue in Part 3, Element 3.8, when examining the impact of transfer programs on the poverty rate.

---

33. For additional information on taxes and other dimensions of economic policy during the Great Depression era, see the supplementary reading "Lessons from the Great Depression," available on the *CSE* website: https://commonsenseeconomics .com/lessons-from-the-great-depression-courtesy-of-cengage/.

In summary, economic analysis indicates that high tax rates, including implicit rates reflecting the loss of transfer benefits, are detrimental. They reduce productive activity, impede both employment and investment, and promote wasteful use of resources. They are an obstacle to prosperity and the growth of income. Moreover, large increases in tax rates during a period of negative or anemic growth can exert a disastrous impact. Thus, if we are going to get the most from our resources, tax rates, particularly marginal tax rates, need to be kept low.

7. Free trade: People achieve higher incomes when they are free to trade with individuals in other countries.

> *Free trade consists simply in letting people buy and sell as they want to buy and sell. Protective tariffs are as much applications of force as are blockading squadrons, and their objective is the same—to prevent trade. The difference between the two is that blockading squadrons are a means whereby nations seek to prevent their enemies from trading; protective tariffs are a means whereby nations attempt to prevent their own people from trading.*[34]

—HENRY GEORGE, NINETEENTH-CENTURY POLITICAL ECONOMIST

The principles involved in international trade are basically the same as those underlying any voluntary exchange. As is the case with domestic trade, international trade makes it possible for each of the trading partners to produce and consume more goods and services than otherwise possible. There are three reasons why this is so.

34. Henry George, *Protection or Free Trade* (New York: Robert Schalkenbach Foundation, 1980).

First, the people of each nation benefit if they can acquire a product or service through trade more cheaply than they can produce it domestically. Resources differ substantially across countries. Goods costly to produce in one country may be economical to produce in another. For example, countries with warm, moist climates, such as Brazil and Colombia, find it advantageous to specialize in coffee production. People in Canada and Australia, where land is abundant and population sparse, tend to specialize in land-intensive products such as feed grains, beef, and sheep. The citizens of Japan, where land is scarce and the labor force highly skilled, specialize in manufacturing such items as cameras, automobiles, and electronic products. Trade permits each of the trading partners to use more of their resources to produce and sell things they generate at a low cost rather than have them tied up producing those things involving a high cost. As a result of this specialization and trade, total output increases, investment expands, and people in each country achieve a higher standard of living than would otherwise be attainable.

Second, international trade allows domestic producers and consumers to benefit from the economies of scale typical of many large operations. This point is particularly important for small countries. For example, trade helps textile manufacturers in countries like Costa Rica, Guatemala, Thailand, and Vietnam enjoy the benefits of large-scale production. If they were unable to sell abroad, their costs per unit would be much higher because their domestic textile markets are too small to support large, low-cost firms in this industry. International trade enables textile firms in these countries to produce and sell large quantities and compete effectively in the world market.

Consumers, too, benefit by purchasing from large-scale producers abroad. Given the huge design and engineering costs of large jet engine airplanes today, for example, no country has a domestic market large enough to permit even a single airplane manufacturer to realize fully the economies of large-scale production. With international trade, however, Boeing and Airbus can sell many more planes, each at a lower cost. As a result, consumers in every nation can fly in planes purchased economically from such large-scale producers.

Third, international trade allows consumers to purchase a wider variety of products at lower prices. Competition from abroad keeps domestic producers on their toes. It forces them to improve the quality of their products and keep costs down. At the same time, the variety of goods available from abroad provides consumers with a much greater array of choices than would be available without international trade.

Governments often impose regulations that restrain international trade. These can be tariffs (taxes on imported goods), quotas (limits on the amount imported), **exchange rate** controls (artificially holding down the **foreign exchange** value of the domestic currency to discourage **imports** and encourage **exports**), or bureaucratic regulations on importers or exporters. All such trade restrictions increase transaction costs and reduce the gains from exchange. As Henry George noted in the quote at the beginning of this section, trade restraints act like a military blockade that a nation imposes on its own people.

Is the United States a free trade country? Many Americans think it is, but that is not entirely true. The United States imposes tariffs of 10 percent or higher on more than one thousand product categories, including apparel, footwear, light trucks, and steel. The United States also imposes quotas on dairy products, sugar, ethanol, cotton, beef, canned tuna, and tobacco. Imports above the quotas are subject to prohibitively high tariffs. In addition, procedures imposed in the aftermath of September 11, 2001, continue to make it both costlier and more time-consuming to clear goods through U.S. Customs.

Noneconomists often argue that import restrictions can create jobs. As we discussed in Part 1, Element 1.11, it is production of value that really matters, not jobs. If jobs were the key to high incomes, we could easily create as many as we wanted. All of us could work one day digging holes and the next day filling them up. We would all be employed, but we would also be exceedingly poor because such jobs would not generate goods and services that people value.

Import restrictions may appear to expand employment because the industries protected from foreign competition may increase in size or at least remain steady. This does not mean, however, that the restrictions expand *total* employment. Remember the secondary effects discussed in Part 1, Element 1.9. When Americans erect tariffs, quotas, and other barriers limiting the ability of foreigners to sell in the United States, they are simultaneously reducing foreigners' ability to buy from Americans. What we buy from people in other countries gives them the purchasing power they need to buy our exports. If foreigners sell less to Americans, they will have fewer of the dollars required to buy from Americans. Thus, import restrictions will indirectly reduce exports, not just imports. Output and employment in export industries will decline, offsetting any jobs "saved" in the protected industries.[35]

Trade restrictions neither create nor destroy jobs; they reshuffle them. The restrictions artificially direct workers and other resources toward the production of things that we produce at a higher cost than others do; they are designed to protect inefficient industries. Output and employment shrink in areas where our resources are more productive—areas where our firms could compete successfully in the world market if not for the impact of the restrictions. Thus, labor and other resources are shifted away from areas of relatively high productivity and moved into areas of low productivity. Such policies reduce both the output and income levels of Americans.

---

35. Many of the "job savers" act as if foreigners are willing to supply us with goods without ever using their acquired dollars to purchase things from us. But this is not the case. People in other countries who export products to us don't want our money; they want what the money can buy. Otherwise, we could just print the dollars we send them to get their goods as cheaply as possible, without fear of inflation, because the dollars would not come back to buy things in our market. But most of the dollars do come back in the form of foreign purchases. Thus, our purchases from foreigners— our imports—generate the demand for our exports.

Some Americans claim that U.S. workers cannot compete with foreigners who sometimes make as little as $2 or $3 per day. This view is wrong and stems from a misunderstanding of both the source of high wages and the law of comparative advantage. Workers in the United States are well educated, possess high skill levels, and work with large amounts of capital equipment. These factors contribute to their high productivity, which is the source of their high wages. In low-wage countries like Mexico and China, wages are low precisely because productivity is low.

Each country will always have some things that it does relatively better than others. Both high- and low-wage countries can benefit from using more of their resources to produce what they do comparatively well—and trade for the rest. If a high-wage country can import a product from foreign producers at a lower cost than it can be produced domestically, importing makes sense. Importing products that are supplied domestically only at high costs frees resources to produce those things that we do well and can supply at a low cost.[36] Trade across nations allows workers in both high- and low-wage countries to produce a larger output than would otherwise be possible. In turn, the higher level of productivity boosts wages across countries.

What if foreign producers were able to provide consumers with a good so cheaply that domestic producers were unable to compete? The sensible thing would be to accept the good and use domestic resources to produce other things. Remember, it is availability of goods and services, not jobs, that determines our living standards. The French economist Frédéric Bastiat dramatically highlighted this point in his 1845 satire "A Petition on Behalf of the Candlestick Makers." The petition was supposedly written to the French Chamber of Deputies by

36. The same logic applies to "outsourcing," undertaking certain activities abroad to reduce cost. If an activity can be handled at a lower cost abroad, doing so will release domestic resources that can be employed in more-productive activities. As a result, output will be larger and income levels higher.

French producers of candles, lanterns, and other products providing indoor lighting. The petition complained that domestic suppliers of lighting were "suffering from the ruinous competition of a foreign rival who apparently works under conditions so superior to our own for production of light that he is flooding the domestic market with it at an incredibly low price; for the moment he appears, our sales cease, all the consumers turn to him, and a branch of the French industry whose ramifications are innumerable is all at once reduced to complete stagnation."

Of course, this rival is the sun, and the petitioners are requesting that the deputies pass a law requiring the closing of windows, blinds, and other openings so that sunlight cannot enter buildings. The petition goes on to list the occupations in the lighting industry that would experience a large increase in employment if using the sun for indoor lighting was outlawed. Bastiat's point in this satire is clear: As silly as the proposed legislation in the petition is, it is no sillier than legislation that reduces the availability of low-cost goods and services to "save" domestic producers and promote employment.[37]

If trade restrictions reduce output and shift employment toward less-productive activities, why are they often adopted? Economic illiteracy provides part of the answer. People often fail to recognize that the trade restrictions cause adverse secondary effects, including higher prices for goods with tariffs and reductions in output and employment in export industries. However, two additional factors contribute to the popularity of trade restrictions.

First, trade restrictions are a special interest issue: They provide benefits to specific businesses and employees in the protected industry at the expense of consumers and suppliers in other industries.

---

37. An abridged version of Frédéric Bastiat's "Competition with the Sun" is available on the *CSE* website: https://commonsenseeconomics.com/supplementals-unfair -competition-bastiat.

Typically, the businesses and unions helped by the trade restrictions are well organized, and their gains are concentrated and highly visible, while consumers, other workers, and other resource suppliers are generally poorly organized and their gains from international trade widely dispersed. Predictably, the organized interests will have more political clout. They will be able to lobby politicians and provide them with campaign contributions and other resources to obtain the trade restrictions.

Furthermore, when products such as steel or lumber are available at lower prices from foreign producers, the adverse impacts on workers who lose their jobs are easy to see. In contrast, the gains to consumers and others helped by the lower prices and freer trade are much less visible. As a result, politicians will often be able to gain politically by supporting the businesses and labor interests benefiting from the restrictions even though they adversely impact the economy as a whole.

Second, politicians may also use trade restrictions in an effort to get a trading partner to behave in a desired manner, particularly in foreign policy. Of course, trade is mutually advantageous, and therefore trade restrictions will impose harm on both trading partners. If the harm is substantial, the restrictions might be used as a tool with which to alter their behavior. For example, the Trump administration imposed tariffs on China to persuade Chinese leaders to be less aggressive militarily. To a large degree, the Biden administration continued with the same policy. Similarly, NATO and other countries imposed various trade restrictions on Russia to punish it for its invasion of Ukraine.

Imposition of trade restrictions against a foreign threat is often popular, but its effectiveness is questionable. Historically, it is difficult to find even a single case where trade restrictions have reduced the threat of conflict and war. Moreover, there is reason to exercise caution in this area. Commerce and the accompanying social interaction can help to promote understanding and break down barriers among trading partners. In contrast, trade barriers often lead to conflict and increased hostility. Frédéric Bastiat is purported to have stated, "When goods don't cross borders, soldiers will."[38]

In recent years, hostility toward international trade appears to be growing in several high-income countries, including the United States. History indicates that this is a dangerous trend. As the economy slowed in the late 1920s, a similar hostility toward trade developed. This led to the passage of the **Smoot-Hawley trade bill** in midyear 1930. This legislation increased tariffs by more than 50 percent on approximately thirty-two hundred imported products. President Herbert Hoover, Senator Reed Smoot, Congressman Willis Hawley, and other proponents of the bill thought higher tariffs would stimulate the economy and save jobs. As Hawley put it, "I want to see American workers employed producing American goods for American consumption."[39]

Today, supporters of trade restrictions in the United States use virtually these same words. The rhetoric sounds great, but the experience of the 1930s indicates that the results are dramatically different. Foreigners responded to the higher tariffs by imposing trade restrictions on American products. International trade plunged and so did output. By 1932 the volume of U.S. trade had fallen to less than half the level prior to the Smoot-Hawley bill. Gains from trade were lost, the tariff revenues of the federal government actually fell, output and employment plummeted, and the unemployment rate soared. Unemployment stood at 7.8 percent when the bill was passed, but it ballooned to 23.6 percent just two years later. The stock market, which had regained al-

38. While Bastiat is often credited with this statement, it cannot be found in his published writings. The nineteenth-century writer Otto T. Mallery made the following similar statement in his *Economic Union and Enduring Peace*: "If soldiers are not to cross international boundaries, goods must do so. Unless the Shackles can be dropped from trade, bombs will be dropped from the sky." For additional details, see Nicholas Snow, "If Goods Don't Cross Borders . . . ," Foundation for Economic Education, October 26, 2010, https://fee.org/resources/if-goods-dont-cross-borders/.

39. As quoted in Frank Whitson Fetter, "Congressional Tariff Theory," *American Economic Review* 23 (September 1933): 413–27.

most all of the October 1929 losses prior to passage of Smoot-Hawley, plunged following its adoption.

More than a thousand economists signed an open letter to President Hoover warning of the harmful effects of Smoot-Hawley, pleading with him not to sign the legislation. He rejected their pleas, but history confirmed the validity of their warnings. Other factors, such as the sharp contraction in the money supply and the huge tax increases of both 1932 and 1936, contributed to the Great Depression. But the Smoot-Hawley trade bill was also a major cause of the tragic events of that era.[40]

Americans will be able to achieve more rapid growth and higher income levels when they trade freely with people in other countries. Restrictions on trade may be good politics, but they are bad economics. Moreover, as the experience of the 1930s illustrates, uninformed political rhetoric and hostility toward trade can lead to catastrophic results.

How Important Are Institutions and Policies?

Economic theory indicates that the seven elements outlined in this part of the book will exert a positive impact on the performance of economies. How big an impact? To answer this question, a measure of institutional quality is needed. In the mid-1980s, the Fraser Institute of Vancouver, Canada, began work on a project designed to develop a cross-country measure of economic freedom. Several leading scholars, including Nobel laureates Milton Friedman, Gary Becker, and Douglass North, participated in the endeavor. The result was the Economic

40. For additional information on the impact of the Smoot-Hawley legislation and other dimensions of economic policy during the Great Depression era, see supplementary reading, "Lessons from the Great Depression," available on the *CSE* website: https://commonsenseeconomics.com/lessons-from-the-great-depression-courtesy-of -cengage/.

Freedom of the World (EFW) index.[41] Now published by a worldwide network of institutes in more than 90 countries, this index measures the extent to which a country's institutions and policies are consistent with economic freedom—that is, with personal choice, private ownership, voluntary exchange, and competitive markets.

The EFW measure uses forty-two separate components to derive ratings in five major areas: size of government, protection of property rights and enforcement of contracts, access to sound money, international exchange, and regulation of credit, labor, and business. Summary ratings on a 0–10 ten scale are available for 123 countries throughout 2000–2019.

To a large degree, the EFW index reflects the seven key elements outlined earlier in this book. To achieve a high EFW rating, a country must provide secure protection of privately owned property, evenhanded enforcement of contracts, and a stable monetary environment. It also must keep taxes low, refrain from creating barriers that deter either domestic or international trade, and rely more fully on markets than government expenditures and regulations to allocate products and resources.

Some might perceive that the EFW index is a measure of "capitalism" at one end of the spectrum and "socialism" at the other. Because these terms are ambiguous, meaning different things to different people, we seldom use them. Strictly speaking, **socialism** implies government ownership of the primary means of production. However, some also use socialism to refer to systems in countries like Denmark, Finland, and Sweden, which have a high level of government expenditures. But a close investigation of these Scandinavian countries reveals each is also characterized by private ownership, free trade, minimal regulation of business, and widespread use of markets. These attributes

41. For additional details, see James Gwartney, Robert Lawson, Joshua Hall, and Ryan Murphy, *Economic Freedom of the World: 2022 Annual Report* (Vancouver: Fraser Institute, 2022); and the website https://www.fraserinstitute.org/economic-freedom.

are virtually the opposite of socialism. The economic organization of Scandinavian countries is vastly different from that of Venezuela, Cuba, North Korea, and China, socialist countries with government ownership in many sectors of the economy.

Similarly, **capitalism** is often a term used to refer to economies that differ substantially in the degree of regulation, price controls, trade restrictions, and security of property rights. In place of such ambiguous terms as "capitalism" and "socialism," the EFW index provides a more accurate measure of the degree to which countries rely on personal choice, voluntary exchange, and market-determined prices, rather than on political decision-making and central planning to allocate available resources and to guide investments.

If the institutional and policy factors outlined here are important, countries with persistently high EFW ratings will achieve better economic outcomes than those countries with persistently low EFW ratings. Let's see if this is the case.

Exhibit 6 presents data on the 2019 per capita income and its growth for the ten countries with the highest and lowest EFW ratings during 2000–2019. Among the 123 countries and jurisdictions for which the EFW data were available over these two decades, the following countries rise to the top of the list of persistently free economies: Hong Kong, Singapore, Switzerland, New Zealand, and the United States. At the other end of the spectrum, Algeria, Republic of Congo, Democratic Republic of the Congo, Myanmar, and Venezuela are at the bottom as the least-free economies.

How do income and growth compare? The average per capita income of the ten most-free economies was $62,476, nearly 14 times the figure ($4,520) for the ten least-free economies. Not only did the ten most-free economies have a substantially higher income level, they also grew more rapidly. The growth rate of per capita GDP of the ten most-free economies averaged 1.7 percent annually during 2000–2019, compared to 1.41 percent for the ten least-free economies.

Exhibit 6

	EFW Rating, 2000–2019	GDP Per Capita 2019, PPP (Purchasing Power Parity) (Constant 2017 International $)	Growth Rate of GDP Per Capita 2000–2019, PPP (Percent, Constant 2017 International $)
10 Highest Rated Countries			
Hong Kong SAR, China	8.94	$59,586	2.64%
Singapore	8.73	$98,412	3.00%
Switzerland	8.54	$70,920	0.94%
New Zealand	8.45	$42,878	1.41%
United States	8.36	$62,631	1.18%
United Kingdom	8.29	$46,406	1.02%
Canada	8.21	$49,007	1.46%
Ireland	8.15	$87,786	3.16%
Australia	8.15	$49,456	1.35%
Denmark	8.08	$57,678	0.87%
Average		$62,476	1.70%
10 Lowest Rated Countries			
Gabon	5.52	$14,950	−0.54%
Niger	5.47	$1,225	1.44%
Central African Republic	5.26	$945	−0.50%
Chad	5.24	$1,580	3.02%
Guinea-Bissau	5.22	$1,939	0.63%
Congo, Democratic Republic	5.07	$1,098	2.02%
Algeria	5.03	$11,511	1.48%
Myanmar	4.79	$5,083	8.42%
Congo, Republic	4.72	$3,843	−0.71%
Zimbabwe	4.47	$3,028	−1.13%
Average		$4,520	1.41%

Sources: J. Bolt and J. van Zanden, "Maddison Style Estimates of the Evolution of the World Economy: A New 2020 Update," Groningen Growth and Development Center, October 2020, https://www.rug.nl/ggdc/historicaldevelopment/maddison /publications/wp15.pdf?lang=en; Gwartney et al., *Economic Freedom of the World: 2021 Annual Report* (Vancouver: Fraser Institute, 2021), https://www.fraserinstitute .org/studies/economic-freedom-of-the-world-2021-annual-report; and World Bank, *World Development Indicators* (2022), https://databank.worldbank.org/source/world -development-indicators.

Exhibits 7a and 7b break the 123 countries into quartiles or four equal groups, arrayed from low to high by their EFW ratings. The 31 countries with the highest average economic freedom rating over the period comprise the top quartile; the 31 with the next highest average ratings make up the next quartile, and so on. The average income level and growth rates for each of the four groups are expressed in terms of a common currency, the 2017 U.S. dollar.

The same pattern emerges in Exhibit 7 as that present in Exhibit 6. The freer economies among the 123 countries both achieve higher per

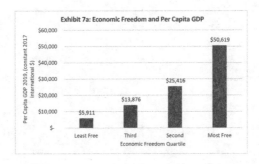

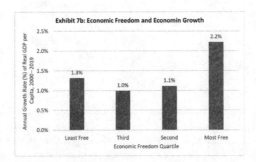

Sources: World Bank, *World Development Indicators* (2022); and Gwartney et al., *Economic Freedom of the World: 2021 Annual Report* (Vancouver: Fraser Institute, 2021).
Note: The growth data were adjusted to control for the change in economic freedom during the period and the initial level of income.

capita income levels and grow more rapidly. The most-free countries had an average 2019 per capita income of $50,619, more than eight times the $5,911 average for the least-free countries. Note the strong positive relationship between economic freedom and per capita GDP across quartiles. Although the figures of Exhibit 7 are not adjusted for other factors that might influence per capita income, more detailed statistical analysis indicates that the strong positive relationship between persistently high levels of economic freedom and income remain after adjustment for other major factors that might influence income levels. Similarly, as Exhibit 7b shows, the average annual growth rate of the top group was 2.2 percent, compared to 1.3 percent for the bottom group. Note the average growth rates of the three least-free quartiles were similar, but all were substantially less than the average for the top quartile.

Some argue that market economies leave the poor behind. So how did the poverty rates in the more-free economies compare with the rate in countries with less economic freedom? The World Bank provides data on extreme and moderate poverty rates. The **extreme poverty rate** is the percentage of the population with an income of less than $2.15 per day, whereas the **moderate poverty rate** is the share of the population with an income of less than $3.65 per day (measured in 2011 international dollars).

Exhibit 8 provides data for both the extreme and moderate poverty rates in 2019, according to economic freedom quartiles arranged from lowest to highest. Clearly, the poverty rates were much lower in the freer economies. The extreme poverty rate in 2019 was 34.1 percent for the least-free economies, but only 0.9 percent in those that were most free. Correspondingly, the moderate poverty rate was 53.2 for the least-free quartile, compared to only 2.0 percent in the most-free quartile. The two middle quartiles had both extreme and moderate poverty rates between those of the least- and most-free economies.

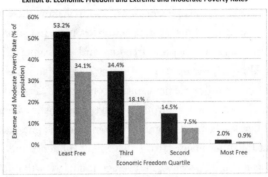

Exhibit 8: Economic Freedom and Extreme and Moderate Poverty Rates

Source: Gwartney et al., *Economic Freedom of the World: 2021 Annual Report* (Vancouver: Fraser Institute, 2021).

Moreover, more detailed analysis indicates that countries moving toward more economic freedom achieved larger poverty rate reductions than did those that were less free. These relationships held even after adjustments for geographic and locational factors, receipt of foreign aid, and political institutions.[42]

It is evident from these data that economic performance is much better in more-free countries. But let's also consider the impact of economic freedom on some broader indicators of quality of life, such as life expectancy and environmental quality.

Exhibit 9 presents the World Bank's life expectancy figures for the countries in the quartile groups. People living in countries with more economic freedom live longer. On average, the life expectancy of persons living in the most economically free quartile of countries was 81.1 years, compared to only 65.9 years for persons living in the least-free quartile of countries. Thus, people living in the freest economies enjoy more than 15 additional years of life relative to those in the least-free quartile.

42. See Joseph Connors, *Global Poverty: The Role of Economic Freedom, Democracy, and Foreign Aid* (PhD diss., Florida State University, 2011).

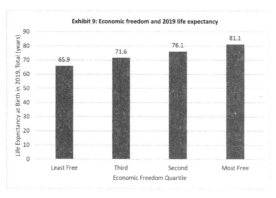

Source: Gwartney et al., *Economic Freedom of the World: 2021 Annual Report* (Vancouver: Fraser Institute, 2021).

What impact does economic freedom have on the environment? The Yale Center for Environmental Law & Policy publishes a comprehensive Environmental Performance Index (EPI) for 180 countries. This index rates the quality and performance of countries in a broad set of environmental areas. The scale of this index ranges from 0 to 100, with higher figures indicating greater environmental quality. Exhibit 10 shows the average EPI score of countries for the economic freedom quartile groups. The average EPI for the most economically free quartile was 73.7, compared to 62.7 for the second-freest quartile, and 52.8 and 45.0 for the two least-free groups. These figures show that there is a strong positive relationship between economic freedom and the quality of the environment. To a large degree, the demand for a cleaner environment increases with income. Therefore, as economic freedom increases per capita income, it also increases the demand for environmental quality. Thus, the positive relationship between economic freedom and the quality of the environment is an expected result.

Does economic freedom guarantee that a country will be able to achieve high income levels? Can a country with little economic freedom nonetheless achieve a high per capita GDP? Examination of

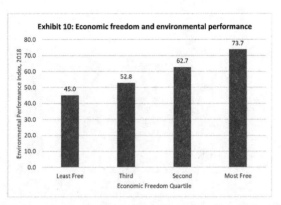

Exhibit 10: Economic freedom and environmental performance

Sources: Gwartney et al., *Economic Freedom of the World: 2021 Annual Report* (Vancouver: Fraser Institute, 2021); and Z. Wendling et al., *The 2018 Environmental Performance Index Report* (New Haven, CT: Yale Center for Environmental Law and Policy, 2018), https://epi.envirocenter.yale.edu/node/36476.
Note: EPI data are missing for Hong Kong and Syria.

the economic freedom and per capita GDP of the 123 countries with EFW data during 2000–2019 sheds light on both questions. These data indicate that, essentially without exception, countries with persistently high economic freedom ratings grow and achieve high levels of income. Conversely, except for a few of the world's leading oil exporters, no country has been able to achieve a high level of per capita income without having a high degree of economic freedom. This close linkage between economic freedom and high per capita income highlights the importance of economic institutions.[43]

The test of a theory is its ability to predict actual outcomes. Both economic theory and the empirical evidence indicate that countries grow more rapidly, achieve higher income levels, and make more progress against poverty when they adopt and maintain policies along the lines outlined in this section. The freer economies also enjoy more lengthy lives, a cleaner environment, and several other contributors to quality

43. See James Gwartney et al., *Economics: Private and Public Choice,* 17th ed. (Boston: Cengage Learning, 2022), chap. 16, Exhibit 10.

of life. Adoption of institutions and policies supportive of economic freedom is a key ingredient for economic growth and development.

Technology, Trade, Entrepreneurship, and the Remarkable Growth of the Past Half Century[44]

Let us return to the historical pattern we described at the beginning of this part of the book. Look back at Exhibit 4. We saw that there was little change in the per capita income of the world prior to 1800. Most people spent their entire lives in villages and farms only a few miles from their places of birth. They had very little knowledge or contact with those living outside of these small areas. The size of markets was small, gains from trade and capital formation minimal, and per capita income hovered near the subsistence level.

But around 1800, technological improvements and capital formation propelled incomes upward. As Exhibit 4 shows, per capita income in the West (the high-income countries of Western Europe, North America, Oceania, and Japan) grew substantially during the 150 years following the start of the Industrial Revolution around 1800. But the situation did not change that much outside the West. Income levels in the rest of the world remained at or near subsistence levels. As recently as 1950, the per person income of developing countries was approximately $4 per day.

During the past half century, however, there has been a remarkable change. The developing countries have grown rapidly. During the past 50 years, the per person income of developing countries increased by an even larger amount than the income of the high-income countries during the 150 years following the Industrial Revolution.

---

44. For a more in-depth analysis of the pattern of income growth during the last one thousand years, see ibid., chap. 17.

What accounts for the remarkable economic progress of the past half century? A huge reduction in the real cost of transportation and communication provides a large part of the answer. Driven by improvements in technology and entrepreneurship, the cost per ton of ocean shipping declined by more than 50 percent during 1974–2016 (adjusted for inflation). The air freight shipping cost per ton-kilometer declined by an even larger amount during the same period. The standardized steel container and mechanization reduced the cost of loading and unloading ocean freighter cargo from $48 per ton in 1956 to 18 cents in 2006,[45] a reduction of 99 percent. The cost reductions for several forms of communication have been so dramatic they are difficult even to estimate. As recently as 1990, international telephone calls were of uncertain quality and cost several dollars per minute. Today, calls involving both audio and video transmission, including conference calls, can be made over the internet at a small fraction of their cost just a few decades ago.

The sharp reductions in transportation and communication costs led to a substantial increase in international trade, increased gains from entrepreneurial activities, and improved economic institutions. These factors enhanced economic performance throughout the world, but the impact in developing countries was particularly dramatic. During the 1960s, international trade as a share of GDP averaged 19 percent of world output. The share increased steadily in the decades that followed, and by 2010 international trade was approximately 50 percent of world GDP, two and a half times the figure of the 1960s.

The lower transportation and communication costs also resulted in larger gains from entrepreneurship. Businesses and entrepreneurs in developing countries can adopt or access at a low cost the successful

45. Both figures are in 2011 U.S. dollars; see A. Hammond, "Heroes of Progress, Pt. 17: Malcom McLean," *Human Progress,* May 3, 2019, https://humanprogress.org/article .php?p=1905.

technologies and practices present in the more advanced economies. As interaction of people across national boundaries and knowledge of successful practices employed elsewhere expanded, gains from these sources soared.

Even the quality of institutions and policies was affected. Reductions in transportation and communication costs provide potential entrepreneurs and investors with greater flexibility and expand the range of country options for locating their business activities. In turn, this increases the incentive of political decision-makers to adopt sound institutions and policies. Thus, in addition to their more direct impacts on the volume of trade and entrepreneurship, lower transportation and communication costs generated positive secondary effects: enhancement of the incentives to remove trade barriers and improve the legal system. As restrictions declined, the quality of the legal system of **less-developed countries** improved.

Some developing countries have grown far more rapidly than others, and some have lagged well behind. Geographic factors, particularly climate and location, have contributed to this variation in economic growth. Jeffrey Sachs of Columbia University has been at the forefront of those arguing that geographic factors, such as people living in hot, humid climates located far from the major markets of Europe, North America, and Asia and having limited access to an ocean coastline, face major economic disadvantages.[46] Hot and humid tropical climatic conditions erode the energy level of workers and increase the risk of disabling and life-threatening diseases such as malaria and yellow fever. Locations distant from the world's major markets make trade more costly and reduce the availability of potential trading partners. Limited access to ocean shipping, particularly when

---

46. See Jeffrey D. Sachs, "Tropical Underdevelopment" (National Bureau of Economic Research Working Paper No. w8119, 2001); and John Luke Gallup, Jeffrey D. Sachs, and Andrew D. Mellinger, "Geography and Environment" (National Bureau of Economic Research Working Paper No. w6849, 1998).

a country is landlocked, further reduces the attractiveness of a country for conducting business and the location of productive activities.

Climate, proximity to world markets, and access to ocean shipping matter. Developing countries with favorable climate conditions and locations closer to the world's major markets have benefited substantially from the sharp reductions in transportation and communication costs. Their trade sectors have grown rapidly and per person income levels have increased substantially. In contrast, countries with hot, disease-prone climates located far from major markets have benefited much less. Predictably, those countries with larger geographic disadvantages have both smaller increases in trade and slower economic growth. Sub-Saharan African countries dominate the list of the world's most geographically disadvantaged countries. Thus, it is not surprising that the growth of per person income in this region has lagged behind that of other developing countries. See Exhibit 4.

During the past half century, the huge reductions in transportation and communication costs and the accompanying growth of international trade have enabled the world to expand production and achieve substantially higher income levels. The change was so dramatic that this period, which began around 1970, may properly be thought of as the Transportation-Communication Revolution. There is widespread recognition of the economic progress that accompanied the Industrial Revolution. In many ways, the Transportation-Communication Revolution of the past half century is even more remarkable. The impact of the former is widely recognized. It is time for the more recent economic revolution to be acknowledged as well.

Conclusion

Part 2 of this book began with the remarkable effects of two revolutions. First, there was the Industrial Revolution, which spurred dramatic economic growth in a group of countries, primarily in Europe. More recently, what we call the Transportation-Communication Revolution spread progress throughout the world by expanding trade and international relationships. Can the economic progress of the past half century be maintained?

Compared to the past, we now have better knowledge and stronger evidence about the types of economic institutions and policies that enhance human progress. However, having knowledge about what works does not mean that sound institutions will necessarily be adopted. Institutions and policies are outgrowths of the political process. Thus, if we want to understand the development of economic institutions, we need to examine the operation of the political process. This will be the focal point of Part 3.

PART 3

*Ten Key Elements of the
Economics of Government*

TEN KEY ELEMENTS OF THE ECONOMICS OF GOVERNMENT

1. Government promotes economic progress by protecting the rights of individuals and supplying a few goods that are difficult to provide through markets.

2. Monopolies and high barriers to entry can prevent markets from achieving ideal efficiency.

3. Public goods and externalities create incentives that encourage inefficiency and waste of resources.

4. Allocation through political voting is fundamentally different from market allocation.

5. Unless restrained by constitutional rules, special-interest groups will use the democratic political process to obtain government favors at the expense of others.

6. Unless restrained by constitutional rules, legislators will run budget deficits and spend excessively.

7. When governments become heavily involved in providing favors to some at the expense of others, inefficiency results and improper, unethical relationships develop.

8. The net gain of transfer recipients is less, and often substantially less, than the amount they receive.

9. The economy is far too complex to be centrally planned, and efforts to do so will result in inefficiency and cronyism.

10. Decentralization can reduce the threat of the abusive exercise of power by central government leaders, increase competitiveness among levels of government, and improve economic efficiency.

Introduction

Economists use the standard of economic efficiency to assess the operation of an economy. When resources are used efficiently, only actions that yield more benefits than costs are undertaken. No action will be undertaken that costs more than it is worth. Put simply, **economic efficiency** means getting the most value from the available resources.

Courses in economics generally explain why markets will fail to achieve ideal efficiency for certain categories of activity and highlight what the government might do to improve the situation. Here we follow this convention: We analyze why markets may fail and consider the potential of idealized political action, but we also apply the tools of economics to the operation of the political process.

Government expenditures now constitute a large share of **national income** in the United States and many other countries. Given the size and scope of this political allocation, understanding how it works is vitally important. Part 3 will use the basic principles of economics to analyze how the political process works, why it will sometimes lead to counterproductive actions, and what might be done to improve its operation. Economists use the term **public choice** when referring to this area of study.[47] Public choice has become an integral part of economics during the past half century.

Democratic governments often use taxes and borrowing to provide transfers, subsidies, and other forms of favoritism to some individuals and businesses. We will analyze this process and explain why the impact of these programs is different, and often substantially different, than most believe. We hope our approach challenges you to think more seriously about the potential and limitations of the political process and what might be done to improve its operation.

1. Government promotes economic progress by protecting the rights of individuals and supplying a few goods that are difficult to provide through markets.

> A wise and frugal government, which shall restrain men from injuring one another, which shall leave them otherwise free to regulate their own pursuits of industry and improvements, and shall not take from the mouth of labor the bread it has earned. This is the sum of good government.[48]
>
> —Thomas Jefferson

Governments play a vitally important economic role. Governments can promote social cooperation and enhance the welfare of the citizenry through the performance of two major functions: (1) the protective function, which provides people with protection for their lives, liberties, and properties; and (2) the productive function, which supplies a

47. James Buchanan was awarded the 1986 Nobel Prize in Economics for his role in the development of public-choice economics. For a clear and comprehensive presentation of public-choice analysis, see Randy Simmons, *Beyond Politics: The Roots of Government Failure* (Oakland, CA: Independent Institute, 2011).

48. Thomas Jefferson, First Inaugural Address, March 4, 1801.

few select goods that have unusual characteristics that make them difficult to provide through markets.

The **protective function** refers to the government's maintenance of
a framework of security and order, including the enforcement of rules
against theft, fraud, and violence. Governments are granted a **monopoly** on the legitimate use of force to protect citizens from each other
and from outsiders. Thus the "protective state" seeks to prevent individuals from harming one another and maintains an infrastructure
of rules that allows people to interact with one another cooperatively
and harmoniously. A legal system that protects individuals and their
property from aggressors, enforces contracts in an unbiased manner,
and provides equal treatment under the law (see Part 2, Element 2.1)
forms the core of this protective function of government.

The protective function is crucially important for the smooth operation of markets. When the government clearly defines and enforces
property rights, market prices will reflect the opportunity cost of resources (discussed in Part 1, Element 1.2), and producers will be
directed to produce the goods and services that are most highly valued by consumers compared to their cost. Moreover, if contracts are
enforced in a way that is efficient and without favoritism, transaction
costs will be low and the volume of trade enlarged. When people and
their property are protected, citizens can have confidence that they
will not be cheated and that the wealth they create will not be taken
from them—by either selfish intruders or by the government itself.
This protection provides citizens with assurance that if they sow, they
will be permitted to reap. When this is true, people will sow and reap
abundantly, and economic progress will result.

In contrast, when the protective function is performed poorly,
problems will abound. Opportunities to get ahead through deception,
fraud, theft, and political favoritism rather than through production
and trade will emerge. Earnings and wealth will be insecure, and
market prices will fail to register the true cost of supplying goods and

services. Incentives to develop resources will be weak, and economic growth will stagnate. Unfortunately, this is precisely the situation in many poor, less-developed countries.

The second primary function of government, the **productive function**, involves the provision of activities difficult to provide through markets. There is both an indirect and direct component of this productive function. The indirect component involves the creation of an environment for the efficient operation of markets through protection of property rights and stable money. As noted, a legal structure that protects property rights and enforces contracts enhances gains from trade and market efficiency. Similarly, monetary arrangements that provide residents with access to money that has stable purchasing power across time reduces uncertainty and facilitates gains from exchange. The provision of a stable monetary and price environment is one of the most important productive functions of government. As discussed in Part 2, Element 2.5, when governments perform this function well, people will invest more, cooperate more fully through trade, and achieve higher income levels.

Sometimes the productive function of government is more direct. There are some goods for which markets are imperfect because it is difficult to establish a one-to-one relationship between payment for and receipt of the good. For example, national defense benefits all citizens. It is jointly consumed by everyone. It would be virtually impossible to provide some citizens with protection against foreign aggressors without simultaneously providing it to all. If national defense were left to markets, they would likely produce too little defense to be fully protective for everyone. As a result, government provision may improve economic conditions. This issue is considered in more detail in Element 3, to come.

In other cases, it may be very costly to monitor usage and collect payments directly from users. When this is the case, it may be inefficient to provide such goods through markets. Roads, particularly those in cities and towns, provide an example. The cost of collecting fees and thereby charging users directly for their use would be exceedingly high. Thus, it is typically more efficient to make most roads available to all and to finance them through taxation.

As we have stressed throughout, getting the most value from our resources requires that actions be undertaken only when the benefits exceed the costs. This principle applies to government as well as market activity. Unfortunately, when government action involves projects financed with taxes or through borrowing, both benefits and costs are difficult to measure. In the marketplace, the choices of buyers and sellers reveal information about benefits and costs. Consumers will not purchase goods unless they value them more than their price. Similarly, producers will not continue to supply goods unless they can cover their costs. But the information provided by the choices of consumers and producers is lost when the government undertakes an activity and finances it with taxes. There are no buyers spending their own money and thereby revealing information about their benefits. Moreover, the revenues paid to the suppliers were extracted through compulsory taxation, and therefore they provide no assurance that the project is valued more than its cost.

Government planners may try to estimate the benefits and costs, but their estimates, to a large degree, will be guesses, because they lack solid information based on the choices of buyers and sellers. Further, in the real world, such benefit-cost calculations will often be influenced by political considerations.

As the quote from Thomas Jefferson introducing this element indicates, it is vitally important for government to restrain people from imposing harm on others (the government's protective function). Economics also indicates that there is a case for government provision of goods that are difficult to supply through markets (the government's productive function). However, as the government moves beyond these activities, the case for still more government weakens. In order to better evaluate the economic role of both government and markets, it is important to develop a deeper understanding of the limitations of markets by applying the tools of economics to the political process.

2. Monopolies and high barriers to entry can prevent markets from achieving ideal efficiency.

If a society is going to get the most out of its resources, the resources must be used efficiently. Competition is central to this efficient use. As previously discussed, competition provides businesses with strong incentives to cater to the views of consumers and produce goods and services economically. If businesses do not provide consumers with value for the price they pay, customers will spend their money elsewhere.

A monopoly exists when there is only a single producer of a good or service for which there are no good substitutes. When this is the case, the producer has an incentive to restrict output and raise price. By producing a smaller quantity and charging a higher price, the firm may be able to earn more profit than it would if resources were being used more productively by producing a larger quantity at a lower price. Inefficiency will result because the monopolist is failing to provide some goods and services that customers value more than their cost of production.

There are two major sources of monopoly: economies of scale and grants of political favoritism. Economies of scale occur when large firms have lower per-unit costs than their smaller rivals. If economies of scale persist as a firm obtains a larger and larger share of the market, a single firm will dominate and become a monopoly. The production of electricity provides an example. As power plants for the generation of electricity become larger, the per-unit cost of generating electricity generally declines. As a result, there is a tendency for a single, large firm to dominate the market. This is why the government usually regulates the prices charged by electric power companies and, in some cases, owns and operates the power plants.

Even where monopolies do not develop, some industries may have only a few dominant firms, usually because the market is costly to enter. A firm may have to produce a large share of the industry output—for example 20 or 25 percent—to achieve a low per-unit cost and compete effectively. When this is the case, there may be room for only four or five firms, all of which experience low per-unit costs. Such markets tend to be dominated by a small number of firms, which have an incentive to collude, raise prices, and act as a monopolist would. Manufacturing industries, such as those making automobiles, television sets, and computer operating systems, are examples of markets dominated by a relatively small number of firms.

But the government itself is sometimes the source of monopoly. Licensing, taxes that favor one group over another, tariffs, quotas, and other grants of privilege reduce the competitiveness of markets. While some of these policies may be well-intentioned, they protect existing firms at the expense of potential rivals, thereby encouraging monopolies and dominant firms.

What can the government do to ensure that markets are competitive? The first guideline might be borrowed from the medical profession: Do no harm. The government should refrain from intervening in markets and making things worse through licensing requirements, discriminatory taxes, and other forms of political favoritism. In the vast majority of competitive markets, sellers will find it difficult or impossible to limit the entry of rival firms (including rival producers from other countries). This means that suppliers cannot limit competition unless government imposes policies to restrict entry or creates rules and regulations that favor some firms.

To promote competition, governments can also prohibit anticompetitive actions such as collusion, the merger of dominant firms in an industry, and interlocking ownership of firms. In this regard, the

United States has enacted a series of "antitrust" laws, most notably the Sherman Antitrust Act (1890) and the Clayton Act (1914), making attempts to monopolize a market and collusion illegal.

The record of government in this area has been mixed, however. On the one hand, government policies have reduced the incidence of collusion and various practices that limit competition. But occupational licensing, regulatory burdens on small businesses, and other laws have almost the opposite effect; they restrict entry into markets, protect existing producers from rivals, and limit price competition. Thus, while high entry barriers and the absence of competition provide the potential for government to improve market performance, some policies actually grant monopoly powers. As we proceed, the underlying reasons for this anticompetitive policy behavior by governments become more visible.

3. Public goods and externalities create incentives that encourage inefficiency and waste of resources.

As we have stressed, if markets are going to allocate resources efficiently, property rights must be well established and producers must be able to capture the benefits of their productive actions. But the nature of some goods makes this difficult. In this element, two categories of economic activity that pose serious challenges to the efficient allocation of resources through markets are considered. They are public goods and externalities.

Public Goods

The nature of some goods makes it difficult for producers to benefit from their production. This is the case with a category of goods that economists call public goods. **Public goods** possess two charac-teristics: (1) jointness in consumption—that is (as we discussed with national defense), providing the product to one party simultaneously makes it available to others; and (2) nonexcludability—that is, it is difficult to exclude nonpaying customers. For example, like national defense, flood control meets the first criterion. Once flood-control de-vices, like dams or reservoirs, are built, everyone in the region benefits. Flood control also meets the second criterion. The supplier of flood control will have trouble charging people for the service, because if it is provided for one, it is provided to all. Thus, because potential provid-ers are unable to establish a one-to-one relationship between payment for and receipt of the good, it will be difficult to provide public goods through markets.

Consumers will have an incentive to become "free riders"—to con-sume the good without helping to pay for it. And when a large num-ber of people become free riders, the good may not be produced (or too little of it may be produced), even when the value derived from its consumption exceeds the cost. In such cases, markets will often fail to produce a quantity of public goods consistent with economic effi-ciency. Flood control, national defense, municipal police protection, and mosquito abatement are examples of public goods. Because these goods are difficult to supply through markets and cover costs, they are often provided by governments.

It is important to note that it is the characteristic of a good, not the sector in which it is produced, that determines whether it qualifies as a "public good." There is a tendency to think that if a good is provided by the government, then it is a public good. This is not the case. Many of the goods provided by governments clearly do not have the charac-teristics of public goods. Medical services, education, mail delivery, trash collection, and electricity come to mind. Although these goods are often supplied by governments, nonpaying customers could be eas-ily excluded, and providing them to one party does not make them available to others. Thus, even if they are provided by governments, they are not public goods.

Most goods and services are private rather than public goods. In the case of private goods, the link between payment and receipt of the good or service can be easily established. Therefore, most products are supplied through markets. Think about this and its importance. Those individuals who pay for a gallon of ice cream, an entertainment system, a smart device, a pair of jeans, or a house enjoy these items and literally thousands of others. Those who do not pay in the marketplace do not enjoy or consume them. Producers in the marketplace continue to supply the products because the price voluntarily paid by you and other consumers covers the costs; those unwilling to pay the price are excluded from consumption. In the case of private goods, government provision is highly unlikely to improve on the efficiency of the market.

Externalities

Sometimes the actions of an individual or group will "spill over" and exert an impact on others, affecting their well-being without their consent. Such spillover effects are called **externalities**. For example, if you are trying to study and others in your home or apartment complex are distracting you with loud music, they are imposing an externality on you. You are an external party—not directly involved in the transaction, activity, or exchange—but you have been affected by it, detrimentally in this case.

The spillover effects may either impose a cost or create a benefit for external parties. When the spillover effects are harmful, they are called external costs. Because costs are imposed on nonconsenting parties, resources are being used to produce goods that are valued less than their full production costs. Economic inefficiency results.

Consider the production of paper. The firms in the market purchase trees, labor, and other resources to first produce pulp and then paper. The manufacturing process using old technologies may emit pollutants into the atmosphere. These pollutants impose costs on residents living around the mills—a sulfuric smell, heavy smog, and breathing issues or other health hazards.

If the residents living near a pulp mill can prove harm and measure it, they could take the mill to court and force the paper producer to cover the cost of their damages. In fact, to prevent that from happening, nineteenth-century paper companies routinely bought up miles of downstream property to let river water dilute the company's effluent.[49] Often, however, people found proving harm and holding specific pulp mills responsible proved difficult and costly. When this is the case, the total costs of the pollution and other external costs will not be reflected through markets. The cost of producing paper will be understated. Inefficiency occurs because units of paper will be produced that are valued less than the costs of their production when external costs are included.

To a large degree, external costs reflect a lack of fully defined and enforced property rights. Because the property right to a resource—clean air, for example—is poorly enforced, the firm does not pay the full cost of using the resource. Thus, the cost of producing goods and services using such resources is understated.

On the other hand, sometimes spillover effects will generate benefits for others. When the spillover effects enhance others' welfare, they are called external benefits. But external benefits can pose problems for markets, too. When the persons or firms that generate the external benefits are uncompensated, they may fail to produce some units even when they are valued more than their production costs.

For example, suppose a pharmaceutical company develops a vaccine

49. Peter Davis, "Theories of Water Pollution Litigation," *Wisconsin Law Review* 3 (1971): 738–816, at 777–80.

providing protection against a deadly virus. The vaccine can easily be marketed to consumers who will benefit directly from it. However, because of the communal nature of viruses, as more and more people take the vaccine, those who haven't bought the vaccine will also be less likely to catch the virus. Yet it will be very difficult for the pharmaceutical companies to capture the benefits derived by the nonusers. As a result, they may produce too little of the vaccine to provide full immunity for the community. Thus, when external benefits are present, market forces may supply less than the amount consistent with economic efficiency.

Perhaps government action can improve the situation. In the case of external costs such as pollution, the government could tax the activities that generate the pollution, and that might lead the person or firm to abate its harmful activities and achieve an output level more consistent with economic efficiency. Similarly, in the case of external benefits, such as the well-being provided by vaccines, government subsidies might spur production, resulting in a more efficient output level.

The potential adverse consequences of externalities can sometimes be controlled without government, however. Let's consider external benefits. Entrepreneurs have an incentive to figure out ways to capture more fully the gains their actions generate for others. The competitive development of golf courses illustrates this point. Because of the beauty and openness of golf courses, many people find it attractive to live near them. Thus, constructing a golf course typically generates an external benefit—an increase in the value of the nearby property. In response, golf course developers have figured out how to capture this benefit. Now they typically purchase a large tract of land around the planned course before it is built. This lets them resell the land at a higher price after the golf course has been completed and the surrounding land has increased in value. By extending the scope of their activities to include real estate as well as golf course development, they can obtain revenues from what would otherwise be external benefits.

As for external costs, simple rules can sometimes help to control them. For example, with respect to disturbing noise from nearby residents, apartment owners often have rules about playing loud music late at night, and they enforce the rules by fining or expelling violators. Manners and social conventions can also play a role. If your roommates are aware that having the television on interferes with your studying, they may have the good manners to turn it off. More broadly, over time it has become "socially unacceptable" for companies to emit pollution that harms people and their environment. There is increasing pressure for companies to be good citizens—and private watchdogs such as environmental groups will publicize their actions if they behave irresponsibly.

So our analysis indicates that public goods and externalities may undermine the efficient operation of markets. Economists use the term **market failure** to describe such situations wherein the existing structure of incentives creates a conflict between personal self-interest and economic efficiency—getting the most out of the available resources. Such market failure encourages self-interested decision-makers to engage in counterproductive rather than productive activities.

This market failure creates the potential for government action to improve economic efficiency. But the political process is merely an alternative form of economic organization. Like markets, it has strengths and weaknesses. We need to know more about how that form of organization works so that it can be compared realistically with markets.[50] We now turn to that topic.

---

50. A. C. Pigou, whom many consider to be the father of welfare economics, makes this same point. In his 1932 classic *The Economics of Welfare* (pt. II, chap. 20, sec. 4), Pigou stated, "It is not sufficient to contrast the imperfect adjustments of unfettered private enterprise with the best adjustment that economists in their studies can imagine. For we cannot expect that any public authority will attain, or will even wholeheartedly seek, that ideal. Such authorities are liable alike to ignorance, to sectional pressure and to personal corruption by private interest. A loud-voiced part of their constituents, if organised for votes, may easily outweigh the whole."

4. Allocation through political voting is fundamentally different from market allocation.

> *The first lesson of economics is scarcity: there is never enough of anything to fully satisfy all those who want it. The first lesson of politics is to disregard the first lesson of economics.*[51]
>
> —THOMAS SOWELL, ROSE AND MILTON FRIEDMAN SENIOR FELLOW
> ON PUBLIC POLICY AT STANFORD'S HOOVER INSTITUTION

The political process is an alternative form of economic organization. It is not a corrective device that can be counted on to provide a sound remedy when problems arise. Even when it is controlled by elected political officials (as opposed to, say, an autocratic regime), there is no assurance that government actions will be productive. This is particularly true when governments become heavily involved in allocating scarce resources toward favored sectors, businesses, and interest groups. As mentioned in the introduction to Part 3, public-choice analysis provides considerable insight into the operation of democratic political decision-making.

Policies favored by a majority do not always make a society better off. Here's a thought experiment: Consider a simple economy with five voters. Suppose three of the voters favor a project that gives each a net benefit of $2 but imposes a net cost of $5 on each of the other two voters. In aggregate, the project generates net costs of $10 against net benefits of only $6. It is counterproductive and will make the five-person society worse off. Nonetheless, if decided by majority vote, it would pass three to two. As this simple example illustrates, majority voting can clearly lead to counterproductive projects, actions that are harmful to the society.

---

51. Thomas Sowell, BrainyQuote.com, retrieved January 14, 2023, from BrainyQuote .com: brainyquote.com/quotes/quotes/t/thomassowe371242.html.

It is useful to compare markets with democratic political allocation, the major alternative form of economic organization. While making the comparison, keep the following four points in mind:

First, in a democracy, the basis for government action is majority
rule. In contrast, market activity is based on mutual agreement and
voluntary exchange. In a democratic setting, when a majority—either
directly or through their elected representatives—adopts a policy, the
minority is forced to pay for its support even if they strongly disagree.
For example, if the majority votes for a new baseball stadium, housing **subsidy** program, or bailout of an automobile company, minority
voters are forced to yield and pay taxes for support of such projects.
Whether they benefit or not, they pay higher taxes, suffer loss of income, and may be harmed in other ways.

The power to tax and regulate makes it possible for the majority to
coerce the minority. There is no such coercive power when resources
are allocated by markets. Market exchanges do not occur unless all
parties agree. Private firms can charge a high price, but they cannot
force anyone to buy their products. Indeed, private firms must provide
consumers with benefits that exceed the price charged in order to attract customers.

Second, there is little incentive for voters to be well-informed about
either candidates or issues. An individual voter will almost never decide
the outcome of an election. It is more likely that a voter will be struck
by lightning on the way to the polling place than cast a decisive vote in
a large city, congressional, or statewide election! So most voters spend
little, if any, serious time and energy studying issues and candidates to
cast well-informed votes. Economists refer to this as the **rational ignorance effect**. Voters are poorly informed, and their failure to obtain
information is rational because it is a virtual certainty that their individual vote will not determine the winner or decide the issue. The data are
consistent with this view. Surveys indicate that most voters do not even
know the names of their congressional representatives and have little or

no idea where candidates stand on issues or what impact government actions or policies (such as agricultural subsidies and trade restrictions) have on the economy.

In sharp contrast to their political decision-making, consumers in the marketplace individually bear the consequences of their decisions on how to spend their money. If they make unsound choices, they directly experience the impact. That fact gives them the motivation to spend their money wisely. When consumers consider the purchase of an automobile, personal computer, gym membership, or thousands of similar items, they have a strong incentive to acquire information to make informed choices.

Third, the political process generally imposes the same outcome on everyone; in contrast, markets allow for diverse representation. Put another way, government allocation results in a "one size fits all" outcome, while markets allow different individuals and groups to "vote" for and receive their desired options. This can be illustrated with schooling.

In the case of government-operated schools, students are assigned to various schools, usually based on zip codes, and a uniform curriculum is established by state and federal officials. In contrast, when allocated by markets, those willing to pay the price find the option that best fits their preferences. As a result, there is more diversity in their choices. While some parents will choose private schools, others will opt for homeschooling. Some will choose schools that stress religious values, while others will opt for education that emphasizes basic skills, cultural diversity, or vocational preparation. This ability to choose makes it possible for more people to obtain goods and services more consistent with their preferences. Markets also avoid the conflicts that inevitably arise when the majority imposes its will on various minorities.

Fourth, market decision-makers and political decision-makers face different incentives. As previously discussed, the profit-and-loss mechanism of a market economy tends to direct resources toward productive projects and away from counterproductive ones. But the political process does not have a similar mechanism, and thus it cannot be counted on to direct resources toward productive activities. This is true even when political decision-makers are controlled through voting. That is because—unless they are constrained by constitutional limits—elected officials will tend to obtain votes by providing favors to some at the expense of others. As the saying goes, if you take from Peter and give to Paul, you can usually count on the support of Paul.

To a large degree, the modern political process can be viewed as a series of "exchanges" between coalitions and politicians. Concentrated interest groups provide politicians with votes, financial contributions, high-paying jobs in the future, and other forms of support in exchange for subsidies, spending programs, and regulatory favors often financed by taxpayers. The rational ignorance effect—the fact that voters choose not to spend the time required to be well-informed—facilitates this process because most voters are unaware of these "political deals." As a result, resources are moved toward lobbying and other favor-seeking activities and away from production and development of better goods and services.

As explained in Elements 3.2 and 3.3 in this part, economic analysis indicates there are cases where markets will fail to allocate resources efficiently. But this is also true of the political process. Put another way, there is government failure as well as market failure. **Government failure** is present when the incentives confronted by political participants encourage counterproductive rather than productive use of resources. Like market failure, government failure reflects a situation in which there is a conflict between what is best for individual decision-makers and what is the best use of resources.

The framers of the United States Constitution understood that even a democratic government might undertake counterproductive actions. Thus, they incorporated restraints on the economic role of government. They enumerated the permissible taxing and spending powers of the central government (Article I, Section 8) and allocated all other powers to the states and the people (Tenth Amendment). They also prohibited states from adopting legislation "impairing the obligation of contracts" (Article I, Section 10). Furthermore, the Fifth Amendment specifies that private property shall not be "taken for public use without just compensation." Over time, however, Supreme Court decisions eroded these restraints, and government control over both individuals and businesses expanded, as did federal control over the states. The remainder of Part 3 in this book will examine the operation of the democratic political process in more detail and consider modifications that might bring political decision-making into greater harmony with economic growth and prosperity.

5. Unless restrained by constitutional rules, special-interest groups will use the democratic political process to obtain government favors at the expense of others.

Democratically elected officials can often benefit by supporting policies that favor special-interest groups at the expense of the general public. Consider a policy that generates substantial personal gain for the members of a well-organized group (for example, an association representing business interests, members of a labor union, or a farm group) at the expense of the broader interests of taxpayers or consumers. While the organized interest group has fewer members than the total number of taxpayers or consumers, the personal benefits derived by their members from the favored policy are generally large. In contrast, while many taxpayers and consumers are harmed by the policy, the cost imposed on each is small, and the source of the cost is often difficult to identify.

Because the personal stake of the interest-group members is substantial, they have a powerful incentive to form alliances to let candidates and legislators know their position on a particular issue. Many interest-group members will decide whom to vote for and whom to support financially almost exclusively based on a politician's stand on a few issues of special importance to them. In contrast, as the rational ignorance effect illustrates, the bulk of voters will be generally uninformed and they will not care much about the harms from the **special-interest issue**, given its minimal impact on their personal welfare.

If you were a vote-seeking politician, what would you do? Clearly you would not get much campaign support by favoring the interests of the largely uninformed and unorganized majority. But you can get vocal supporters, campaign workers, and, most important, campaign contributions by favoring the position of the special interest. In the age of media politics, politicians are under strong pressure to support special interests, tap them for campaign funds, and use the contributions to project a positive candidate image on television and the internet. Politicians unwilling to play this game—those unwilling to use the government treasury to provide well-organized interest groups with favors in exchange for political support—are seriously disadvantaged. Given these incentives, politicians are led as if by an invisible political hand to reflect the views of special-interest groups, even though this often leads to policies that, summed across all voters, waste resources and reduce our living standards. Economists refer to this bias in the political process as the **special-interest effect**.

The power of special interests is further strengthened by logrolling and pork-barrel legislation. **Logrolling** is the practice of vote trading between politicians to get the necessary support to pass desired legislation. **Pork-barrel legislation** is the bundling of unrelated projects benefiting many interests into a single bill. Both logrolling and pork-barrel legislation often make it possible for counterproductive projects benefiting concentrated interests to gain legislative approval.

Exhibit 11 illustrates how pork-barrel politics and vote-trading reinforce the special-interest effect and lead to the adoption of counterproductive projects. In this simple example, a five-member legislature is considering three projects: (1) a sports stadium in District A; (2) construction of an indoor rainforest in District B; and (3) subsidies for ethanol that generate benefits for the corn farmers of District C. For each district, the net benefit or cost is shown—that is, the benefit to the district minus the tax cost imposed on it. The total cost of each of the three projects exceeds the benefits (as shown by the negative number in the total row at the bottom of the table). Therefore, each is counterproductive.

If these counterproductive projects were voted on separately, each would lose by a four-to-one vote because, for each option, only one district would gain and the other four would lose. However, when the projects are bundled together through either logrolling (representatives A, B, and C could agree to trade votes) or pork-barrel legislation (all three programs could be incorporated into a single bill), they can all pass even though all are inefficient. This can be seen by noting that the total combined net benefit is positive for representatives A, B, and C. Given the weak incentive for voters to acquire information, those harmed by pork-barreling and other special-interest policies (such as D and E, in this case) are unlikely to even be aware of them. Thus, the incentive to support special-interest projects, including those that

Exhibit 11: Trading Votes and Passing Counterproductive Legislation

Net Benefits (+) or Costs (-) to Voters in Equal Size Districts

Voters of District	Sports Stadium	Indoor Rainforest Project	Ethanol Subsidy	Total
A	$100	-$30	-$30	$40
B	-$30	$100	-$30	$40
C	-$30	-$30	$100	$40
D	-$30	-$30	-$30	-$90
E	-$30	-$30	-$30	-$90
Total	-$20	-$20	-$20	-$60

are counterproductive, is even stronger than is implied by the simple numeric example of Exhibit 11.

Market exchange is a win-win, positive-sum activity: Both trading partners expect to gain or the exchange will not occur. In contrast, "political exchange" can be a win-lose, negative-sum activity, wherein the voting majority gains but the minority loses more. Here, there is no assurance that the gains of the winners will exceed the losses imposed on others.

The tendency of the unrestrained political process to favor well-organized groups helps explain the presence of many programs that reduce the size of the economic pie. Consider the case of the roughly twenty thousand American sugar growers. For many years, the price of sugar paid by American consumers has been 50–100 percent higher than the world sugar price because of the federal government's price support program and highly restrictive quotas limiting the import of sugar. As a result of these programs, sugar growers gain about $1.7 billion, or approximately $85,000 per grower. Most of these benefits are captured by large growers whose owners have incomes far above the national average. On the other hand, each year sugar consumers pay between $2.9 billion and $3.5 billion, or approximately $25 per household, in the form of higher sugar prices.[52] As a result, Americans are worse off because their resources are wasted in producing a good we are ill-suited to produce and one that could be obtained at a substantially lower cost through trade.

---

52. See Jared Meyer and Preston Cooper, "Sugar Subsidies Are a Bitter Deal for American Consumers," *Economic Policies for the 21st Century at the Manhattan Institute,* Manhattan Institute, June 23, 2014, https://manhattan.institute/article/sugar-subsidies-are-a-bitter-deal-for-american-consumers. In recent years candy manufacturers and other major users of sugar have been moving to Canada, Mexico, and other countries where sugar can be purchased at the world market price. Illustrating our earlier discussion of trade, the import restrictions that "saved" jobs in the sugar-growing industry caused job losses in other industries, particularly those that use sugar intensely.

Nonetheless, Congress continues to support the sugar program, and it is easy to see why. Given the sizable impact on their personal wealth, it is perfectly sensible for sugar growers, particularly the large ones, to use their wealth and political clout to help politicians who support their interests. This is precisely what they do. During each election cycle, the sugar lobby contributes millions to Democratic and Republican candidates and political-action committees. In addition, the sugar growers spend millions more on lobbying. A single firm, the American Crystal Sugar Company, typically contributes about one-third of the total. In contrast, it would be irrational for the average voter to investigate this issue or give it any significant weight when deciding for whom to vote. In fact, most voters are unaware that this program costs them money. Thus, politicians gain by continuing to subsidize the sugar industry even though the policy wastes resources and reduces the wealth of the nation.

The special-interest effect often leads to counterproductive government action favoring specific industries over consumers. The Merchant Marine Act, popularly known as the Jones Act, provides another example. The Jones Act, passed in 1920, mandates that goods shipped from one American port to another must be transported on ships that were built in the United States, owned by an American firm, and that at least three-fourths of each ship's crew members must be American. But the cost of building modern ocean ships in the United States and operating them primarily with an American crew often doubles or even triples shipping costs. While the Jones Act benefits those in the American shipping industry, it increases the cost of shipping products among American cities, thereby harming American consumers.

Thus, goods that could be transported more economically by water are sent by rail, truck, or air. Moreover, shipments between American cities often are routed via a foreign port in order to evade the Jones Act and realize gains from the lower shipping costs of foreign vessels. For example, shipments to and from Gulf Coast cities like Houston or New Orleans to East Coast cities like New York and Boston are often routed through countries like Jamaica and the Bahamas. Similarly, cruise ships from West Coast cities to Alaska make stops in Canada in order to circumvent the Jones Act. These roundabout routes not only increase cost, they also waste fuel and generate more pollution than would otherwise be the case. The higher shipping costs accompanying the Jones Act are particularly harmful to those living in Alaska and Hawaii because they have few alternatives other than using U.S. ships for obtaining and selling goods. Why isn't this highly inefficient act repealed? The answer is obvious: The concentrated interests in the shipping business have more political clout than the disorganized consumers who are harmed by the legislation.

The primary business of modern politics has become to extract resources from the general public in order to provide favors to well-organized voting blocs in a manner that will create a voting majority. Consider the following: Taxpayers and consumers spend approximately $20 billion annually to support grain, cotton, tobacco, peanut, wool, and dairy programs, all of which have a structure like the sugar program's. The political power of special interests also explains the presence of tariffs and quotas on steel, shoes, textiles, and many other products. Federally funded irrigation projects, banking bailouts, and subsidies to sports stadiums, ethanol producers, and airports in specific districts—the list goes on and on—are all policies politically motivated by the special-interest effect rather than the net benefits to Americans. While each of these programs imposes only a small drag on our economy, together they expand the federal budget, waste resources, and significantly lower our standard of living.

The special-interest effect also tends to stifle innovation and restrict the competitive process. Older, more established businesses with stronger records of political contributions, better knowledge of lobbying techniques, and closer relationships with powerful political figures are, predictably, more mature and have more political clout than new upstarts, entrepreneurs, and family-owned businesses. They will use their influence to deter new rivals and squash innovations that threaten them.

Consider the experience of Uber, which uses technology to bring willing drivers together with potential ground-transportation passengers. Consumers searching for ground transportation request cars via their smart devices, and the Uber app immediately provides a price, wait time, and ride-sharing options. Uber also provides feedback information about drivers to potential passengers and vice versa. The technology reduces transaction costs. The process of getting to and from a location is often faster and cheaper than traditional taxi services. As Uber entered markets in large cities throughout the world, the traditional taxi industry fought hard for and often achieved legislation prohibiting the use of the ride-sharing technology, keeping passengers from getting lower-priced rides and many drivers from earning income.[53] As a result, the gains from the innovative technology and expansion in the volume of exchange were slowed.

The experience of Tesla, an electric car manufacturer, provides another example of existing producers using the political process to deter the entry of a newcomer. Tesla's business model was based on the sale of its autos directly to consumers. But a well-organized interest group, the established auto dealers, lobbied state legislatures demanding that they adopt laws prohibiting manufacturers from selling their cars directly to consumers. Approximately half of the states adopted prohibitions on such direct sales. These laws made it much more difficult for Tesla to enter the auto manufacturing market.

The special-interest effect is a major source of the growth of government and counterproductive political action. Politicians spend significant time catering to interest groups and seeking political con-

53. See Holman W. Jenkins Jr., "How Uber Won the Big Apple," *Wall Street Journal*, July 24, 2015, www.wsj.com/articles/how-uber-won-the-big-apple-1437778176.

tributions, then use the funds to pursue narrow interests rather than society's interests. The relationship between political decision-makers and interest groups is not only a major source of economic inefficiency, it contaminates and weakens political democracy.

The framers of the Constitution of the United States understood the problems arising from the power of special interests. They called the interest groups "factions." The Constitution sought to limit their access to the federal treasury. Article I, Section 8, specifies that Congress is to levy taxes only for programs that promote the common defense and general welfare. For many years, this clause restrained the use of general tax revenues to provide benefits to subgroups of the population at the expense of the general populace. However, through time, court decisions and legislative acts have altered its meaning. Thus, as it is currently interpreted, the Constitution does little to deter the political power of well-organized interest groups.

6. Unless restrained by constitutional rules, legislators will run budget deficits and spend excessively.

> *The attractiveness of financing spending by debt issue to the elected politicians should be obvious. Borrowing allows spending to be made that will yield immediate political payoffs without the incurring of any immediate political cost.*[54]
>
> —JAMES BUCHANAN, 1986 NOBEL LAUREATE

When government's spending exceeds revenues, a budget deficit results. Governments generally issue interest-earning bonds to finance their budget deficits. These bonds comprise the **national debt**. An

54. James Buchanan, *The Deficit and American Democracy* (Memphis, TN: P. K. Steidman Foundation, 1984).

annual budget deficit increases the size of the national debt by the amount of the deficit. In contrast, when government revenues exceed spending, a **budget surplus** is present. This allows the government to pay off bondholders and thereby reduce the size of its outstanding debt. Basically, the national debt represents the cumulative effect of all the prior budget deficits and surpluses.

Prior to 1960 almost everyone—including the leading figures of the major political parties—assumed the U.S. federal government would operate with its budget balanced except perhaps during war. There was widespread implicit agreement—much like a constitutional rule—that the deficits and surpluses relative to the size of the economy would be small.

The Keynesian revolution changed all of this. The English economist John Maynard Keynes (pronounced "canes") developed a theory that provided both an explanation for the length and severity of the Great Depression and a remedy for preventing such events in the future. During the 1940s and 1950s, the Keynesian view swept the economics profession, and it soon dominated the thinking of intellectual and political leaders. According to Keynesian analysis, government spending and budget deficits could be used to promote a more stable economy. Keynesians argued that rather than balancing the budget, the government should run budget deficits during periods of recession and shift toward a budget surplus when there was concern about inflation.

While the effectiveness of Keynesian fiscal policy is a point of controversy, its impact on the federal budget is clear. Freed from the **balanced budget** constraint, politicians have consistently spent more than they were willing to tax. During the sixty-three years between 1960 and 2023, the federal government ran fifty-nine deficits and four surpluses. Exhibit 12 shows the path of the federal deficit measured as a share of GDP during this era. While the deficits have been larger during recessions, perpetual deficits have been the norm. The federal deficit averaged about 2 percent of GDP between 1960 and 1980, and the figure was even larger during the 1980s. The deficits were smaller during the 1990s, and surpluses were even achieved from 1998 to 2000. But the era of deficit control was exceedingly short. The surpluses quickly evaporated, and deficits soared to new highs, reaching 10 percent of GDP during the recession of 2008–2009 and spiking to 15 percent during the pandemic of 2020–2021.

Deficits push the national debt upward. Largest budget deficits will even increase the debt as a share of GDP. Measured as a share of GDP, the outstanding federal debt rose from 58 percent in 2000 to 70 percent in 2008, before soaring to 135 percent in 2021. The federal debt as a share of GDP remains historically high.

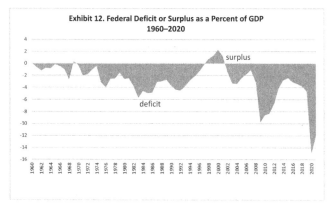

Source: U.S. Office of Management and Budget and Federal Reserve Bank of St. Louis, *Federal Surplus or Deficit as Percent of Gross Domestic Product* [FYFSGDA188S], retrieved from FRED, Federal Reserve Bank of St. Louis, June 27, 2022, https://fred.stlouisfed.org /series/FYFSGDA188S.

The political attractiveness of spending financed by borrowing rather than taxation is predictable. It reflects what economists call the **shortsightedness effect**: the tendency of elected political officials to favor projects that generate immediate, highly visible benefits at the expense of future costs that are less visible. Legislators have an incentive to spend money on programs that benefit the voters of their district and special-interest groups that will help them win reelection. They do not like to tax, because taxes impose a visible cost on voters. Budget deficits and borrowing allow politicians to supply voters with immediate benefits without imposing higher taxes. Thus, deficits are natural outgrowths of democratic politics unrestrained by commitment to a balanced budget.

The unconstrained political process plays into the hands of well-organized interest groups and encourages politicians to increase spending to gain benefits for a few at the expense of many. For example, each member of Congress has a strong incentive to fight hard for expenditures beneficial to district constituents. In contrast, there is little incentive for a legislator to be a spending "watchdog," for two reasons. First, such a watchdog would incur the wrath of colleagues because a spending restraint would make it more difficult for them to deliver special programs for their districts. They would retaliate by providing little support for spending in the watchdog's district. Second, and more important, the benefits of spending cuts and deficit reductions that the watchdog is trying to attain (for example, lower taxes) will accrue equally to voters in the other 434 districts. Thus, even if successful, the constituents of the watchdog's district will reap only a small fraction of the benefits.

Perhaps the following illustration will help explain why it is so difficult for the 435 representatives and 100 senators in Congress to bring federal spending and the budget deficit under control. Suppose these 535 individuals go out to dinner knowing that after the meal each will receive a bill for 1/535th of the cost. No one feels compelled to order less, because the restraint will exert little impact on each person's share of the total bill. Why not order shrimp for an appetizer, entrees of steak and lobster, and a large piece of cheesecake for dessert? After all, the extra spending will add only a few pennies to each person's share of the total bill. For example, if one member of the dinner party orders expensive items that push up the total bill by $50, that person's share of the cost will be less than 10 cents (1/535th of $50). What a bargain! Of course, the member will have to pay extra for the extravagant orders of the other 534 diners, too. But that's true no matter what he or she orders. The result is that everyone ends up ordering extravagantly and paying more for extras that provide little value relative to cost.[55]

The shortsightedness effect also explains the government's un-funded liabilities. The future benefits promised to senior citizens un-der the Social Security and Medicare programs are far greater than the payroll tax revenues that provide their financing. These unfunded liabilities are another form of debt. In fact, the debt implied by the un-funded Social Security and Medicare liabilities is many times the size of the official national debt. As the baby boomers continue to move into retirement and out of the labor force, spending on Social Security and Medicare will outstrip the revenues for their finance, further complicat-ing the debt liability of the federal government.

What will happen if the federal government does not bring its fi-nances under control? As a nation's debt gets larger and larger relative to the size of its economy, there will be repercussions in credit markets. Extending loans to the government of a country with a large ratio of debt to GDP is risky. As a result, the highly indebted government will have to pay higher interest rates. In turn, the higher interest costs will make it even more difficult for the government to keep within its bud-get and keep taxes at reasonable levels.

If the debt continues to rise relative to income, investors will be-come more and more reluctant to buy the bonds issued by the United States Treasury. Eventually a financial crisis will result—either out-right default by the government or financing the debt by money cre-ation and inflation. In either case, there will be a destructive impact on the economy. This has occurred in other countries, such as Greece, that have failed to control government finances. The United States is not immune to the laws of economics.

55. We are indebted to E. C. Pasour Jr., emeritus professor of economics at North Carolina State University, for this example.

The bias of the political process toward debt financing and unfunded future obligations is a time bomb. If it is not corrected, it will result in an economic crisis: debt obligations that cannot be met. Efforts to meet these obligations with higher taxes or money creation will lead to inflation, a severe reduction in income, or both. Control of government debt, both the outstanding national debt and the unfunded promised benefits, is unlikely to happen without a change in the political rules to make it more difficult for politicians to spend and promise more than they are willing to tax. There are several ways this could be done. The Constitution could be amended to require the federal government to balance its budget, following the lead of most state governments. Or a constitutional amendment could require two-thirds or three-fourths approval by both houses of Congress for spending proposals and increases in the federal government's borrowing power. Or the current year's spending might be limited to last year's level of revenues. Proposed constitutional rule changes of this kind would both improve the efficiency of government and avert a future catastrophic debt crisis.

7. *When governments become heavily involved in providing favors to some at the expense of others, inefficiency results and improper, unethical relationships develop.*

The tool of politics (which frequently becomes its objective) is to extract resources from the general taxpayer with minimum offense and to distribute the proceeds among innumerable claimants in such a way as to maximize the support at the polls. Politics, so far as mobilizing support is concerned, represents the art of calculated cheating or, more precisely, how to cheat without being caught.[56]

—JAMES R. SCHLESINGER, FORMER SECRETARY OF DEFENSE

56. James R. Schlesinger, "Systems Analysis and the Political Process," *Journal of Law & Economics*, October 1968, 285.

There are two ways individuals can acquire wealth: by production and **plunder**. People can get ahead by producing goods or services of value and exchanging them for income. This positive-sum method of acquiring income helps both trading partners and enhances the wealth of society. But sometimes people will try to get ahead through plunder, the taking from others without their consent. Of course, the victims of plunder will lose what the plunderer gains. But, in addition, where plunder is feared, potential victims will employ resources to defend themselves against it. In a society in which burglary is common, for example, people will buy more locks, use more security services, demand more police, and even design their homes in ways to discourage theft. The costs imposed on the citizenry will be greater than the gains obtained by those engaging in plunder. In contrast to positive-sum exchange activities, plunder is a negative-sum activity. It not only fails to generate additional income but also consumes resources, reducing the wealth of the society.

Governments promote **economic prosperity** when they encourage production and exchange and discourage plunder. When effective laws and their enforcement make it difficult to take from others, either via crime or use of political action, few resources will flow into those actions. Moreover, the resources employed defending against plunder will also be small.

In the modern world, however, government itself has become a major plunderer. Governments provide subsidies and favors to some by taking resources from taxpayers, by borrowing, and by shuffling budget allocations. While technically not theft, because it is done through laws, it is still a negative-sum activity that harms the citizenry and slows economic growth.

In the United States, transfers and subsidies now account for more than half of the federal budget. Social Security and health-care subsidies comprise the bulk of the transfers. More than 2,300 subsidy programs are funded by the federal government. That is more than twice the number in the 1980s.[57] Numerous activities are subsidized, including irrigation of arid lands, ethanol-enriched gasoline, mortgage loans, export of aircraft, low-cost housing, small business start-ups, production of wind and solar power, and production of agricultural goods ranging from corn and cotton to peanuts and wheat—to list just a few.

Subsidies and government favoritism are dangers to both political democracy and economic efficiency. There are several reasons why this is the case.

First, the subsidies encourage businesses to spend more time searching for favoritism in Washington and less time developing better and more economical products. Predictably, an increase in the availability of government favoritism will strengthen the power of special interests and encourage deception. To obtain more government funds and gain advantages relative to rivals, businesses and other favor-seekers will tie their interests to popular objectives, such as increasing employment, reducing poverty, improving environmental quality, and lessening dependence on foreigners. Even when their actions are motivated by financial gain and political power, interest groups will have a strong incentive to claim they are seeking to achieve broader, more popular objectives than is actually the case.

Second, subsidies to some firms and sectors distort market prices, placing others at a disadvantage. Some of the unsubsidized firms will be driven out of business or fail to enter the market because they can't compete with subsidized rivals. The result is a diversion of resources from businesses dependent on market consumers to those favored by politicians.

Third, and perhaps most important, the subsidies and favoritism

57. See Chris Edwards, "Cutting Federal Spending," Cato Handbook for Policy Makers, 2022. Available at: Cato Institute. https://www.cato.org/cato-handbook -policymakers/cato-handbook-policymakers-9th-edition-2022/cutting-federal -spending.

will create an improper, unethical relationship between business and political officials. "Corporate welfare" and "crony capitalism" are thereby encouraged, and the interests of the taxpayer are compromised. The greater the degree of corporate welfare (that is, the more numerous the government subsidy programs directed toward business), the greater the flow of resources into favor-seeking activities. (Note: Economists often use the term **rent-seeking** to describe this favor-seeking by businesses and other groups.) As politics replaces markets, the economy will be increasingly characterized by cronyism, corruption, and counterproductive activities, and economic growth will fall below its potential.

Increasingly, the governments of the United States and other high-income democratic countries use taxes and borrowing to provide subsidies and other favors to specified voting blocs in exchange for political contributions and support. In a statement widely attributed to Scotsman Alexander Tytler, he argues:

> *A democracy cannot exist as a permanent form of government. It can only exist until the voters discover that they can vote themselves largesse from the public treasury. From that moment on, the majority always votes for the candidates promising the most benefits from the public treasury with the result that a democracy always collapses over loose fiscal policy.*[58]

Once businesses and other interest groups become heavily involved in providing politicians with support in exchange for subsidies and favoritism, these forces will be very difficult to restrain. As government favoritism grows and both the recipients and politicians become

---

58. Others attribute this statement to Lord Thomas Macaulay. The author cannot be verified with certainty. For additional information on this topic, see Loren Collins, "The Truth About Tytler," at www.lorencollins.net/tytler.html.

more dependent on it, transfer spending will grow and resources will move away from productive activities. Moreover, deceitful behavior, unethical relations, and even corruption will become commonplace. There will be upward pressure on taxes, budget deficits will expand even further, and the politically manipulated economy will stagnate. Unless the constitutional protection of property rights and limitations on the spending, subsidizing, and borrowing activities of government are restored, democratically elected politicians will continue to enact programs that waste resources and impair the general standard of living. As illustrated by the case of Greece—whose government overspent itself into a debt crisis in 2010—this path will eventually lead to excessive debt and economic collapse.

8. The net gain of transfer recipients is less, and often substantially less, than the amount they receive.

To noneconomists, **income transfers** look like an effective way to help targeted beneficiaries. However, economic analysis indicates that transferring income to a group of recipients to improve their long-term well-being is very difficult. As is often the case in economics, the unintended secondary effects explain why this proposition is true.[59]

Three major factors undermine the effectiveness of income transfers. While the process may be most vivid in the case of direct income transfers like welfare assistance, the same types of forces occur when the benefits are agricultural subsidies or grants to individuals or corporations.

First, an increase in government transfers will generally reduce the incentive of both the taxpayer-donor and the transfer recipient to earn. Under many transfer programs, as the recipients' incomes rise, the mag-

59. See James Gwartney and Richard Stroup, "Transfers, Equality, and the Limits of Public Policy," *Cato Journal*, Spring/Summer 1986, for a detailed analysis of this issue.

nitude of the transfer is reduced (because the recipients are now better off). Recipients will have less incentive to earn because additional earnings will increase their net incomes by only a fraction—and in many cases only a small fraction—of the additional earnings. Similarly, as taxes increase to finance additional transfers, taxpayers have less incentive to make the sacrifices needed to produce and earn and more incentive to invest in tax shelters to try to hang on to money earned. Thus, neither transfer recipients nor taxpayers will produce and earn as much as they would in the absence of the transfer programs. As a result, economic growth will be slowed.

To see the negative effect of almost any transfer policy on productive effort, consider the reaction of students if a professor announces at the beginning of the term that the grading policy for the class will be to redistribute the points earned on the exams so that no one will receive less than a C. Under this plan, students who earned A grades by scoring an average of 90 percent or higher on the exams would have to give up enough of their points to bring up the average of those who would otherwise get Ds and Fs. And, of course, the B students would also have to contribute some of their points as well, although not as many, to achieve a more equal grade distribution.

Does anyone doubt that at least some of the students who would have made As and Bs will study less when their extra effort is "taxed" to provide benefits to others? And so would the students who would have made Cs and Ds study less, since the penalty they paid for less effort would be cushioned by point transfers they would lose if they earned more points on their own. The same logic applies even to those who would have made Fs, although they probably weren't doing very much studying anyway. Predictably, the outcome will be less studying, and overall achievement will decline.

The impact of tax-transfer schemes will be similar: less work effort and lower overall income levels. Income does not just happen; it is something that people produce and earn. Individuals earn income as they provide goods and services to others willing to pay for them. We can think of national income as an economic pie, but it is a pie whose size is determined by the actions of millions of people, each using production and trade to earn an individual slice. It is impossible to redistribute income without simultaneously reducing the work effort and innovative actions that generate the income.

Second, competition for transfers will erode most of the long-term gains of the intended beneficiaries. Governments must establish a criterion for the receipt of income transfers and other political favors. If they do not do so, the transfers will bust the budget immediately. Generally, the government will require a transfer recipient to own something, do something, or be something. For example, the recipient of unemployment compensation must be out of a job, and a company must have a limited number of employees to qualify for a small-business grant or loan. Once the criterion is established, many people will modify their behavior to qualify for the "free" money or other government favors. As they do so, their net gain from the transfers declines.

Think about the following: Suppose that the United States government decided to give away a $100 bill between 9:00 A.M. and 5:00 P.M. each weekday to all persons willing to wait in line at the teller windows of the Department of Treasury. Long lines would emerge. How long? How much time would people be willing to take from their leisure and their productive activities to wait in line? A person whose time was worth $15 per hour would be willing to spend about six hours waiting for the $100 bill. But others whose time was worth less, say $10, $8, or $5 per hour would wait longer—ten hours or more. And everyone would find that the time waiting consumed much of the value of the $100 transfer. If the proponents thought the program would make the recipients $100 better off, they would have been wrong.

This example illustrates why the intended beneficiaries of transfer programs are not helped as much as most perceive. When beneficiaries must do something (for example, wait in line, fill out forms, lobby government officials, take an exam, endure delays, or contribute to selected political campaigns) to qualify for a transfer, much of their potential gain will be lost as they seek to meet the qualifying criteria. Similarly, when beneficiaries must own something (for example, land with a wheat production history to gain access to wheat program subsidies, or a license to operate a taxicab to get a subsidy), people will bid up the price of the asset needed to acquire the subsidy. The higher price of the asset, such as the taxicab license or the land with a history of wheat production, will capture the value of the subsidy.

In each case the potential beneficiaries will compete to meet the criteria until they dissipate much of the value of the transfer. As a result, the recipient's net gain will generally be substantially less than the amount of the transfer payment. Indeed, the net gain of the marginal recipient (the person who barely finds it worthwhile to qualify for the transfer) will be very close, if not equal, to $0.

Consider the impact of the subsidies (grants and low-cost loans) to college students. These programs were designed to make college more affordable. But the subsidies increase the demand for college, which pushes tuition prices upward. About 60 percent of the increases in transfers to students was passed through in the form of higher tuition prices according to a 2017 report from the Federal Reserve Bank of New York. Put another way, for every $3 increase in student subsidies, colleges and universities raised tuition by $2.[60] It is no coincidence that as the grant and loan aid programs for college students have increased substantially since 1990, tuition and other expenses of college have increased far more rapidly than the general level of prices. Furthermore, the subsidy programs have contributed to a glut of college students entering the job market, which has reduced their employment prospects as well as their future

60. See Lucca, David O., Nadauld, Taylor, & Shen, Karen (2017), *Credit Supply and the Rise in College Tuition: Evidence from the Expansion in Federal Student Aid Programs* (Federal Reserve Bank of New York Staff Reports, no. 733).

earnings. When the secondary effects—higher college costs and less attractive employment opportunities—are taken into consideration, the net benefits to college students are substantially less than the transfers.

Transfer programs can even leave intended beneficiaries worse off. The Homestead Act of 1862 illustrates this point. Under this legislation, the federal government provided a land plot of 160 acres (later expanded to up to 640 acres in parts of the West) to settlers who staked a claim, built a house on the land, and stayed for five years. This option attracted many, but it was not easy to survive in the early West, even with 160 acres. Thus, more than 60 percent of the land claims were abandoned before the five years lapsed.[61] In essence, this transfer program encouraged people to settle the land before it was economical to do so, and as a result, many of the homesteaders suffered severe financial losses.

More recently, as discussed in Part 2, Element 2.4, government regulations designed to make housing more affordable encouraged lenders to extend more loans with little or no down payment to homebuyers who could not qualify for conventional mortgage loans. The impact of these regulatory subsidies was much like those of the Homestead Act: high default rates, foreclosures, and financial troubles for many of the intended beneficiaries.

There is a third reason for the ineffectiveness of transfers. Transfer programs reduce the adverse consequences suffered by those who make imprudent decisions, reducing their motivation to avoid adversity. For example, government subsidies of insurance premiums in hurricane-prone areas reduce the personal cost of individuals protecting themselves against losses. But there is a cost to society. Because the subsidy makes the purchase of hurricane insurance cheaper, more people will build in hurricane-prone areas than would be true if they had to pay the

61. Fred A. Shannon, "The Homestead Act and the Labor Surplus," *American Historical Review* 41 (July 1936): 637–51.

full cost. As a result, the damage from hurricanes is greater than would otherwise be the case.

The impact of unemployment compensation is similar. The benefits make it less costly for unemployed workers to refuse existing offers and, instead, keep looking for better jobs. Therefore, workers engage in more lengthy job searches, pushing the unemployment rate upward.[62]

The War on Poverty illustrates how difficult it is to help the intended beneficiaries. When the War on Poverty was declared in the mid-1960s, President Lyndon Johnson and other proponents of the program argued that poverty could be eliminated if only Americans were willing to transfer a little more income to the less fortunate members of society. They were willing, and income-transfer programs expanded substantially. Measured as a proportion of total income, transfers directed toward the poor or near-poor (for example, Aid to Families with Dependent Children, food stamps, and Medicaid) doubled during the 1965–1975 period. Since 1975, anti-poverty income transfers have continued to grow as a share of national income.

No doubt, the proponents of the War on Poverty programs were motivated by lofty objectives. However, as we have stressed, good intentions do not guarantee the desired outcome. As Exhibit 13 shows, the poverty rate was declining rapidly prior to the War on Poverty. The share of families in poverty declined from 32 percent in 1947 to 13.9 percent in 1965. The downward trend continued for a few more years, reaching 10.1 percent in 1970. In the late 1960s, only a few years after the War on Poverty transfers were initiated, the declining trend in the poverty rate came to a halt. Since 1970, the poverty rate of families has

62. For evidence on this point, see Lawrence Katz and Bruce Meyer, "The Impact of the Potential Duration of Unemployment Benefits on the Duration of Unemployment," *Journal of Public Economics* 41, no. 1 (February 1990): 45–72. Also see Daniel Aaronson, Bhashkar Mazumder, and Shani Schechter, "What Is Behind the Rise in Long-Term Unemployment?," Federal Reserve Bank of Chicago, *Economic Perspectives* (Second Quarter 2010): 28–51.

fluctuated within a relatively narrow range between 8 percent and 12 percent. The poverty rate was 11.8 percent in 2010, and by 2020, just before the pandemic, it declined to approximately 9 percent. These rates are only slightly lower than the figure when the War on Poverty programs were initiated. Given that the 2020 income per person, adjusted for inflation, was two-and-a-half times the level of the late 1960s, this lack of progress in reducing poverty is startling.

Exhibit 13: Percent of Familes Below Poverty Rate

Source: U.S. Census Bureau, Current Population Survey, *Annual Social and Economic Supplements,* 1960 to 2022 (CPS ASEC).

The calculation of the official poverty rate does not include noncash benefits such as those of food, health care, and housing. If noncash benefits were counted as income, the family poverty rate would be about 3 percentage points lower. However, the pattern is still the same as that in Exhibit 13. When noncash benefits are counted as income, the family poverty rate in 2022 is still almost the same as in 1970.

Why haven't the anti-poverty transfer programs been more effective? The transfers generate three unintended secondary effects that slow progress against poverty.

First, the income-linked transfers reduce the incentive of low-income individuals to earn, move up the income ladder, and escape poverty. There are more than seventy-five means-tested government programs (for example, food supplements, Medicaid, housing subsidies, school lunches, and child health-care insurance) that target the poor for assistance. Benefits from most of these programs are scaled down and eventually eliminated as the recipients' earnings rise. As a result, many low-income recipients get caught in a poverty trap. If they earn more, the combination of the additional taxes owed and transfers lost means that they get to keep only 10, 20, or 30 percent of the additional earnings. In some cases, the additional earnings may even reduce the recipient's net income. This poverty trap reduces the incentive for many low-income recipients to work, earn more, acquire experience, and move up the job ladder. To a large degree, the transfers merely replace what would have been earned income, and the net gains of the recipients are much less than the transfer spending.

Second, transfer programs that significantly reduce the hardship of poverty also reduce the opportunity cost of risky choices. Dropping out of school or the workforce, childbearing by teenagers and unmarried women, divorce, abandonment of children by fathers, and drug use often lead to poverty. As more people choose these high-risk options, it is very difficult to reduce the poverty rate. Isabel Sawhill and Ron Haskins of the Brookings Institution find evidence that a person can reduce the chances of living in poverty from 12 percent to 2 percent by doing just three basic things: completing high school (at a minimum), working full-time, and getting married before having a child.[63] When young people choose these options, it is unlikely that they will spend any significant time in poverty. This is a vitally important point that educators, parents, guardians, and others need to discuss with young people, many of whom are making these life-changing decisions.

Third, government anti-poverty transfers crowd out private charitable efforts. When people perceive that the government is providing for the poor, action by families, churches, and civic organizations becomes less urgent. When taxes are levied and the government does more, predictably, private individuals and groups will do less. Yet pri-

---

63. Ron Haskins and Isabel V. Sawhill, *Opportunity Society* (Washington, DC: Brookings Institution Press, 2009).

vate givers have real advantages over government transfers: They can see the real nature of the problem more clearly, are often more sensitive to recipients' lifestyles, and typically focus their giving on those making a good effort to help themselves.

From an economic viewpoint, the poor record of transfer programs, ranging from farm price supports to anti-poverty programs, is not surprising. When the secondary effects are considered, economic analysis indicates that it is extremely difficult to help the intended beneficiaries over the long term.

9. The economy is far too complex to be centrally planned, and efforts to do so will result in inefficiency and cronyism.

> The man of system . . . is apt to be very wise in his own conceit. . . . He seems to imagine that he can arrange the different members of a great society with as much ease as the hand arranges the different pieces upon a chess-board. He does not consider that the pieces upon the chess-board have no other principle of motion besides that which the hand impresses upon them; but that, in the great chess-board of human society, every single piece has a principle of motion of its own, altogether different from that which the legislature might chuse to impress upon it. If those two principles coincide and act in the same direction, the game of human society will go on easily and harmoniously, and is very likely to be happy and successful. If they are opposite or different, the game will go on miserably, and the society must be at all times in the highest degree of disorder.[64]

—ADAM SMITH

64. Adam Smith, *The Theory of Moral Sentiments,* Glasgow ed. (Indianapolis: Liberty Fund [1759], 1976): 233–34. Also available at https://www.econlib.org/library /Smith/smMS.html.

As previously discussed, governments can often coordinate the provision of public goods—a small class of goods for which it is difficult to limit consumption to paying customers—better than markets can. Many people also argue that government officials can manage all, or most, of the economy better than markets can. The proponents of central planning claim that the general populace would be better off if government officials used taxes, subsidies, mandates, directives, and regulations to centrally plan and manage the key sectors of the economy. Central planning replaces markets with government allocation. It can involve direct command and control, as under the old Soviet system. But it can also occur when elected political officials substitute their verdicts for those of consumers, investors, and entrepreneurs directed by market forces.

It is easy to see why central planning has appeal. Surely, it makes sense to plan. Aren't elected officials and government experts more likely to represent the "general welfare" of the people than business entrepreneurs are? Won't government officials be "less greedy" than private businesses would be? The attractiveness of central planning among those who lack knowledge of public choice and its implications for the operation of the political process is understandable. Economics, however, indicates that central planning will be inefficient. Five major reasons explain why this is the case.

First, central planning merely substitutes politics for market decisions. Real-world central planners (and the legislators who direct them) are not a group of omniscient selfless saints. Inevitably, the subsidies and investment funds allocated by planners will be influenced by political considerations. Think how this process works even when decisions are made democratically.

Expenditures will have to be approved by the legislature (say, the Congress of the United States). Various business and unionized labor interests will lobby for investment funds and subsidies. Legislators will be particularly sensitive to those in a position to provide campaign contributions or to deliver key voting blocs. This process will favor older firms with more lobbying experience and political clout, even if they are economically weak, over newer growth-oriented firms. In addition, legislative committee chairs will often block various programs unless other legislators agree to support projects that benefit their constituents and favored interest groups (that is, "pork-barrel" projects). Given this **incentive structure**, only a naive idealist would expect this politicized process to result in less waste, more wealth creation, and a better allocation of investment funds than markets.

Second, the incentive of government enterprises and agencies to control expenditures and supply goods efficiently is weak. Rather than serving customers to build their agencies, they rely on a government budget. Predictably, the directors of government organizations will be motivated to pursue a larger budget. A larger budget will provide funding for expansion, salary increases, additional spending on clients, and other factors that will make life more comfortable for the managers. Managers of government enterprises and agencies, almost without exception, will try to convince legislators that their activities are producing goods or services that are enormously valuable to the general public and, if they were just given more funds, they would do even more marvelous things for society. Moreover, they will argue, if the funding is not forthcoming, people will suffer and the outcome will be disastrous. It will be difficult for legislators and other government planners to evaluate such claims.

Further, the incentive of directors and managers of public-sector enterprises to produce efficiently and keep costs low is weak. Unlike private owners, public sector managers do not gain much from improved efficiency and lower costs. There is nothing comparable to private-sector profit that provides evidence that a government agency or enterprise is well managed. In the private sector, bankruptcy eventually weeds out inefficient producers. But in the public sector, there is no parallel mechanism that forces unsuccessful programs to be shut down. In fact, poor performance and failure to achieve objectives are often used as an argument for increased government funding! For example, the police department will use a rising crime rate to argue for additional law-enforcement funding. Similarly, if the achievement scores of students are declining, public school administrators will use this failure to argue for still more funds. Given the strong incentive of government enterprise managers to expand their budgets, and the weak incentive to operate efficiently, government enterprises can be expected to have higher per-unit costs than comparable private firms.

Third, there is every reason to believe that investors risking their own money will make better investment choices than central planners spending the money of taxpayers. Remember, an investor who is going to profit must discover and invest in a project that increases the value of resources. The investor who makes a mistake—that is, whose project results in losses—will bear the consequences directly. In contrast, the success or failure of government projects seldom exerts much impact on the personal wealth of government planners. Even if a project is productive, the planner's personal gain is likely to be modest. And if the project is wasteful—if it reduces the value of resources—this failure will exert little negative impact on the income of planners. They may even be able to reap personal gain from wasteful projects that channel subsidies and other benefits toward politically powerful groups, who will then give their agency or enterprise added political support. Given this incentive structure, there is no reason to believe that government planners will be more likely than private investors to discover and act on projects that increase society's wealth.

Fourth, the efficiency of government spending will also be undermined because the budget of an unconstrained government is something like a common pool resource. As we saw in Part 2, Element 2.1, private ownership provides a strong motivation to take the future effects of current decisions into consideration. But when money and resources are owned in common, there is little motivation to consider the future. For example, fish in the ocean are owned in common until someone catches them, and as a result, many species are on the verge of depletion because of overfishing. All in the fishing industry would be better off if the fish were harvested less rapidly so there would be more opportunity for their populations to reproduce. But because of the common ownership, each fisherperson knows that fish not caught today will be harvested by someone else tomorrow. Thus, there is little incentive for anyone to reduce today's catch so more fish will be available in the future.

Similarly, when interest groups are "fishing" (that is, lobbying political planners) for government spending, they have little incentive to consider the adverse consequences of higher taxes and additional borrowing on future output. The proponents of each spending project may recognize that future output would be greater if taxes were lower and **private investment** higher. But they will also recognize that if they do not grab more of the government budget, some other interest group will. Given these incentives, inefficient spending projects and perpetual budget deficits are an expected result. We saw in Element 3.6 the growing problem of the United States' chronic government budget deficits.

Fifth, there is no way that central planners can acquire enough information to create, maintain, and constantly update a plan that makes sense. We live in a world of dynamic change. Technological advances, new products, political unrest, changing demand, and shifting weather conditions are constantly altering the relative scarcity of both goods and resources. No central authority will be able to keep up with these changes, politically assess them, and/or provide enterprise managers with sensible instructions. Government planners have neither the information nor the incentive to plan efficiently.

Central planning often generates unintended secondary effects and outcomes that differ substantially from what was promised. As Adam Smith indicated more than two and a half centuries ago, individuals have minds of their own, what Smith calls "a principle of motion." See his quote at the beginning of this element. Because citizens have minds of their own, their actions often generate unanticipated secondary effects. Examples abound. When the Chinese government instituted a one-child policy in the 1980s, potential parents disproportionally aborted females, leading to a gender-imbalanced population. As a result, males now constitute nearly 60 percent of the Chinese population under age thirty-five.

Secondary effects have also led to undesired planning outcomes in the United States. In the early 1990s, Congress requested that housing planners take action to increase home ownership among those in the middle-and lower-income brackets. Government planners responded by lowering down payment requirements and credit standards for a person to obtain a mortgage loan, actions that encouraged people to take out larger loans than they could comfortably afford. With time, this led to unintended side effects: rising mortgage defaults and **foreclosure rates**, the bankruptcy of several lending institutions, a financial crisis, and the severe recession of 2008–2009.

Central planning outcomes can also be affected by conflicts among the central planners of various nations. The efforts of the Biden administration to reduce the supply and phase out the use of fossil fuels provide a vivid example. When the Biden administration assumed the presidency in 2021, it eliminated construction of key pipelines, prohibited fracking (a process that extracts more oil and gas than conventional drilling) on government lands, and terminated drilling in a slice of Alaska's Arctic National Wildlife Refuge. It imposed regulations to curtail the use of fossil fuels while expanding subsidies for wind and solar energy. Although the costs of wind and solar energy have come down over the years, both wind and solar still rely heavily on subsidies. Also, they are less reliable than oil and gas and must always have backup power from other sources such as fossil fuels.

As a result of these policies, the cost of energy-intensive production in the United States rose. At the same time, Chinese central planners were following policies designed to keep energy costs low. In 2021 and 2022, the Chinese were building two coal-powered plants per week. While coal is relatively cheap, it is the dirtiest of the major fossil energy sources. Thus, while the U.S. central planners were increasing energy costs, the Chinese were reducing them. As a result, energy-intensive production shifted from the United States, which has high costs but low carbon-dioxide emissions, to China, which has low costs but higher emissions. Worldwide carbon dioxide emissions increased—an outcome that was the opposite of what the U.S. planners intended. Moreover, the reductions in U.S. output of petroleum pushed the world price of crude oil and natural gas higher, thereby enriching the treasuries of petroleum exporters such as Russia, providing it with additional funding for its war against Ukraine. The world is complex and therefore outcomes often differ from the intentions of the planners.

Central planning almost always leads to entrenchment of political power. This is true even when the policies are counterproductive. Consider the case of Venezuela. The central planning policies of the Socialist Party have led to a two-thirds reduction in the output of the nationalized petroleum industry, hyperinflation, increasing poverty, and falling living standards. In recent years, four million people, more than 10 percent of the population, have left the country. Nonetheless, the Socialist Party continues to maintain its dominant political position.

The situation in California is similar. California politicians constantly stress that their policies will help the poor, reduce income inequality, and make the rich pay their "fair share." California's 13 percent top marginal income tax rate is the highest in the nation.[65] The

---

65. Chris Edwards, "Capital Gains and State Damage from Federal Tax Increases," Available at: Cato Institute, https://www.cato.org/blog/capital-gains-state-damage -federal-tax-increases, April 11, 2020.

state spends more than $100 billion on welfare annually, more than any other state.[66] Its housing market is one of the most, if not *the* most, regulated in the country. Despite all of this government planning, California's poverty and homelessness rates are the highest in the nation.[67] But the government planning has worked politically. The dominance of the Democratic Party in California has expanded in recent decades and, for all practical purposes, it is now a one-party state.

During the 1970s and 1980s, many intellectuals and media sources believed that government planning and "industrial policy" provided the keys to economic growth. Economists Paul Samuelson and Lester Thurow were among the leading proponents of this view. They argued that market economies faced a dilemma: They would either have to move toward more government planning or suffer the consequences of slower growth and economic decline. The collapse of the Soviet system and the poor performance of the Japanese economy have largely eroded the popularity of this view.

What are the implications of public choice and the record of government planning? Nobel laureate F. A. Hayek provides the answer to this question. In his acceptance speech for the Nobel Prize, F. A. Hayek stated:

> *If man is not to do more harm than good in his efforts to improve the social order, he will have to learn that in this, as in all other fields where essential complexity of an organized kind prevails, he cannot acquire the full knowledge which would make mastery of the events possible. He will therefore have to use what knowledge he can achieve, not to shape the results as*

---

66. Michael D. Tanner, "Welfare Reform." Available at: https://www.cato.org/study/welfare-reform.

67. Michael D. Tanner, "An Overview of Poverty and Inequality in California, 2021." Available at: https://www.cato.org/study/overview-poverty-inequality-california#introduction.

the craftsman shapes his handiwork, but rather to cultivate growth by providing the appropriate environment, in the manner in which the gardener does this for his plants.[68]

In other words, the economy is far too complex to be micromanaged. Instead, as stressed in Part 2, the best strategy to achieve growth and prosperity is the establishment of sound institutions and long-range policies. They will create an environment in which individuals pursuing their own interests will undertake productive, wealth-creating activities.

10. Decentralization can reduce the threat of the abusive exercise of power by central government leaders, increase competitiveness among levels of government, and improve economic efficiency.

The primary purpose of government is to secure and protect the rights of individuals. The government is granted a monopoly on the legitimate use of force in order to protect the rights of individuals against those who would use force to threaten, take, or damage the person or property of another. But, as history illustrates, the coercive powers of government, particularly those of the central government, also pose a potential danger to the rights of individuals. This is why political power needs to be both limited and divided.

It can be divided horizontally among the executive, legislative, and judicial branches of government. Each provides a check on the power of the other two branches. Political power can also be divided vertically among the central, state or provincial, and local levels of government. Decentralization reduces the power of political leaders, such

68. F. A. Hayek, "Pretence of Knowledge," Nobel Prize Lecture in Economics, Stockholm, Sweden, December 11, 1974.

as presidents, prime ministers, and legislative leaders, who exercise power at the central government level.

Decentralization and expansion in the role of state and local governments relative to the central government can help protect citizens from exploitation. This is because it is much easier to escape the oppressive powers of state and local governments than a central government. It is much easier to move to another location within a country to escape high taxes and poor government services than to move out of a country. Decentralization makes it easier for citizens to choose the "exit option" and find a location providing government services and taxes more to their liking. In turn, this ability to move enhances the incentive of state and local officials to be more sensitive to the concerns of their residents.

Decentralization increases competitiveness within government. As we have stressed throughout, competition among business firms protects consumers against high prices, shoddy merchandise, poor service, and rude behavior. When firms serve their customers poorly, they lose business to rivals providing consumers with a better deal. Competition is a disciplinary force, and it can improve performance, reduce costs, and stimulate innovative behavior in government, just as in the private sector.

Decentralization and variations in the activities of state and local governments also can provide citizens with a broader range of options for goods and services offered through the political process, enhancing their ability to obtain government services more consistent with their preferences. Just as people differ regarding how much they want to spend on housing or automobiles, they will also have different views concerning expenditures on public services. Some will prefer higher levels of services and be willing to pay higher taxes for them. Others will prefer lower taxes and fewer government services. Some will want to fund government services with taxes, while others will prefer greater reliance on user charges. Within the framework of a decentralized political system, individuals will be able to group together with others desiring similar combinations of government services and taxes, and this grouping will make it possible for a larger number of people to obtain services more consistent with their preferences.

Moreover, the movement of people among the decentralized governmental units will also help improve efficiency. If a government levies high taxes (without providing a parallel quality of service) and regulates excessively, some individuals and businesses that make up the tax base will choose the exit option. Americans move a great deal, nearly 40 million each year. Moreover, their movements are not in a random pattern.

Between 2003 and 2013, the populations of the nine states without a personal income tax grew by an average of 3.7 percent as the result of immigration from other states. During the same period, the nine states with the highest income tax rates lost an average of 2 percent in population.[69] Changes in employment also provide insight into the pattern of population movements. From 2000 to 2022, employment in the nine states without an income tax increased by 25.3 percent, more than twice the 10.2 percent growth of the high-tax states. Among the four most populous states, employment between 2000 and 2022 increased in the low-tax states of Texas and Florida by 41 percent and 36 percent respectively, compared to only 16 percent and 4 percent in the high-tax states of California and New York. These movers are sending a message to high-taxing, poorly run governments. Like businesses that realize losses when they fail to serve their customers, democratic governments lose citizens when they serve them poorly.

69. Stephen Moore, Arthur B. Laffer, and Joel Griffith, "1,000 People a Day: Why Red States Are Getting Richer and Blue States Poorer," Heritage Foundation, May 5, 2015. The nine states with the highest personal income taxes are California, New York, Hawaii, Iowa, Minnesota, New Jersey, Oregon, Vermont, and Wisconsin. The nine states without personal income taxes are Florida, Nevada, New Hampshire, South Dakota, Tennessee, Texas, Washington, Wyoming, and Alaska.

In summary, decentralization allows people to move toward governmental units that provide desired public services at a low cost. In turn, the movements of voters will help keep governments in line with the preferences of citizens.

However, if competition among decentralized governments is going to serve the interests of citizens, it must not be stifled by the policies of the central government. When the national government subsidizes, mandates, and regulates the bundle of services provided by state and local governments, it undermines the competitive process among them. The best thing the central government can do is perform its limited functions well and remain neutral with regard to the operation and level of services of state, regional, and local governments. Like private enterprises, units of government prefer protection from rivals. There will be a tendency for governments to seek a monopoly position. Therefore, competition among governments does not evolve automatically. It must be incorporated into the political structure. This is what the American founders were attempting to do when they designed the U.S. Constitution and the federal system of the United States. Unfortunately, many of the built-in factors have eroded or been weakened through the years, and the central government is now substantially larger than state and local governments.

Is there a country that typifies the idealized decentralization model outlined here? Switzerland comes close. Switzerland is a small landlocked country surrounded by European powers. Its geographic size is half that of the state of South Carolina, and its population is less than Georgia's. It is mountainous and has little fertile agricultural land.

In spite of its small size, the Swiss government is highly decentralized, and political power is divided both horizontally and vertically. There are twenty-six cantons (twenty full cantons and six so-called half cantons) that operate as independent states with substantial powers to restrain the central government. Any eight cantons can call for a popular referendum to repeal an action of the central government. There are two legislative branches of the central government—the Council of States and the National Council. The members of the Council of States are elected by majority vote with two members from each of the twenty full cantons and one from each of the six half cantons. In contrast, the National Council is based on proportional representation. This difference in how members of the legislative branches are elected reduces the power of political parties and makes it more difficult to obtain legislative approval at the central level. In Switzerland, there is no chief executive with powers similar to those of a president or prime minister. The central executive branch is directed by a seven-member council selected by the legislative bodies. The taxing powers of the central government are limited, which explains why more than half of total tax revenue and 80 percent of the income tax revenues are raised at the canton and municipal government levels. Switzerland's decentralized structure has served it well. Even though it has little in the way of natural resources, it has the highest per capita income among the industrial countries and ranks among the world's freest economies.

Markets, Politics, and Improving the Operation of Government

> *There is enormous inertia—a tyranny of the status quo—in private and especially government arrangements. Only a crisis— actual or perceived—produces real change. When that crisis occurs, the actions that are taken depend on the ideas that are lying around. That, I believe, is our basic function: to develop alternatives to existing policies, to keep them alive and available until the politically impossible becomes politically inevitable.*[70]
>
> —MILTON FRIEDMAN, 1976 NOBEL LAUREATE

70. Milton Friedman, *Capitalism and Freedom* (Chicago: University of Chicago Press, 2002).

We have examined the operation of both markets and the political process. While both have shortcomings, the empirical evidence indicates that countries with more economic freedom and greater reliance on markets grow more rapidly and achieve higher income levels. See Part 2, Exhibits 6 through 10. Why is this the case? Incentives provide the answer. Markets create a powerful force for individuals and businesses to serve others, providing others with goods and services they value highly relative to cost. In a market economy, income is earned by helping others. If you want to earn a lot of income, you had better figure out how to help others a lot. Even though this attribute is seldom recognized, perhaps because people are unaware of it, markets motivate people to undertake actions that promote human progress. As Adam Smith noted nearly 250 years ago, the invisible hand of market prices directs self-interested individuals to undertake actions that promote the general welfare.

Of course, political allocation is the alternative to markets. There are two general structures of democratic political regimes: presidential and parliamentary. Under presidential systems, the president is directly elected by the voters. The president is the head of the executive branch of government and appoints cabinet members, typically subject only to approval by a legislative body, to manage the operation of government in various areas. The United States is an example of a country with a presidential system. Under a parliamentary system, members of the parliament are elected and then they select the executive leader, who is typically called the prime minister. The parliament, acting in conjunction with the prime minister, also selects cabinet members who manage various areas of the government. The prime minister serves at the discretion of the parliament and can be replaced at any time. Canada and the United Kingdom provide examples of countries with a parliamentary system.

Regardless of whether the political system is presidential or parliamentary, political allocation of resources, even in democratic countries, often leads to a conflict between personal interests and the general welfare. Voters have little incentive to cast a well-informed vote. Politicians and political parties, seeking to assemble a majority coalition, have a strong incentive to use debt financing, money creation, and hidden taxes to conceal the cost of resources extracted from the citizenry. The extracted resources can then be used to provide subsidies and other forms of favoritism to "buy" the support of various voting blocs. But the political favoritism encourages business, labor, and other interest groups to shift resources away from productive activities toward rent-seeking designed to get more of the government favors. Political allocation may sound like a great idea, but the real-world results are unattractive. Unconstrained democracy undermines economic efficiency and leads to interest-group politics, cronyism, excessive debt, and conflict among the citizenry.

What could be done to minimize the adverse consequences of democracy? What would a political structure more consistent with economic progress look like? These are complex questions, but key aspects can be outlined. First, political power must be both divided and constrained. The American founders were keenly aware of this point. They established two legislative branches, one based on population and the other on statehood, each designed to check the power of the other. Political power was further divided among three separate branches—the legislative, executive, and judicial. As Lord Acton stated, "Power corrupts, absolute power corrupts absolutely." If tyranny is to be avoided, power must be divided and checked.

Second, decentralization of political power is also highly important. However, there is a strong tendency, even in democratic countries, for political power to become more centralized. Centralization increases the oppressiveness of government because it reduces the ability of people to vote with their feet: to move to areas offering a combination of taxes, spending, and regulation more consistent with their preferences. The American Constitution sought to constrain centralization by limiting the powers of the federal government to those specified in Article I, Section 8 of the Constitution. However, as the U.S. case illustrates, constitutional restraints tend to erode with time. Thus, structural factors are also needed to constrain the centralization of government.

One way this might be done is to require larger majorities for approval of projects at higher levels of government. For example, while a simple majority could approve action at the local level, a three-fifths majority could be required for legislative approval at the state level and two-thirds for approval at the federal level. This reform would strengthen federalism and help to correct the tendency of power and control to flow toward the central government. Further, the supermajority requirements for approval at state and federal levels would mean that broad agreement, not just a simple majority, would be required before a project could be undertaken at these levels. This would help to minimize another deficiency of unconstrained democracy: the ability of special interest groups to obtain government favors at the expense of taxpayers, consumers, and other citizens.

Third, debt financing must be constrained. Both economic analysis and recent history indicate the political process is biased toward debt because it enables politicians to increase spending without having to levy taxes, which impose a more visible cost on voters. If this bias is ignored, predictably shortsighted politicians will expand debt to levels that undermine prosperity, as they did in Greece. In the United States, most state governments confront a balanced budget requirement, although borrowing may be permitted for capital projects. However, there are no constitutional restrictions on federal borrowing, and in recent years, the federal debt as a share of the economy has grown to levels even greater than those of World War II. A constitutional supermajority requirement (for example, two-thirds or three-fourths) approval for Congress to finance spending with debt would help correct this deficiency.

Fourth, money of stable value is essential for the smooth operation of markets. Monetary policymakers need to be made more accountable for their failure to maintain approximate price stability. One way this could be done is to require that those individuals in charge of monetary policy—the Board of Governors of the Federal Reserve in the United States—resign if they fail to keep the inflation rate within a specified range, for example, 0 to 3 percent. This type of provision makes monetary policymakers' responsibilities clear and holds them accountable should they fail. New Zealand has already adopted policy along these lines.

These changes would provide people with protection against the oppressiveness of centralized power, strengthen federalism, and help bring government spending and borrowing under control, while limiting the inclination of politicians to serve special interests and to undermine personal freedom. Taken together, the changes would be a positive step toward the restoration of government based on mutual agreement rather than the power to plunder. We have no doubt that they would assure growth and prosperity for future generations.

We are aware that structural changes like those outlined above are unlikely to be adopted in the immediate future. We also recognize that, other than a small number of public-choice economists, few people even think about the problem of how the political process works and what might be done to make it work better. Opinion leaders and the media focus on who is gaining political power and totally ignore the adverse consequences of how that power is exercised.

Thus, getting people to think seriously about the structure of government and what might be done to improve its operation will be a challenge. But economic analysis tells us that the United States and several other democratic countries are on unsustainable paths. If change does not occur, a crisis is likely and that may create an opportunity for constructive change. See the quotation from Milton Friedman at the beginning of this section.

However, history indicates there is a tendency to be too pessimistic.

Entrepreneurial discovery is a powerful force for human progress. Past crises have been avoided and doomsday scenarios falsified as the result of entrepreneurial discoveries. Remember, the whale-oil crisis ended with the discovery of kerosene. The "running out of oil" crisis has been avoided decade after decade by entrepreneurial discovery of new petroleum supplies and development of substitutes. Even if constructive reforms are minimal and counterproductive political policies continue, economic growth and higher living standards, perhaps at a slower rate, may continue as the result of entrepreneurial discoveries.

Looking Ahead

Parts 2 and 3 focused on national prosperity. The final section of this book will focus on personal prosperity. It will consider practical things you can do that will help you better prepare for the future and achieve a more prosperous life.

PART 4

Twelve Key Elements of Practical Personal Finance

TWELVE KEY ELEMENTS OF
PRACTICAL PERSONAL FINANCE

1. Discover your comparative advantage.

2. Cultivate skills, attitudes, and entrepreneurship over your lifetime.

3. Budget to provide the most value from your income.

4. Manage credit and debt wisely.

5. Spend strategically.

6. Pay into an emergency fund every month.

7. Put the power of compound interest to work.

8. Diversify: Don't put all your eggs in one basket.

9. Indexed equity mutual funds can help you outperform the experts.

10. Adjust your asset mix to match the timing of financial goals.

11. Reduce risk when making education, housing, and other investment decisions.

12. Use insurance to manage risk.

Introduction

Compared to Americans a couple of generations ago and their contemporaries worldwide, today's Americans have incredibly high income levels. Yet many are under financial stress. How can this be? The answer is that financial insecurity is mainly the result of the choices we make, not the incomes we earn.

If you do not take charge of your finances, they will take charge of you. As Yogi Berra, the great American philosopher (and late baseball star) said, "You've got to be very careful if you don't know where you are going, because you might not get there." In other words, each of us needs a plan. If we don't have one, we may end up where we do not want to be. The twelve elements in this part form the core of a practical plan. They focus on practical suggestions—things that you can do immediately—that will help you make better financial decisions whatever your current age, income level, or background.

Often, personal finance and investment decisions seem totally divorced from the world of economics. But they are not. As illustrated in Part 1, Element 1.4, the law of comparative advantage, which explains why countries benefit from specializing in the activities they do best, also explains why you as an individual can benefit from specialization in things you do well that are valued highly by others. Similarly, when it comes to building wealth over time, entrepreneurship, financial account-ability, career planning, and investment in capital (especially human capital) are as important for individuals as they are for countries.

The twelve-element plan outlined here is basic and practical. It will not make you a Wall Street wizard or an instant millionaire, but it will help you avoid major financial errors and provide the basic steps to building wealth. More sophisticated plans are available. However, the search for perfection is often the enemy of positive action. Individuals who think they don't have the time or the expertise to develop a sound financial plan may fail even to apply simple guidelines that can help them avoid major financial troubles. These elements will provide you with the knowledge to get started right away.

Life is about choices. Our goal is to enhance your ability to choose options that can help you lead a comfortable and rewarding life. John Morton, an associate of ours and one of the nation's leading economic educators, states:

> *I always told my students that life is not a lottery and life is not a zero-sum game. Your success will not take away from anyone else's success. Your success depends on your choices and choices have consequences.*[71]

Before examining how you can make better financial choices and get more from the resources available to you, we want to share a couple of thoughts about the importance of money and wealth. There is more to a rewarding life than making money. When it comes to happiness,

71. This quotation was provided in correspondence with the authors. John Morton was a legendary economics instructor at Homewood-Flossmoor High School in the Chicago area. He was also the founder and president of the Arizona Council on Economic Education and vice president for program development for the Council for Economic Education. Literally tens of thousands of students have used his *Advanced Placement Economics* book in their preparation for the AP exams in economics.

nonfinancial assets, such as a good marriage, family, friends, fulfilling work, religious convictions, and enjoyable hobbies, are far more important than money.[72] Thus the single-minded pursuit of money and wealth makes no sense.

At the same time, however, there is nothing unseemly about the desire for more wealth. This desire is not limited to those who are only interested in their personal welfare, narrowly defined. Many people would like more wealth so they can donate more to religious, cultural, and charitable organizations, or do more to help elderly parents. No matter what our objectives in life, they are easier to achieve if we have less debt and more wealth. Thus, all of us have an incentive to improve our financial decision-making. These twelve guidelines can help us do so.

1. Discover your comparative advantage.

The principle of comparative advantage is used most often to explain why international trade makes it possible for people in different countries to achieve higher living standards. As illustrated in Part 1, Element 1.4, specialization based on comparative advantage makes it possible for trading partners to produce more and achieve a higher income level. The principle of comparative advantage is just as important when individuals are considering occupational and business opportunities. Think about the relationship between your skills and opportunity costs. To pick one extreme, suppose that you are better than everyone else in every productive activity. Would that mean that you should

---

72. Arthur Brooks, a professor at Harvard Business School and Harvard Kennedy School, is one of the leading scholars on the determinants of happiness. For an overview of his views, see "A Formula for Happiness," *New York Times*, December 14, 2013, at nytimes.com/2013/12/15/opinion/sunday/a-formula-for-happiness .html?pagewanted=all&_r=0.

try to spend some time on each activity? Or to go to another extreme, someone could be worse than everyone else. Would that individual be unable to gain from specialization because he or she would be unable to compete successfully in anything? The answer to both questions is no.

No matter how talented you are, you will be relatively more productive in some areas than others when opportunity costs are taken into account. Similarly, no matter how poor your ability to produce, you will be able to produce some things at a lower cost than others. You will be able to compete successfully in some areas and can gain by specializing where you have a comparative advantage. Your comparative advantage is determined by your relative abilities, not your absolute abilities. Some people start out with fewer advantages than others, but even those who are less advantaged can do extremely well if they make the effort and apply themselves intelligently. You need to take charge of your career development and plan how you can best develop your talents and use market cooperation to achieve your goals. No one else cares more about your personal success than you do. Neither does anyone else know more about your interests, skills, and goals.

We usually think of costs as something that should be kept as low as possible. But, remember, costs reflect the highest valued opportunity given up when we choose an option. Thus, when you have attractive alternatives, your choices will be costly. Should you take that part-time job at Starbucks to have more money while you're a student? Or should you take an extra course so that you can complete your college degree more quickly? Both options are attractive. Furthermore, as you improve your skills and your opportunities become even more attractive, the choice among options will be more costly.

In contrast, your costs will be low when you have very few good choices. For example, a very effective way of reducing the cost of reading this book is to get thrown in jail with it so that reading it is the only opportunity you have other than staring at the walls. This is obviously a bad idea. It would reduce the cost of doing one thing (a very desirable thing, in our opinion) by eliminating your opportunity to do many other attractive things. You make yourself better off by increasing your opportunities, not by reducing them.

Young people are encouraged to get a good education so they will have more attractive opportunities later in life. But this is the same as encouraging them to increase the costs of all the choices they make. A good education will generally increase your productivity and the amount employers are willing to pay you. This will enhance your earnings, but it also means you will have to turn down some attractive offers.

Sound career decision-making involves more than figuring out those things that you do best. It is also vitally important to discover where your passions lie—those productive activities that provide you with the most fulfillment. If you enjoy what you do and believe it is important, you will be happy to do more of it and work to do it better. Thus, competency and passion for an activity tend to go together. Moreover, real wealth is measured in terms of personal fulfillment. For example, the authors of this book have found it satisfying to find answers to economic questions and to express what we know in ways that can help others better understand the corners of the world that we have examined professionally. Even though the hours are sometimes long, we find most of those hours enjoyable. What we do is not for everyone. But, for us, with our interests, the joys of what we do more than make up for the rough patches.

2. *Cultivate skills, attitudes, and entrepreneurship over your lifetime.*

In a market economy, financial success reflects one's ability to provide others with value. This is true for both employees and businesses. If you want to achieve high earnings, you had better figure out how to provide others with services they value highly.

As previously stressed, improved knowledge, higher skill level, and experience generally increase productivity and enhance one's ability to provide valuable services to others. As a result, investments in human capital—education, training, and other forms of skill acquisition—can improve both productivity and earnings. But other personal attributes also influence productivity. Two of the most important are personal attitudes and entrepreneurial thinking. The importance of these two attributes as a source of productivity is closely related to what psychologists call emotional intelligence (EQ). Many psychologists now believe that EQ is more important than IQ as a determinant of personal success.[73] Even economists often overlook these two vitally important sources of personal productivity. Let's consider each of them.

How does one's personal attitude impact productivity and success? Consider the following simple thought experiment: Suppose an employer is evaluating two potential employees. The first has the following set of attributes: honesty, dependability, persistence, reliability, trustworthiness, respect for others, desire to learn and improve, and ability to work with others. The second has a different set: disrespect for others, poor reliability, quarrelsome, contempt for education, vulgarity of speech, blaming others for problems, and dishonesty. If you were the employer, which would you hire? Predictably, most would hire the first candidate because those attitudes are success-oriented. Other things being constant, employees with these positive attitudes are usually more productive. In contrast, the second set of attributes are failure-oriented. They will undermine productivity and the ability of the employee to work with others.

---

73. See Janae Ernst, "How Can I Improve Emotional Intelligence (EQ)?," *Performance Magazine*, February 12, 2021, https://www.performancemagazine.org/emotionally-intelligent-eq-part-1/.

If you want to be successful, you need to cultivate, develop, and strengthen the first set of attributes. They need to become habits—the core values of your life. Equally important, you need to cast the second set out of your life. Do not let anyone, including friends, convince you that any of the failure attributes are "cool." They are paths to trouble, and you do not want to go down those routes.

There is some good news here: You can choose the success attitudes rather than the failure ones. Moreover, you can do so regardless of your family background, current income, educational level, or choice of career. Your attitudes will exert a huge impact on your future financial success. Positive attitudes will help you overcome other disadvantages, such as a poor education or a financially restricted childhood.

Of course, if you choose the failure attitudes, you can blame others—your family, your neighborhood, the schools you attended, or society in general. These factors may influence your choices, but they do not determine them. Your attitude characteristics are under your control. If you grew up in a troublesome environment, it may be more difficult to attain and maintain these attitudes. But a person who overcomes a negative environment is admired and respected by almost all. A troublesome background can even help launch your success if you choose to develop positive attitudes.

Some of you may be thinking, "My attitudes are my own business. No one is going to tell me what to do or change my behavior." Suppose a business owner, let's call him Sam, has this perspective. Sam ignores the wishes of consumers and instead provides what he thinks consumers should value. Sam is free to make this choice. However, if he does so, he will pay a price in the form of losses and business failure. Similarly, potential employees are free to "do their own thing." They can ignore how their attitudes and behavior affect productivity and employability. But, like the business that ignores the desires of consumers, people who ignore how their attitudes and behavior influence their productivity will pay a price in the form of poor opportunities, low earnings, and more spells of unemployment. None of us is an island unto ourselves. If we want others to provide us with income, we need to cooperate and make our services valuable to them.

The bottom line is straightforward: Success-oriented attitudes are a highly important determinant of financial success. You cannot buy these attitudes. Neither can someone else provide them to you. You must choose them and integrate them into your life. Further, if you do so, it is a near certainty that you will have a substantial degree of economic success. But the opposite is also true: If your life is largely a reflection of the failure set of attributes, it is a virtual certainty that your future will be characterized by financial troubles and personal bitterness.

Entrepreneurial thinking is also a personal attribute that can enhance your productivity. While entrepreneurship is often associated with business decision-making, in a very real sense all of us are entrepreneurs. We are constantly making decisions about the development and use of knowledge, skills, and other resources under our control. Our financial success will reflect the outcome of these choices.

If you want to be financially successful, think entrepreneurially. Put another way, focus on how to develop and use your talents and mobilize available resources to provide others with things that they value highly.

Once you begin to think entrepreneurially—to think about how you can increase the value of your services to others—do not underestimate your ability to achieve success. Entrepreneurial talent is often found in unexpected places. Who would have thought that a middle-aged, milkshake-machine salesman, Ray Kroc, would revolutionize the franchising business and expand a single McDonald's restaurant in San Bernardino, California, into the world's largest fast-food chain? Did anyone in the 1960s expect Sam Walton to take a couple of small stores in Arkansas and transform them into the largest retailer in America during the 1990s? How could anyone have anticipated that Jeff Bezos, starting an online bookstore in his garage in 1994, would expand Amazon into the world's largest retailer? These are high-profile cases, but the same pattern occurs over and over. Successful self-employed professional and business leaders often come from diverse backgrounds that appear to be largely unrelated to the areas of their achievement.

Self-employed entrepreneurs are disproportionately represented among the wealthy. While the self-employed constitute about one-sixth of the labor force, they account for two-thirds of America's millionaires. Four major factors contribute to the financial success of self-employed entrepreneurs. First, they are good at identifying and acting on attractive opportunities that have been overlooked by others. Second, they are willing to take risks. Greater risks and higher returns go together. To a degree, the higher incomes of self-employed entrepreneurs are merely compensation for the uncertainties accompanying their business activities. Third, they have high investment rates. Self-employed business owners often channel large shares of their incomes into the growth and expansion of their businesses. Fourth, they generally love what they do and therefore work long hours.[74]

Perhaps most important, employees can gain by "thinking like entrepreneurs." Just as the incomes of business entrepreneurs depend on their ability to satisfy customers, the earnings of employees depend on their ability to make themselves valuable to employers, both current and prospective. If employees want to achieve high earnings, they need to develop skills, knowledge, attitudes, and work habits that are highly valued by others.

Development and use of your talents in ways that provide large benefits to others is a key to financial success. It is also central to what Arthur Brooks calls "earned success," the central component of

74. Thomas J. Stanley, *The Millionaire Mind* (Kansas City, MO: Andrews McMeel Publishing, 2000).

happiness and life satisfaction.[75] No one can give you earned success; you must achieve it. Earned success is present when your education, work, and lifestyle choices reflect the purpose of your life. Throughout our careers, we have asked our students what they want to do with their lives. In one form or another, the response is nearly always the same: I want to do things that will make the world a better place to live. Of course, individuals will differ with regard to how they plan to do so. But, regardless of their plans, a positive set of attitudes and an entrepreneurial thought process will enhance their ability to live a meaningful and rewarding life.

3. Budget to provide the most value from your income.

Money is only a tool. It will take you wherever you wish, but it will not replace you as the driver.[76]

—Ayn Rand

Most financial insecurity today is the product of unwise choices. Spending more than you earn, building up debt without concern for how to repay it, lack of budgeting, and other unwise financial habits create havoc and cause stress. A commitment to budgeting is key to obtaining a healthy financial life, building wealth, and achieving your personal goals. People, like nations, build wealth through saving and investment. But successful building of wealth also takes strategic planning. There must be a plan in place to guide how the spending, saving, and investment are directed toward wealth creation. For the individual

75. Harvard professor Arthur C. Brooks wrote several articles and columns on this topic. A good summary can be found on an American Enterprise Institute video, December 14, 2013, https://www.youtube.com/watch?v=sDH4mzsQP0w.

76. Ayn Rand, *Atlas Shrugged* (New York: Random House, 1957), 411.

or household, that plan is a **budget**. A budget helps you channel your funds toward sound spending, regular saving, and diversified investments in a manner that will provide you with the most value from your income. Think of your budget as your wealth GPS. It will direct you to your goals or alert you when you're veering away from them.

Effective budgeting is an ongoing process, not a one-time event. It is comprised of two specific actions. First, you must create the initial budget that is simply a document that identifies all of your planned or expected spending for a period of time. Most people create a monthly budget, but a yearly budget is also common. It is important to carefully consider all of your spending, not just the highly visible spending like groceries, car payments, and rent or mortgage. Don't forget about birthday gifts, license tag renewal fees, streaming subscriptions, and oil changes for your car. Estimate your monthly or annual income, then identify where you are going to spend every penny. We recommend zero-based budgeting, which means that saving and investment are specific items in your budget, not just the leftover balance (if there is any).

The second action is documentation of actual spending and making needed budget adjustments. Keeping track of all spending and placing it into the categories of your budget provides valuable information about your habits and the progress made toward achievement of your financial goals. Tracking your spending will also help you develop a better, more precise budget in the future. For example, if you fail to include a spending item or two in your initial budget, when that actual spending is observed, you can then make sure to include it in your new budget next time. Suppose you budget $100 for restaurant meals for the month but then realize that you actually spent $150. You will know to either change your budget or your spending to account for this difference. The documentation of your actual spending provides you with a feedback mechanism that will help you make adjustments to your budget and spending in the future.

Budgeting your income and monitoring your behavior will help you evaluate your spending and direct it toward the categories that will provide you with the most overall value. Four simple steps will get you on the path to financial stability: Begin immediately, set goals, get tools, and design a budget to meet your goals.

Step 1. Start now and increase the likelihood of success! Don't fool yourself into thinking that budgeting is only for people with jobs or high salaries or that you'll start "later." Children receiving allowance, students receiving support from their parents, and people without direct incomes should still budget and develop goals. Budgeting will not be easier when you are older or when you are earning more money. In fact, it will probably be more complex. It is easy to procrastinate. People who budget, spend their money wisely, and save for the future generally started early when their incomes were relatively low.[77]

Step 2. Set goals. Incentives matter. Recognize this in your personal life, and let your goals drive your actions. Set short-, medium-, and long-term financial goals and incorporate them into your budget. Short-term milestones can be achieved within the next year and provide immediate gratification. Depending on your situation, they might include the elimination of the credit-card debt on your highest-interest-rate loan, a significant increase in your emergency fund for coverage of unexpected expenditures, or money for an upgrade of your phone or other technological device. Midterm goals are achieved over a longer period—anywhere between one and three years. Purchasing a pre-owned car with cash, putting 20 percent down on a home or condo, and building a solid savings account leading to a well-diversified portfolio are examples of goals that will generally require more time to achieve. Finally,

77. Thomas Stanley and William D. Danko point out in their bestseller *The Millionaire Next Door* (Atlanta: Longstreet Press, 1996) that the most common characteristic of millionaires is that they have lived beneath their means for a long time. Over half of them never received any inheritance, and fewer than 20 percent received 10 percent or more of their wealth from inheritance (p. 16).

saving and investing for your children's college and for retirement, and paying off student loans or a home **mortgage** provide examples of longer-term goals many will want to pursue.

As indicated earlier, saving and investing should be specific categories in your budget. The sooner you start spending strategically, saving, and investing, the more wealth you will build. What is not so obvious is how much more wealth you can accumulate by starting early. Even the smallest amount saved or invested today can make a very big difference. Consider the following long-range plan:

Start regularly saving $2 a day for two years when you turn twenty-two years of age. That's probably not as much as you will spend on coffee, bottled water, snacks, or have in loose change at the end of the day. Then from your twenty-fourth until your twenty-sixth birthday, begin saving $3 a day. That's just a dollar more, and your income will probably have increased. Between the ages of twenty-six and thirty, bump up your savings amount to $4 per day. By not spending this amount daily and putting it aside in an account with a positive rate of return, you won't cramp your style much. By the time you reach thirty, you will have saved $9,490, plus the interest received—quite a nice sum. Saving $2, $3, or $4 a day really adds up.

But here's the real surprise. By the time you retire at age sixty-seven, the saving from just this early nine-year period can add more than $150,000 to your wealth if invested wisely, and that's in today's purchasing power. This will be the case if you earn a real rate of return of about 7 percent—what the stock market has yielded historically (more on this rate of return and the power of compound interest in future elements). Morcover, if you start early, you are far more likely to continue with a regular savings plan throughout your life.

Step 3. Use budgeting tools. Don't re-create the wheel by starting with a blank piece of paper to develop a budget. With today's websites, spreadsheets, and apps, budgeting has never been easier. A plethora of resources exist at little or no money cost. Literally, they are available at your fingertips. Conduct an internet search for "budgeting tools," and find numerous high-quality and secure budgeting options. Choose one that helps you become meticulous in logging your expenses and income, keeps your financial goals in front of you, issues payment reminders, helps you control any impulses to spend outside your budget, and links you to options on how to achieve those goals. Make a habit of using your selected budgeting tool. Keeping track of your spending and income can be easy with the right tools. For more on budgeting basics and suggestions for creative consumption and savings plans, visit commonsenseeconomics.com/supplementals/.

Step 4. Devise a plan of action. Create a personal budget with actual and proposed items to achieve your goals. Although we constantly think about all the things we "need" to buy, there are very few things most of us are required to have beyond adequate food, clean water, basic shelter, and simple clothes. The best way to see where you can begin to achieve your goals is by listing your "needs" and separating them from your "wants." Reduce your wants to make way for savings and investing, and for devising a plan within your budget to meet your short-, medium-, and long-term goals. This places you in the driver's seat of your financial life.

An architect does not build a house without a blueprint. A surgeon does not effectively remove a patient's appendix without coordinating her plans with the other members of the medical team. An athlete does not end up competing at the Olympics without committing to a philosophy of success long before reaching the Olympics. Developing a detailed plan of action, sticking to it, and updating it when necessary are essential if you are going to succeed in all aspects of life, including your financial life.

Each budgetary item needs to be evaluated within the context of the others. Since you have limited income, increased spending in one area translates into decreased spending in another, unless new sources of income are identified. As stressed in Part 1, every choice has an opportunity cost. Consider yours when making a spending decision. Examine the big picture through your budgetary lens. Figure out your monthly basics: Show how much you earn, pay in taxes, save, invest, spend, and face in debt.

Regardless of your occupation, income, or position in life, the two actions in the budgeting process—creation of your budget and tracking and adjusting your spending to improve your welfare—will help you systematically examine and guide your spending to get where you want to go. Make your plan crystal clear and become the CEO of you. Commit to creating a budget that organizes your spending, controls your debt, provides emergency funds, helps you meet various financial goals, and supplies funds for investing.

Dave Ramsey, one of the nation's leading financial advisors, highlights the importance of making a personal commitment to forming sound money habits. He claims, "The thing I have discovered about working with personal finance is that the good news is that it is not rocket science. Personal finance is about 80 percent behavior. It is only about 20 percent head knowledge."[78] After reading the entirety of Part 4, you will have the head knowledge. Are you ready to focus and commit to aligning your consumption, saving, borrowing, and earning decisions with those that promise financial stability and lead to a rewarding life?

4. Manage credit and debt wisely.

Imprudent use of credit cards and debt can be a huge stumbling block to financial success. Although many people use credit carefully, others act as if an unused balance on a credit card is like money in the bank. This is blatantly false and dangerous thinking. An unused balance on

---

78. See Dave Ramsey, BrainyQuote.com, https://www.brainyquote.com/quotes/dave _ramsey_520281.

your credit card merely means that you have some additional borrowing power; it does not enhance your wealth or provide you with more money. It is best to think of your credit card as a means of using what you have in your checking account. If you have funds in your checking account, you can use your credit card to access those funds—if you pay off the bill every month. If you don't have sufficient funds in your account, don't make the purchase.

While credit cards and their electronic counterparts (such as PayPal and Apple Pay) are convenient to use, they are also both seductive and costly methods of borrowing. Your outstanding credit-card balance is a loan—a debt that must be repaid. Because credit cards make it easy to run up debt, they are potentially dangerous. Some people seem unable to control the impulse to spend when there is an unused balance on their cards.[79] If you have this problem you need to take immediate action! You need to stop using credit for spending you cannot afford. Get your hands on a pair of scissors and cut up all of your credit cards. If you do not, they will lead to financial misfortune.

Making purchases on your credit card makes it look as though you are buying more with your money, but the bill invariably comes due. This presents another temptation: the option to send in a small payment to cover the interest and a tiny percentage of the balance and keep most of your money to spend on more things. If you choose this option and continue to run up your balance, however, you will quickly confront a major problem—the high interest rates being charged on the unpaid balance. Interest charges of 15 to 18 percent on credit-card debt are common. These rates are far higher than most people, even

---

79. Some may need creative methods of controlling impulse purchases with a credit card. If this is the case, economist and financial advisor William C. Wood suggests that you freeze your credit card inside a block of ice in your refrigerator. By the time the ice thaws, your impulse to buy may have cooled. For an excellent book on personal finance written from a Christian perspective, see William C. Wood, *Getting a Grip on Your Money* (Downers Grove, IL: Inter-Varsity Press, 2002).

successful investors, can earn on their savings and investments. As we shall see in later elements, you can become wealthy earning 7 percent per year on your investments. Unfortunately, high interest rates on outstanding debt will have the opposite impact. Paying 15 to 18 percent on your credit-card debt can drive even a person with a good income into financial distress.

Consider the example of Sean, a young professional who decides to take a few days to relax in the Bahamas. The trip costs Sean $1,500, which he puts on his credit card. But instead of paying the full amount at the end of the month, Sean pays only the minimum, and he keeps doing so for the next ten years, when the bill is finally paid off. How much did Sean pay for his trip, assuming an 18 percent interest rate on his credit card? He pays $26.63 per month for 120 months, or a total of $3,195.40. So Sean pays his credit-card company more than he paid for the air travel, hotel, food, and entertainment.

Sean could have taken the trip for a whole lot less by planning ahead and starting to make payments to himself before the trip, instead of making payments to the credit-card company after the trip. By saving $75 a month at 5 percent per year in compound interest (we will discuss compound interest in Element 7) for twenty months, Sean could have had $1,560.89 for the trip, and not the $3,195.40 he ended up paying (including interest) for the same trip (but taken earlier) on the credit card. In other words, by saving and planning to make his trip, instead of running up credit-card debt to pay for it, Sean could take two trips for less than what he ended up paying for one on credit.

In some cases, you may already have a sizable credit-card bill. The very first thing anyone who has credit-card debt and is serious about achieving financial success should do is *pay that debt off,* from savings if necessary. It would have been better if you had avoided that debt, but it does provide an opportunity for you to get a very high return: Every dollar you save to pay down a credit-card debt effectively earns an interest rate of 18 percent, or whatever you are paying on the debt.

Look at it this way. If you put a dollar in an investment that is paying 18 percent, then one year from now it has added $1.18 to your net worth. If you save a dollar to pay off your credit-card debt, then one year from now it has also added $1.18 to your net worth. Your debt will be that much lower—first, from the dollar you saved that reduced your debt initially and, second, from the 18 cents you would have otherwise owed in interest.

Does it ever make sense for an individual or family to purchase a good on credit? The answer is "yes," but only if the good is a long-lasting asset and if the borrowed funds are repaid before the asset is worn out. This way you pay for a good as you use it.

Very few purchases meet these criteria. Three categories of major expenditures come to mind: housing, automobiles, and education. If maintained properly, a new house may provide useful life for forty or fifty years into the future. Under these circumstances, the use of a thirty-year mortgage to finance the expenditure is perfectly sensible. Similarly, if an automobile can reasonably be expected to be driven five or six years, there's nothing wrong with financing it over a four-year period.

When long-lasting assets are still generating additional income or a valuable service after the loans used to finance their purchase are repaid, some of the loan payments are actually a form of savings and investment, which will enhance the net worth of a household. Like housing, investments in education generally provide net benefits over a lengthy time period. Young people investing in an education through debt financing may reap dividends in the form of higher earnings. The educational investment will be a good one if, over the next twenty or thirty years, the higher earnings are sufficient to pay off the borrowed funds. But there are risks here: If the additional education does not increase your future earnings, at least not by much, it may be exceedingly difficult to repay the borrowed funds. (Note: This issue will be considered in more detail in Element 11 of this part.)

Financing an item over a time period lengthier than the useful life of the asset forces you to pay in the future for something that will no longer be of value to you. As a result, you will be forced to reduce your future consumption. Further, this strategy increases your indebtedness and you will become poorer in the future.

For most households the implications of this guideline are straightforward: Do not borrow funds to finance anything other than housing, automobiles, and education. Furthermore, make sure that funds borrowed for the purchase of these items will be repaid well before the expiration of the asset's useful life. Application of this simple guideline will go a long way toward keeping you out of financial trouble.

How can you tell if you are managing your credit and debt wisely? Here are two general guidelines. First, no single monthly debt payment should be greater than 28 percent of your monthly gross income. Second, all combined debt payments should be no greater than 36 percent of your monthly gross income. Even if you follow these two, your credit score is the primary indicator. Your **FICO score**, created by the Fair Isaac Corporation, is the most widely used metric. With a range of 300 to 850, it is used by banks and other financial institutions to assess risk and determine the interest rate you will pay on loans. It is also used by potential employers to assist in hiring decisions. Maintaining a consistently high score will greatly enhance your wealth-building potential. You may access your credit report from each of the three nationwide credit bureaus every twelve months without charge by visiting annualcreditreport.com.

5. Spend strategically.

Most of us would like to have more in the future without having to give up much today. Many, including those with incomes well above average, do two things that undermine this objective. First, as we saw in the previous element, they go into debt to buy things before they can afford them. Second, they insist on buying items before carefully considering alternatives.

As we saw in Element 3 on budgeting, make sure your purchases are within your budget. Ask yourself the following questions before buying: Is this purchase taking me toward or away from my goals? What will my life be like with the purchase? What will it be like without it? Is this a need or a want? Am I simply replacing an item I already have that is still usable, or am I obtaining something new? Are there any alternatives?

You can stretch your money by buying used items when they will serve you almost as well as new ones. The problem with buying things new is that they depreciate or decline in value almost immediately. Thus, while new items can be purchased, they cannot be owned as new items for long. Almost as soon as an item is purchased, it becomes "used" in terms of market value.

Buying things that are used—or, in today's parlance, pre-owned—can lead to substantial savings. Consider the cost of purchasing a new automobile compared with a used one. Suppose you buy a brand-new car for $28,000 and trade it in after one year; you will receive about $18,000, or $10,000 less than you paid for it. If you drove the car 15,000 miles, then your depreciation cost—the cost to you of the decline in the car's value—is about 66 cents per mile.

But instead of buying a new car, you can buy one that is a year old from a dealer. You will pay about $20,000. This is $8,000 less than it cost new (and about $2,000 more than the original owner received from the dealer).

Given how long cars last if you take care of them, you should easily be able to get excellent service from your used car for eight years, at which time you can probably sell it for about $2,000. If you drove 15,000 miles per year, your depreciation cost per mile will be $18,000/120,000 miles, or just 15 cents. This is 51 cents per mile less than the cost of driving a new car every year. Staying with the assumption that you drive 15,000 miles a year, the depreciation saving from the used car is $7,650 every year. Of course, your repair bills may be somewhat higher after the car is a few years old, but even if they average $1,650 a year (very doubtful), you will still save $6,000 each year by sacrificing that new car smell.

Many other items are just as functional used as new and often much less expensive. Clothes, furniture, appliances, refurbished phones, and toys come immediately to mind. You may want to spend some time at garage sales or secondhand stores. Given the value of your time, however, there are other ways to find used items. Online options such as Craigslist, Facebook Marketplace, eBay, and apps provide alternatives that reduce time spent and transaction costs. In a few "touches," you can find items that are both in excellent condition and priced significantly below retail. Of course, there are some cases when buying new is economical. We are merely encouraging you to consider the potential savings that can often be derived from used purchases without giving up much in terms of consumer satisfaction. Look for opportunities to get more value from your money.

6. Pay into an emergency fund every month.

We have talked about the value of saving for your future. But you also need an emergency fund. What is that? Life has an endless string of surprise occurrences: a flat tire, a leaking roof, your phone dies—just to name a few.[80] We can't predict which ones will occur or when. But we can predict that over any long period of time, each of us will confront such costly items. Thus, it makes sense to plan for them. This is what your emergency fund is for. It will help you deal with unexpected bills

---

80. Professor William C. Wood calls such items "SIT expenditures." Wood indicates that "'SIT' stands for two things: (1) sit down when you get an unexpected bill; and (2) surprises, insurance and taxes."

that could otherwise put you under severe emotional stress and into a financial bind. An emergency fund also equals a financial-freedom fund. The emotional and mental stress of the unexpected event will be difficult to deal with. An emergency fund makes the finances simply an inconvenience.

The alternative is to wait until the surprise events occur and then try to devise a plan to deal with them. This will generally mean running up credit-card balances or some other method of borrowing funds on highly unfavorable terms. Then you must figure out how you're going to cover the interest charges and eventually repay the funds. All of this leads to anxiety that is likely to result in unwise financial decisions.

How much should you set aside regularly to deal with such events? One approach would be to make a list of the various surprises of the past year and estimate how much each one cost you. Think about car repairs, unexpected travel, doctor's visits, a home appliance replaced—anything that you didn't expect to happen last year. Add the costs up, divide that number by twelve, and begin channeling that amount monthly into your emergency fund. Another approach is to save three to six months of expenses. In other words, imagine you lose all income for three months. Is your emergency fund large enough to replace the income and cover expenses?

You might even want to pay a little more into the account just in case you confront higher future spending in this area. After all, if you pay too much into the account, you can build up a little cushion. If eventually the funds in the account become larger than necessary, you can shift the surplus into investments. The key point is to consider the monthly allocations into your emergency fund as a mandatory rather than an optional budget item. Thus, they should be treated just like your mortgage payment, electric bill, and other regular expenditures.

An emergency fund allows you to purchase a little peace of mind rather than worry about the financial bumps of life. With such a fund you will be able to deal confidently with expenditures that, while unpredictable as to timing, can nonetheless be anticipated with a fair degree of accuracy. During periods when your surprise expenditures are below average, the balance in your emergency fund will grow. When the surprise expenditures are atypically large, the funds in your account will be drawn down, but you can remain calm because you are prepared. This is an important element of what it means for you to "take charge of your money" rather than allowing "money to take charge of you."

7. Put the power of compound interest to work.

Compound interest is the most powerful force in the universe.[81]

—ALBERT EINSTEIN

In Element 3 earlier in this part, we emphasized the importance of budgeting regularly, saving habitually, and spending your money effectively. There are two major reasons for starting earlier rather than later. First, as discussed, those who yield now to the many excuses not to start budgeting, saving, and spending wisely will have a hard time doing so later. But in this element we want to talk more about the second reason to begin saving right away: the big payoff that comes from starting early.

A small head start in your savings program leads to a substantial increase in the payoff when the savings is directed into investment. Recall the example in Element 3 of the additional retirement wealth a young person could have by saving a modest amount from age twenty-two to thirty. Giving up just a little less than $9,500 in purchasing power for those nine years can easily add over $150,000 to retirement

81. Mignon McLaughlin, BrainyQuote.com, supposedly quoting Albert Einstein, www.brainyquote.com/quotes/quotes/m/mignonmcla158995.html. There is some controversy about whether this statement was actually made by Albert Einstein, but he clearly made similar statements highlighting the power of compound interest.

wealth at age sixty-seven. The key to converting a small amount of money now into a large amount later is to start saving immediately to take full advantage of the "miracle of compound interest."

Compound interest is not really a miracle, but sometimes it seems that way. While easy to explain, the results are truly amazing. Compound interest is simply earning interest on interest. If you don't spend the interest earned on your savings this year, the interest will add to both your savings and the interest earned next year. By doing the same thing each year in the future, you then earn interest on your interest on your interest, and so on. This may not seem like much, and for the first few years it doesn't add that much to your wealth. But before too long your wealth begins growing noticeably, and the larger it becomes, the faster it grows. It's like a small snowball rolling down a snow-covered mountain. At first it increases in size slowly. But each little bit of extra snow adds to the size, which allows even more snow to be accumulated, and soon it is huge and growing rapidly.

The importance of starting your savings program early is explained by how compound interest sets the stage for the later accelerating effect. The savings you make right before retirement won't add much more to your retirement wealth than the amount you save—a little but not much. The snowball that starts near the bottom of the mountain won't be much bigger when it stops rolling. So the sooner you start saving, the more time that early savings will have to grow, and the more dramatic the growth will be.

Consider a simple example. Assume a sixteen-year-old is reading this book and decides to act on some of what she's read. She sets goals, budgets, and strategically makes decisions in such a way that she reduces her spending by $7.50 per day. So, if our teenager—let's call her Olivia—alters her decisions just a little, she will save $2,737.50 a year. Suppose that instead of spending this amount on something else, Olivia invests it in a mutual fund that provides an annual rate of return of 7 percent in real terms—that is, after adjusting for inflation. (Note: This 7 percent return is approximately equal to the annual rate of return of the **Standard & Poor's (S&P) 500 Index**, an index of the five hundred largest U.S. firms that mirrors the performance of the overall stock market.) As Exhibit 14 illustrates, if Olivia keeps this up for ten years, when she is twenty-six she will have accumulated $37,823 from savings of $27,375. Not bad for a rather small sacrifice.

But this is just liftoff; the payoff from compound interest is merely getting started. If Olivia keeps this savings plan going until she is thirty-six, she will have $112,225 from savings of $54,750. Continuing until she is forty-six will find her with $258,586 from savings of $82,125. And now the afterburners really start kicking in. By the time Olivia is fifty-six she will have $546,501 from saving contributions of $109,500. As Exhibit 14 shows, when she retires at age sixty-seven, she will have $1,193,512 from direct contributions of only $139,613. Thus, by choosing a slightly different spending pattern and investing the funds, Olivia accumulates nearly $1.2 million in retirement benefits—and this figure is in dollars with today's purchasing power![82]

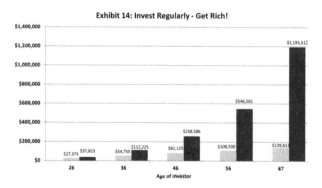

Exhibit 14: Invest Regularly - Get Rich!

Source: Authors' calculations. Assumes altering spending habits to save $7.50 per day and earning interest of 7 percent per year.

82. Our calculations assume that your investments yield a return of 7 percent every year. Obviously, this is unlikely to happen. Even though you can expect an average annual return of approximately 7 percent, this return will vary from year to year. This can make a difference in how much you accumulate at retirement, but the difference is likely to be small.

Alternatively, consider what would happen if Olivia continued her original spending habits from age sixteen to twenty-six, then altered her habits and started allocating the $7.50 per day into an investment fund. It is good that she made the changes, and she will still benefit from the savings. But by postponing her investing program by ten years, instead of having $1,193,512 at age sixty-seven, Olivia will have only $587,494. Delaying a fifty-one-year investing program by ten years costs Olivia $606,018 at retirement!

You don't have to give up much in order to enlarge your savings. Making small sacrifices in consumption can yield powerful results. Instead of buying the premium cup of coffee every morning, purchase the generic one or make a cup at home. Instead of eating lunch at a restaurant every day, bring your lunch one or two days a week. Skip the soft drink or beverage at a restaurant and drink water. Carpool or take the bus to work once a week to save gas money. Everyone can find small changes in their consumption habits to save money.

Again, our point is not that you should live a miserable life of austerity and sacrifice so that you can be rich when you retire. Where's the advantage in becoming rich in the future by living in poverty until the future arrives? Instead, we are stressing that anyone can have a high standard of living and still accumulate a lot of wealth, because it does not take much savings to get a big payoff. Of the $1,193,512 Olivia accumulated by altering her spending, only $139,613 came from reducing her consumption. Indeed, people who save and invest will be able to consume far more than those who do not. At retirement—or sooner—Olivia can start spending her wealth and end up having much more than if she had never saved.

All it takes is an early savings program, a little patience, knowing how to get a reasonable return on your investments (see the next two elements), and taking advantage of the power of compound interest.

8. Diversify: Don't put all your eggs in one basket.

The two most common financial investments are stocks and bonds. Let's make sure you understand the nature of these two instruments. **Stocks** represent ownership of corporate businesses. Stock owners are entitled to the fraction of the firm's future net revenues represented by their ownership shares. If the future net revenues of the business are expanding, the stockholders will gain. The gains of stockholders typically come in the form of either dividends (regular payments to owners) or appreciation in the value of the stock. But there is no assurance the business will be successful and earn income in the future. If unsuccessful, the value of the firm's stock will decline. While the stockholders are not liable for the debts of the corporation, they may lose all of the funds used to purchase the stock. (Note: "Equity" is another term for stock.)

Bonds provide businesses, governments, and other organizations with a convenient way to borrow money. These organizations acquire funds from bond purchasers in exchange for the promise (and legal obligation) to pay interest and repay the entire **principal** (amount borrowed) at specified times in the future. As long as the organization issuing the bond is solvent, the bondholder can count on the funds being repaid with interest.

All investments involve risk. The market value of a corporate stock investment can change dramatically in a relatively short period of time. Even if the **nominal return** is guaranteed, as in the case of high-quality bonds, changes in interest and/or inflation rates can substantially change the value of the asset. If you have most of your wealth tied up in the ownership of a small number of corporate stocks (or even worse, a single stock), you are especially vulnerable. The experiences of those holding a large share of their assets in the **equities** of firms such as Blockbuster, Sears, and JCPenney illustrate this point.

You can reduce your risk through **diversification**—holding a large number of unrelated assets. Diversification puts the law of large numbers to work for you. While some of the investments in a diversified **portfolio** will do poorly, others will do extremely well. The performance of the latter will offset that of the former, and the rate of return will converge toward the average.

For those seeking to build wealth without having to become involved in day-to-day business decision-making, the stock market can provide attractive returns. It has done so historically. During the last two centuries, corporate stocks yielded a real return (real means adjusted for inflation) of approximately 7 percent per year, compared to a real return of about 3 percent for bonds.[83]

The risk with stocks is that no one can ever be sure what they will be worth at any specified time in the future; inevitably there will be periods over which the market value of your investments is falling, only to rise months or years later. But that risk, known as volatility, is a big reason why stocks yield a significantly higher rate of return than savings accounts, money-market certificates, and short-term government bonds, all of which guarantee you a given amount in the future. Since most people value the additional certainty in the yields that bonds and savings accounts provide over stocks, the average return on stocks has to be higher to attract investors away from their less risky counterparts with more predictable returns.

Mutual funds can help investors diversify and reduce risk. Mutual funds simply combine the funds of a group of investors and channel them into various categories of investments, such as stocks (equities),

83. A 7 percent real rate of return may not sound like much compared to what some stocks, such as Dell and Microsoft, have yielded. But a 7 percent compounded rate of return means that the value of your savings will double every ten years. In contrast, it will take thirty-five years to double your money at a 2 percent interest rate, the approximate after-tax return earned historically by savings accounts and money-market mutual funds. Note: You can approximate the number of years it will take to double your funds at alternative interest rates by simply dividing the yield (the average annual return on your money) into seventy. This is sometimes referred to as the Rule of 70.

bonds, real estate, or treasury bills. Thus, there are a variety of mutual-fund categories.

An **equity mutual fund** channels the funds of its investors into the stock of many firms. These funds provide even small investors with an economical way to achieve diversity and reduce risk. The risks of stock market investments are substantially lowered if one continually adds to or holds a diverse portfolio of stocks over a lengthy period of time, say thirty or thirty-five years. Historically, when a diverse set of stocks has been held over a lengthy time frame, the rate of return has been high and the variation in that return has been relatively small. Regular payments into an equity mutual fund holding a diverse set of stocks provide investors with a low-cost method of investing in the stock market.

Diversification will reduce the volatility of investments in the stock market in two ways. First, when some firms do poorly, others do well. An oil price decline that causes lower profits in the oil industry will tend to boost profits in the airline industry because the cost of airline fuel will decline. When profits in the steel industry fall because steel prices decline, the lower steel prices will tend to boost the profits in the automobile industry.

Second, diversification can help protect you against a change in general economic conditions. A recession or an expansion will cause changes in the value of the stocks of almost all firms. But diversification reduces the volatility in the value of your investments because a recession is worse for some firms and industries than others, and a boom is better for some than for others. For example, the recession that harms Neiman Marcus may boost sales and profits for Walmart, at least relative to most firms.

Some employers offer retirement programs—such as a 401(k) plan—that will match your purchases of the company stock (but not investments in other firms) or will allow you to purchase the company stock at a substantial discount. Such a plan makes purchasing the stock of your company attractive. If you have substantial confidence in the company, you may want to take advantage of this offer. After a holding period, typically three years, these plans will often permit you to sell the purchased shares and use the proceeds to undertake other investments. As soon as you are permitted to do so, you should choose this option. Failure to do so will mean that you will soon have too many of your investment eggs in the basket of the company for which you work. This places you in a position of double jeopardy: Both your employment and the value of your investments depend substantially on the success of your employer. Do not put yourself in this position.

We can summarize the importance of stock investments and diversity this way: To achieve their financial potential, individuals must channel their savings into diversified investments that yield attractive returns. In the past, long-term investments in the stock market have yielded high returns. Equity mutual funds make it possible for even small investors to hold a diverse portfolio, add to it monthly, and still keep transaction costs low. Investing in a diverse portfolio over a lengthy period of time reduces the risk of stock ownership to a low level. All investments have some uncertainty. But if the past century and a half are any guide, we can confidently expect that over the long haul, a diverse portfolio of corporate stocks will yield a higher real return than will savings accounts, bonds, certificates of deposit, money-market funds, and similar financial instruments. Ownership of stock through mutual funds is particularly desirable for young people saving for their retirement years.

9. Indexed equity mutual funds can help you outperform the experts.

Many Americans refrain from investments in stocks because they feel they do not have either the time or expertise to identify businesses that are likely to be successful in the future. They are correct about the difficulties involved in forecasting the future direction of either individual stocks or a broad measure of their average price. No one can say for sure what will happen to either the price of any specific stock or the general level of stock prices in the future.

Most economists accept the **random-walk theory**. According to this theory, current stock prices reflect the best information that is known about the future state of corporate earnings, the health of the economy, and other factors that influence stock prices. Therefore future changes of stock prices will be driven by surprise occurrences, things that people do not currently anticipate. By their very nature, these factors are unpredictable. If they were predictable, they would already be reflected in current stock prices.

Why not pick just the stocks that will do well, as Apple, Google, and Microsoft have, and stay away from everything else? That is a great idea, except for one problem: The random-walk theory also applies to the prices of specific stocks. The prices of stocks with attractive future profit potential will already reflect these prospects. The future price of a specific stock will be driven by unforeseeable changes and additional information about the prospects of the firm that will only become known over time. Countless factors affect the future price of a particular stock, and they are constantly changing in unpredictable ways. The price of Apple stock could be driven down, for example, because of an idea a high-school kid is working on in his basement right now. Thus, there is no way that you can know ahead of time which stocks are going to rocket into the financial stratosphere and which ones are going to fizzle on the launchpad or crash after takeoff.

You may be able to improve your chances a little by studying the stock market, the details of particular corporations, and economic trends and forecasts. For most of us, however, the best option will be to channel our long-term (that is, our retirement) savings into an equity mutual fund. **Exchange traded funds (ETFs)** are similar to mutual funds that are traded on market exchanges.

There are two broad categories of equity mutual funds: managed funds and indexed funds. A **managed equity mutual fund** is one in which an "expert," the fund's portfolio manager, decides what stocks will be held and when they will be bought and sold. The fund manager is almost always supported by a research staff that examines both individual companies and market trends in an effort to identify those stocks that are most likely to do well in the future. The manager seeks to pick and choose the stockholdings of the fund in a manner that will maximize the fund's rate of return.

The second type of fund, an **indexed equity mutual fund**, merely holds stocks in the same proportion as their representation in broad indexes of the stock market, such as the S&P 500 or the Dow Jones Industrial Average. Very little trading is necessary to maintain a portfolio of stocks that mirrors a broad index. Neither is it necessary for index funds to undertake research evaluating the future prospects of companies. Because of these two factors, the operating costs of index funds are substantially lower, usually 1 or 2 percentage points lower, than those of managed funds. As a result, index funds charge lower fees, and therefore a larger share of your investment flows directly into the purchase of stock.

An equity mutual fund indexed to a broad stock market indicator, such as the S&P 500, will earn approximately the average stock market return for its shareholders. What is so great about the average return? As noted earlier, historically the stock market has yielded an average real rate of return of about 7 percent. That means that the real value of your stockholdings doubles approximately every ten years. That's not bad. Even more important, the average rate of return yielded by a broad index fund beats the return of almost all managed mutual funds when comparisons are made over periods of time, such as a decade. This is not surprising, because, as the random walk theory indicates, not even the experts will be able to forecast consistently the future direction of stock prices with any degree of accuracy.

Over the typical ten-year period, the S&P 500 has yielded a higher return than 85 percent of the actively managed funds. Over twenty-year periods, mutual funds indexed to the S&P 500 have generally outperformed about 98 percent of the actively managed funds.[84] Thus the odds are very low, about 1 to 50, that you or anyone else will be able to select an actively managed fund that will do better than the market average *over the long run.*

Just because a managed mutual fund does well for a few years or even a decade, it does not follow that it will do well in the future. For example, the top twenty managed equity funds during the 1980s outperformed the S&P 500 Index by 3.9 percentage points per year over the decade. But if investors entering the market in 1990 thought they would beat the market by choosing the "hot" funds of the 1980s, they would have been disappointed. The top twenty funds of the 1980s underperformed the S&P 500 Index by 1.2 percentage points per year during the 1990s. Similarly, the average return of the top twenty managed equity funds from 1990 to 1999 outperformed the S&P 500 Index by 3.1 percentage points per year; but from 2000 to 2009 those same funds underperformed the S&P 500 Index by 1.3 percentage points per year.[85] For the twenty-five-year period 1993–2017, the S&P 500 Index yielded an annual rate of return of 9.7% compared to an annual return of 8.6% for the average managed equity fund.[86]

These examples actually understate the advantage of a mutual fund indexed to the S&P 500 compared to a managed equity fund because of the survivorship bias. The S&P 500 index is highly unlikely to go out of business, but over the time period relevant to saving for retirement, a managed fund is quite likely to shut down. A mutual fund can disappear for two reasons, both related to poor performance: It may

84. See Jeremy J. Siegal, *Stocks for the Long Run,* 3rd ed. (New York: McGraw Hill, 2002), 342–43.

85. See Burton Malkiel, *A Random Walk Down Wall Street: The Time-Tested Strategy for Successful Investing* (New York: W. W. Norton, 2015), 177–78. For additional evidence that a mutual fund yielding a high rate of return during one period cannot be counted on to continue to do so in the future, see Mark M. Carhart, "On Persistence in Mutual Fund Performance," *Journal of Finance* 52, no. 1 (March 1997), 57–82.

86. See Malkiel, *A Random Walk* (2020), 173.

be shut down with the remaining value of the fund distributed to its owners or it may be merged into another managed fund with a better record. Although there are thousands of managed mutual funds today, in 1970 there were only 358. Burton Malkiel followed those funds through 2013. During these forty-three years, 274 funds—over 75 percent of the total—ceased to exist. Out of the remaining 84, only 4 had outperformed the S&P 500 index by 2 percentage points or more on an annual basis.[87]

The stock market has historically yielded higher returns than other major investment categories, and index funds make it possible for the ordinary investor to earn these returns without worrying about trying to pick either individual stocks or a specific mutual fund. Of course, there will be ups and downs and even some fairly lengthy periods of declining stock prices. Therefore, many investors will want to reduce equities as a percentage of their asset holdings as they approach retirement (see the following element). But, based on a lengthy history of stock market performance, the long-term yield derived from a broad index of the stock market can be expected to exceed that of any other alternative, including managed equity funds.[88]

As Exhibit 15 illustrates, when held over a lengthy time period, a diverse holding of stocks has historically yielded both a high and relatively stable rate of return. Data for the highest and lowest average annual real rate of return derived from broad stock market investments for periods of varying length between the years 1871 and 2019 are shown here. The exhibit assumes that the investor paid a fixed amount annually into a mutual fund that mirrored the S&P 500

87. Malkiel, *A Random Walk* (2015), 177–78.

88. Even those investing in index funds should obtain some advice from experts. There are tax and legal considerations, such as taking advantage of tax-deferred possibilities, establishing wills and trusts, making wise insurance choices, and so on, which do require input from specialists.

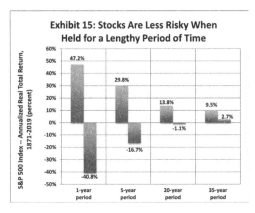

Source: Linqun Liu, Andrew J. Rettenmaier, and Zijun Wang, *Social Security and Market Risk* (National Center for Policy Analysis Working Paper No. 244, July 2001). The returns are based on the assumption that an individual invests a fixed amount for each year in the investment period. Data are updated through 2019.

Index.[89] Clearly, huge swings are possible when stocks are held for only a short time period. During the 1871–2019 period, the single-year returns of the S&P 500 ranged from 47.2 percent to −35.5 percent. Even over a five-year period, the compound annual returns ranged from 29.8 percent to −16.7 percent.

However, note how the "best returns" and "worst returns" converge as the length of the investment period increases. When a thirty-five-year period is considered, the compound annual return for the best thirty-five years between 1871 and 2019 was 9.5 percent, compared to 2.7 percent for the worst thirty-five years. Thus, the annual real return of stocks during the worst-case scenario was about the same as the real return for bonds. This high and relatively stable long-term return makes stocks a particularly desirable method of investing for retirement.

Here is the most important takeaway from this element: Do not

89. See Liqun Liu, Andrew J. Rettenmaier, and Zijun Wang, *Social Security and Market Risk* (National Center for Policy Analysis Working Paper No. 244, July 2001). The stock market changes of recent years do not alter the data of Exhibit 15.

allow a lack of time and expertise to keep you out of equity invest-ments. You do not have to do a lot of research or be a "super stock picker" in order to be a successful investor. Regular contributions into an indexed equity mutual fund will provide you with attractive returns on long-term investments with minimal risk. For most, these invest-ments will be an important ingredient of a sound retirement plan. Ev-ery large reputable investment firm will have several indexed equity mutual funds from which to choose. Each firm may have a slightly dif-ferent name for their fund, so be sure to read the description to deter-mine the one that best fits your needs.

10. Adjust your asset mix to match the timing of financial goals.

When making long-term investments, such as the funds allocated into a retirement plan, a stock index fund is generally your best investment. While the long-term return of stocks is substantially greater than bonds, the value of the latter is more stable over short time periods. As the time approaches when the funds from an investment plan may be needed, it will make sense to shift funds toward investments of more stable value. Given a five-year horizon, purchasing a bond that matures in five years, at which point you will receive your initial investment plus interest, is a relatively safe investment. As a general proposition, buy bonds that mature at about the time you will need the funds, per-haps for a down payment on a home or income during retirement.

The primary risk of owning bonds is inflation, which lessens the value of both the principal and the fixed-interest payments. This risk may be reduced through the ownership of **TIPS (Treasury Inflation-Protected Securities)**. TIPS pay a market-determined fixed interest rate set at the time they are purchased, plus an annual adjusted yield for the rate of inflation during the life of the bond. When people expect inflation, the initial fixed interest rate of TIPS will tend to be lower than the rate for regular U.S. Treasury securities. If the actual rate of inflation is higher than was expected, TIPS will generally yield a higher rate of return than regular Treasury securities, but the opposite will be the case when the actual rate of inflation is less than what was expected. Thus, TIPS provide the bondholder with protection against an unanticipated surge in the inflation rate. TIPS are particularly attractive for retirees seeking to generate a specific stream of real purchasing power from their assets. However, their short-term value will also be influenced by changes in interest rates and how policy is expected to impact the future rate of inflation. Therefore, we recommend that one consult with a financial advisor before investing heavily in TIPS.

An additional risk associated with bonds is the impact of changes in interest rates. Suppose you buy a $1,000 thirty-year bond that pays 5 percent interest. This bond promises to pay you $50 in interest every year for thirty years, at which time it matures and you get $2,500. But if the overall or general interest rate increases to 10 percent soon after you buy this bond, then your bond will immediately fall in value to about one-half of what you paid for it. The reason? At a 10 percent interest rate, an investor can get $50 in interest every year by buying a $500 bond. So $500 is about all anyone will be willing to pay for your $1,000 bond. Of course, if the interest rate drops to 2.5 percent soon after you buy your thirty-year 5 percent bond, then its price will approximately *double* in value. But this is more volatility (or risk) than you want to take if you are saving for something you expect to buy in five years.

How long should a portfolio consist of stocks, and when should the move to bonds be made? That depends on the length of time before you want to access the investment funds. As we suggested above, relatively short-term investments may do best in bonds exclusively. For example, a young couple saving in order to place 20 percent down to buy a house may be better off avoiding the stock market entirely—for that portion of their savings *only*—and investing it in bonds. That is because purchasing a house or condominium often involves saving for just a few years. In contrast, a couple might save for eighteen years to finance a college education for a newborn, or thirty-five to forty-five years to build up savings for their retirement. In these two cases, equities should be an important part of, or perhaps the entire, investment fund for most of the saving years.

The parents of a newborn who begin saving right away for the child's college education have more years to build wealth and to diversify the risk of capitalizing on stocks to build it faster. In that case, having some of that college portfolio in equities may make sense. However, as the plunge in stock prices during the Great Recession of 2008–2009 and the market decline in 2022 illustrates, even with an eighteen-year horizon, stockholdings involve risk. Again, investors seeking to reduce risk in their college funds can do so by holding fewer stocks and more bonds, especially as the time approaches when the funds will be needed.

As people earn more and live longer, saving for retirement expenses becomes ever more important. We don't want to drastically, and negatively, alter our lifestyle upon retirement; and we cannot afford to outlive our retirement nest eggs. For the saver whose retirement is more than ten years ahead, a diversified portfolio of stocks, such as a mutual fund indexed to the S&P 500, probably makes the best investment portfolio. For the more conservative saver, having 10, 20, or even 40 percent of one's portfolio in bonds will generally provide more stability in the value of one's retirement assets, even though total returns will probably be lower in the end.

As the need for retirement income approaches, it is prudent for all but the most wealthy among us to begin to switch an all-stock portfolio gradually into bonds. When that switch should begin depends partly on when and how much monthly income is needed during retirement. For those individuals with a large portfolio or a good pension income relative to their retirement income needs, much of their savings can be left longer in equities to maximize expected total return. The goal of switching to bonds is primarily to avoid the need to sell stocks at temporarily low prices. The sooner you expect to turn to your portfolio to meet monthly living expenses, the more important it is to reduce risk by moving strategically and gradually into bonds.

With regard to retirement investments, it is also vitally important to consider the tax treatment of both your investment contributions and retirement income. There are two broad types of retirement plans: traditional plans and Roth IRA plans. Traditional plans include individual retirement accounts (IRAs), 401(k) plans offered by employers, and equivalent 403(b) plans provided by nonprofit organizations. For traditional plans, the contributions into retirement investment accounts are deductible against your taxable income at the time of the contribution. Thus, your tax bill during the current year will be lower. As the result of the tax saving during the current year, your after-tax income will fall by less than your contribution into the traditional plan. In such plans, the taxes on the contributions into your retirement account, as well as the earnings from these investments, are cast into the future. That is, they are tax-deferred until they are withdrawn during retirement. This will be particularly advantageous if you expect to be in a lower tax bracket during your retirement years.

In contrast, the contributions into a Roth IRA are not tax deductible. Thus, there is no tax advantage at the time the contributions are made. However, the value of your investments grows tax-free in Roth IRAs. Thus, during your retirement years, both the contributions and investment earnings of a Roth IRA can be withdrawn without any payment of taxes.

Summarizing, the value of Roth IRA investments grows tax-free, while the contributions and earnings from traditional plans are tax-deferred. Under certain conditions, a tax break in the future can more than make up for the fact that your after-tax income during your working years will be less with a Roth than with a traditional IRA or 401(k). At first glance, a Roth IRA will probably be better for you if you believe your current marginal income tax rate is about the same or lower than what you expect it to be when you are making withdrawals during retirement. In contrast, a traditional IRA or 401(k) will generally be a better option if you believe your current tax rate is higher than it is likely to be during your retirement years. Nonetheless, factors other than present and future income (and tax rates) can also be important. Further, there are income and maximum contribution limits that sometimes apply. Thus, you should seek some impartial and expert advice before making a decision about the type of IRA that will be best for you.

Our advice to those seeking to prepare for future retirement can be summed up this way: Start saving for retirement early, stay with diversified portfolios of stocks until the need for funds is near enough in time to justify gradual shifts toward lower-risk, lower-return assets such as bonds, and take advantage of the favorable tax treatment provided for retirement plans.

11. Reduce risk when making education, housing, and other investment decisions.

Many reading this book will soon be making important decisions regarding what to do after completing high school. Should you go to college, acquire vocational training, or enter the labor force immediately? If you go to college, which one will you choose? Should you select a two-year or four-year, private or public, or in-state or out-of-state school? How will you choose a major? Which college provides you with the most attractive options? These are important investment choices, and tens of thousands of dollars and hours of potential emotional satisfaction are at stake. Thus, it is crucially important that your educational choices are well-informed. As you make educational choices, here are some important factors to consider.

While college may be a desirable option, it is not for everyone. Going to college is costly. If a student incurs the time and money cost of going to college for a couple of years, then drops out without a diploma, the investment is unlikely to be an attractive one. The biggest risk for a student considering postsecondary education is the possibility of a negative return on his or her investment. This would occur if the higher earnings achieved from the education are less than the costs involved in obtaining the education.

According to the Bureau of Labor Statistics (BLS), the median annual earnings in 2022 for workers holding bachelor's degrees were over $30,100 higher than for those who only had a high school diploma.[90] But there is substantial variation in the earnings of college graduates. The actual earnings after graduation depend on many factors, including the skills acquired, college major, and the overall demand and supply conditions of a particular labor market. According to Payscale.com, which has compiled the world's largest database of salary profiles, the college majors with the highest earnings potential include engineering, interaction design, applied economics and management, building science, and actuarial mathematics. At the other end of the scale, majors for which the typical earnings are low include child and family studies, education, social work, exercise science, athletic training, music, and culinary arts.[91]

It is risky to borrow a large sum of money to finance an education expected to result in low future earnings. As we indicated in Elements 1 and 2 earlier in this part, it is important to choose a work activity that you enjoy. But your choice needs to be well-informed. Search for and discover the expected earnings in the occupations for which you are training. We want you to make informed choices that will lead to the

90. U.S. Department of Labor, Bureau of Labor Statistics, "Employment Projections," October 30, 2023, https://www.bls.gov/emp/tables/unemployment-earnings -education.htm.

91. Payscale, Inc., *College Salary Report,* 2023, www.payscale.com/college-salary -report/majors-that-pay-you-back/bachelors.

largest possible return on your educational investment—including the personal satisfaction you derive from the employment.

Let's consider why students sometimes choose educational options that result in negative returns. First, many students have unrealistic expectations about future earnings accompanying career choices. With inflated expectations, they may be willing to pay more for their education than what their future earnings can support. You should investigate resources to keep informed of labor market conditions and earnings potential. In addition to Payscale.com, the BLS *Occupational Outlook Handbook* (*OOH*) is a valuable source. This online handbook provides information on hundreds of occupations, including their requirements, job outlook and growth prospects, and median pay. Having realistic expectations about future income is a vital ingredient for making better decisions about postsecondary education.

Second, many students underestimate the cost of education. The total cost of education includes the direct cost of tuition, books, fees, and room and board. But don't forget about opportunity costs. Going to school, even part-time, means giving up current income from a job. Make sure to properly account for the total cost of education.

Third, students overuse debt. Some view the student loan check as free money and borrow too much. Many young people are ill-prepared to judge how difficult it will be to squeeze the funds for repayment of student loans out of their monthly budget after graduation. Assuming a 3 percent interest rate, you will pay $345 per month for fifteen years to repay $50,000 in loans. You will pay $518 per month for fifteen years to repay $75,000, and $691 per month to repay $100,000. Will your future earnings be sufficient to make the monthly payment on your student loans within the context of your overall budget? Think seriously about this issue prior to taking out a student loan.

We are not saying that you should never borrow to finance education. There are times when this option makes sense. Like any other form of debt, student loan debt requires repayment of principal plus interest and fees. A variety of student loan programs exist. Investigate them carefully to decide what's best for you.

To further minimize education risks, students and their parents can pursue other options to finance education. As a general guideline, develop a financial plan that has debt as the last option. Start with a college savings plan. Students and parents can start their own savings plans or consider the relative benefits of contributing to a government-sponsored qualified tuition program. These programs come in two forms. The first is a prepaid tuition plan, which allows participants to pay a predetermined tuition amount for future education. The second is an investment plan (referred to as a 529 plan) usually comprised of mutual funds, where withdrawals made for qualified educational expenses are tax-free.

Scholarships and grants are also available. They are particularly attractive because they do not have to be repaid. High school guidance offices and the internet are loaded with scholarship and grant lists. Make time to search for them. Each will have a specific set of instructions, eligibility requirements, and deadlines. Factor all of these options into your decision to invest in education and choose a path that makes sense for you given market considerations.

In addition to education, the purchase of a home is perhaps the most important investment decision each of us will confront during a lifetime. For most, a home purchase will be their largest investment, at least initially. Buying a home you can afford in a desirable location and keeping it well maintained can be a good investment. But there are potential pitfalls. Examination of the following factors will help you avoid the worst problems.

First, carefully consider the "own versus rent" option. Many people immediately conclude that purchasing is a better option than renting, because purchasing can build home equity. They reason that their money is wasted on rent going into the landlord's pocket when it could be put to work creating equity, helping to build the homeowner's net worth as the mortgage is paid off and the market value of the property appreciates. However, during the first few years of a mortgage, almost all of the monthly payment is for interest and very little is actually building equity. In most cases, you will accumulate little or no equity during your first three years of ownership. You will simply pay the bank interest instead of paying rent to a landlord.

Second, buying and selling real estate is expensive, and therefore it is not a good idea to purchase a house unless you expect to live in it at least three years. In most states, Realtor commissions are 6 percent or more of the sale price. Closing costs on a mortgage are typically several thousand dollars. If you sell the house within a few years after the initial purchase, the transaction costs are likely to be greater than your equity.

Third, do not buy a house until you have saved for a 20 percent down payment. If your down payment is less than 20 percent, you will have to pay mortgage insurance, which increases your monthly payment. (Mortgage insurance protects the lender from losses that occur when a person defaults on payments.) Also, do not use a mortgage with a low "teaser interest rate" to purchase your home. These rates are followed by sharply escalating interest rates, which will substantially increase your monthly mortgage payment after the initial period has expired.

Fourth, just because you can afford a mortgage payment doesn't mean you can afford the house. The mortgage is the first and most obvious payment made each month. However, home ownership requires other regular payments and obligations that you need to consider. If they are not included in the mortgage as escrow, property taxes must be paid. Homeowner's insurance is required. The roof may leak one day, the hot-water heater, dishwasher, or clothes dryer may break down, the air-conditioning unit or plumbing system may need repair, or any number of other items may result in maintenance costs. You may need a lawn mower and other equipment to maintain your yard. These are all regular expenses you can expect as a homeowner. You need to factor them into your monthly budget when examining whether home ownership makes sense for you.

Lastly, as you build up equity in your house, do not take out another mortgage or borrow against your equity in order to increase your current consumption. Housing prices go down as well as up. After the housing crisis of 2008–2009, many people were "upside down" or "under water" with their housing. That is, the appraised value of their home was less than the outstanding mortgage. Some people incurred huge losses when they sold their homes. Others simply couldn't afford to sell at a loss and kept the home, hoping for a market rebound. Still others went through the painful process of foreclosure. Thus, safety dictates that it is important to maintain a sizable equity in your home.

Living by the guidelines presented above will encourage you to live within your means, economize on housing, and minimize the risks involved in housing decisions. Now let's turn to other potential investments.

While education and housing are likely to be the largest investments you'll make, other investment opportunities will emerge. There are precautions to take when considering which ones to seize. It is important to recognize that when making investments, you are vulnerable; you must think about whether your interests are aligned with the party offering the investment. Whenever you are offered something that seems to be an extremely attractive proposition, it pays to step back and carefully examine the incentives behind why this proposition is being presented to you. Borrowers looking for money to finance a project will initially turn to low-cost sources such as bank loans. Finding individual investors like you and promising a high rate of return makes no sense if financing is available from bank lenders and other investment specialists. High potential returns on any investment inevitably come with high risk; that is, there is a high probability of failure. If banks and professional investors are not interested in the investment, you should ask yourself, "Why should I be?"

The interests of those selling investment alternatives are often substantially different from yours. While you want to earn an attractive return, they are likely to be primarily interested in the commission on the sale or earnings derived from management fees or a high salary related to the business venture. Put bluntly, their primary interest is served by getting their hands on your money. They do not necessarily seek to defraud you; they may well believe that the investment is a genuine opportunity with substantial earning potential. But, no matter how nice they are, how well you know them, or how much it appears that they want to help you, their interests are different from yours. Moreover, once they have your money, you will be in a weak position to alter the situation.

Today, Bitcoin and other cryptocurrencies are assets that use blockchain technology to facilitate peer-to-peer transactions in a virtual world without borders. Everything is tracked and recorded from inception forward, without fees or requiring financial intermediaries. Data on transaction history and the entities involved in crypto exchanges are difficult to change once recorded, authenticated, and validated in a decentralized public ledger. This makes counterfeiting and double counting cryptos nearly impossible. On the flip side, governments don't offer market oversight and leave the users of cryptocurrencies to protect themselves from any losses. Plus, their risks are too new to price and insure privately. They are speculative assets. They are relatively novel and are not recognized by governments as legal tender. Proceed with caution if you introduce them into your investment portfolio.

How can you tell beforehand whether an investment is a wise one? There is no "silver bullet" that can assure positive results from all investment decisions. But there are things you can do that will help you avoid investment disasters costing you tens of thousands of dollars. The following six guidelines are particularly important.

1. If it looks too good to be true, it probably is. This is an old cliché, but a valid one. Some investment marketers may be willing to do just about anything to obtain your money, because once they do, they are in charge and you are vulnerable.

2. Deal only with parties that have reputations to protect. Established companies with solid reputations will be reluctant to direct their clients into unsound investments.

3. Never purchase an investment solicited by telephone, email, or social media. Such marketing is a technique used by those looking to prey on individuals who are easy targets. Do not let yourself be a victim of scams. Never share personal information with people you do not explicitly trust. Your social security number, date of birth, cell phone number, and postal address should be carefully guarded.

4. Do not allow yourself to be forced into a quick decision. Take time to develop an investment strategy. Never let yourself be pressured into having to hastily decide something.

5. Do not allow friendship to influence an investment decision. Numerous people have been directed into bad investments by their friends. If you want to keep a person as your friend, invest your money with an objective third party.

6. If high-pressure marketing is involved, keep your money and run. Attractive investments are sold without the use of high-pressure marketing techniques. If you already have a substantial portfolio, there may be a place in it for high-risk investments, including **"junk" bonds** and precious metals.

But those investments must come from funds that you can afford to lose. If you are looking for a sound way to build wealth, most of your funds should be in more routine lower-risk investments, helping you establish a well-diversified portfolio.

12. Use insurance to manage risk.

Life involves risks. The risks of life range from the small and financially insignificant, like receiving poor service at a restaurant, to the large and financially devastating, such as a severe illness or having your home destroyed by a tornado. While you cannot eliminate risk, you can take steps to reduce and manage it.

You can make choices that will reduce risks. Not texting while driving reduces the chance of being involved in an accident. Wearing a seat belt lowers the chance of injury if you are involved in a collision. Installing smoke detectors and a security system decreases the likelihood of your residence burning down or getting burglarized. Decreasing sugar consumption and eating low-cholesterol foods reduce the chance of illness and disease. However, while your choices can reduce risk, it cannot be eliminated.

How can you manage risk and protect yourself from the most adverse consequences? Insurance can reduce the financial loss resulting from damages to possessions (such as your home or car), an illness, loss of income, or other harmful events. Insurance provides a way for a group of people to pool payments and share risks in order to offset the losses of members actually damaged by an adverse event. The principle of sharing risk is often forgotten because individuals pay premiums to an insurance company and have no interaction with the group members. The insurance company is an intermediary, or middleman, in the risk-sharing process. The company collects premiums from each member of the group (its policyholders), then disburses payments when a covered loss occurs.

To understand how risk sharing works, imagine the following situation: You and four associates go to a restaurant for lunch and expect that the total bill will be $200. The five of you agree to instruct the waitress to randomly give the check to one of you at the end of the meal, and that person will pay the entire amount. You and the other group members can then choose between two options: (1) take a chance, and hope you are not selected to pay the $200 bill; or (2) pay a premium of $40 to an insurer, who will pay the $200 bill if you are selected. Many people will prefer option 2 because it is less risky. While you have to pay the $40 premium, you protect yourself against the 20 percent possibility of having to pay the entire $200 bill.

Of course, insurers providing the risk-sharing service incur costs. They will have to assess risks, formalize agreements, collect premiums, examine and validate claims, and process payments. These handling and processing costs will have to be covered, in addition to the costs of the risk. Thus, the insurance premiums will have to be somewhat higher than the expected costs of the loss. For example, if an insurance company were going to provide members of our lunch group with protection against the 20 percent chance that they might end up with the $200 bill, it would have to charge each a little more than $40, perhaps $44, in order to have an incentive to offer the service.

Insurance reduces risk because it spreads over a larger group of people the burden of unfortunate events that a few experience. In the lunch situation, the $200 bill is coming with certainty. The uncertainty comes from not knowing which member of the group will receive it. A larger group will increase the amount of the potential loss but will also reduce the chance of any individual member receiving the bill.

When it comes to large sums, most of us are risk averse. That means we are willing to pay a premium in order to reduce the adverse consequences of various events. Buying insurance is one way of reducing exposure to risks.

Insurance, however, is not always cost-effective. You should think carefully about whether it makes sense for you to insure against a risk. Yes, you should insure against events that, if they occur, will impose severe financial hardship. A severe illness that prevents you from working for an extended period of time, a car accident, or a flood that damages your home are examples. However, insuring against relatively small adverse events, such as a breakdown of an appliance or television, is generally not cost-effective. Providing the risk-sharing service will be expensive relative to the potential harm. Thus, it will generally be more economical to accept these risks and use an emergency fund (see Element 6 in this part) to plan for and cover the cost of these risks. In contrast, automobile, housing, and health-care insurance are usually cost-effective. In these cases, the cost of spreading the risks over a group of people is generally low relative to the potential damages of an adverse event. We now turn to those topics.

Most states require car owners to maintain some level of automobile insurance. Make sure to check with your insurance company so that you meet the minimum requirements. Customers will pay a premium based on a number of factors. Those include the driver's record, characteristics of the driver, the type of automobile, and the specific coverage limits and deductibles of the policy. A deductible is the amount the customer must pay first before any insurance coverage applies. For example, a $500 deductible means the customer must pay $500 before the insurance policy will pay for a loss. Generally, the higher the deductible, the lower the premium. Coverage is the maximum amount the policy will pay in the event of a loss.

An auto policy is typically structured with a few basic coverages, or types of loss. Collision pays for damages to your car in the event of an accident. Comprehensive pays for noncollision damages, such as theft, vandalism, and acts of nature, like a tree branch falling on your windshield. Liability coverage comes in two forms. First, it pays others for damages to their person or vehicle caused by the operation of your automobile. Second, it pays damages to you and your passengers for medical expenses and death benefits. For example, liability coverage of $500,000 means the most the insurance will pay in the event of a loss is $500,000, even if the actual loss is greater. When purchasing insurance, you should consider carefully the size of your coverage limits and deductible levels. For example, when choosing the size of your deductible, you will want to consider the degree of hardship imposed by payment of the deductible amount if an adverse event should occur.

As just discussed in Element 11, housing is often the largest investment people will make. It makes sense to insure against the loss of your biggest asset. Similar to auto policies, housing insurance will have deductibles and coverage limits. Housing insurance typically has three basic kinds of coverage. The first pays for damages to the house and other structures, such as a detached garage or shed. The second pays for damages to the personal property of the homeowner—that is, the items inside the house. The third pays for liability. It covers other people who may get injured at your home. As in the case of auto insurance, if you choose a higher deductible, your premiums will generally be lower. You should carefully analyze how much risk to bear yourself.

Health-care insurance can be a complicated issue because of the financing and payment methods for customers and the variety of plans available. Some people obtain their insurance through their employers, while others buy directly from insurance companies. Some people pay all of their premiums, while others have third parties pay (for example, the government or employer). Plans vary, including health maintenance organizations (HMOs), health savings accounts (HSAs), preferred provider organizations (PPOs), Medicare, and Medicaid. In the United States, the Patient Protection and Affordable Care Act, enacted by Congress in 2010, added further complexity by mandating broader coverage and implementing a system of taxes, penalties, and subsidies. In other countries, there is complete government control of the health-care systems. The complexities surrounding health-care insurance and international comparisons of systems are beyond the scope of this book, but we want to make a few principles clear.

The payments made for health-care insurance come in four forms. First, premiums (or taxes) are paid to obtain the coverage offered by the plan. Second, a deductible may apply. Third, there is the copay, which is a fee for a particular service, such as a doctor office visit or prescription. Copays typically range from $10 to $100. Fourth, coinsurance is the percent of the medical bill the customer must pay. For example, a plan may require the customer to pay 20 percent of the bill for a hospital stay or medical procedure.

Competition in health-care insurance is generally more restricted than for other forms of insurance, which means consumers will have fewer options available. Also, unlike most other insurance, consumers typically can make changes to their plan only once a year. This makes it more difficult to put together a plan that meets your needs. You may be forced into some coverage for a period of time that you don't want or cannot use. Even with these restrictions, you will have some choices to make about how much risk to assume yourself and how much you can share with others.

There are circumstances in which having insurance protection actually increases the likelihood of a harmful event. This is known as **moral hazard**. Consider the following two scenarios: Rachel trades in her twelve-year-old car and buys the most recent model, which has all the latest technological advances and safety devices. Since Rachel feels safer in the new car, she might actually drive a little less carefully knowing that her chance of becoming injured in a collision is lower because of the safety devices. Jacob's mother insists he wears a helmet, knee and elbow pads, and long pants when he rides his skateboard. Emboldened with a sense of security and protection, Jacob might attempt more dangerous jumps and maneuvers on his skateboard knowing that an injury is less likely. Under both scenarios, the risk increases because of the change in behavior from feeling safer.

Other types of insurance to consider, but not covered here, include life, disability, and long-term care. After evaluating your personal choices that determine the level of risk in your life, carefully analyze the risks you cannot avoid but can reduce through the effective use of insurance. It makes sense to insure against risks with large potential adverse effects, but when the potential financial damages are small, it is generally best to either absorb their cost in your monthly budget or cover them with money from your emergency fund. The most important objective of an insurance strategy is to prevent devastating financial losses.

Concluding Thoughts

Besides being economists and educators, all of the authors are also parents. In addition to leaving a legacy of knowledge to our students and other readers of this book, we wish to positively influence our children's lives. We encourage you to do the same.

Parents want their children to be successful, not just financially, but in all aspects of life. Financial security tends to elevate general well-being by making necessities attainable and eliminating worry about fulfilling basic needs. Those who develop the habits of working diligently, setting goals and achieving them, and avoiding the temptations of instant gratification by considering the future consequences of current choices are typically more successful in all walks of life than those who don't. There are many ways to instill these attributes in your children. Getting them started on an earnings and savings program at an early age is one of them.

One of the most important ways to teach young people responsibility is by helping them understand that money is earned; it is not manna from heaven. Instead of just giving your children an allowance, pay them for performing certain tasks around the house and for achieving educational goals. Couple these payments with some discussion explaining that the money you earn is a measure of how well you help others. Money is not just a means of getting more of what you want; it is also a measure of your contribution to helping others get more of what *they* want. The best way to earn more money is by serving others and finding ways to make them better off. This entrepreneurial lesson will pay important dividends during your children's careers, no matter what those careers turn out to be.

Of course, you will buy your children many things without requiring that they earn the money for them. But even when you are paying for your children's purchases, it is possible to provide them with an understanding of the costs and trade-offs that are inherent in all expenditures. Throughout their lives, all of our children will have to decide how they are going to spend limited incomes. If they spend more on one item, they will have to spend less on others. We all have to make trade-offs. Beginning at an early age, we need to teach our children about this reality and provide them with experiences that will help them learn to choose wisely.

To a large degree success in life is about setting goals, working hard to achieve them, figuring out how to make your services useful to others, saving for a specific purpose, and spending money wisely. These are the key ingredients for success. Economics provides the recipe for how to live a more fulfilling life.

We are now at the end of a journey. Throughout this book, our goal has been to provide you with information and tools that will help you live a more successful life. It is our hope that today you will start on a new journey—that you will earnestly resolve to take control of your life and choose options more consistent with success.

Acknowledgments

The authors would like to express their appreciation to several key people who contributed to this project. We are very pleased to welcome Jane Shaw Stroup to the author team. She was helpful with earlier editions of the book and played a more prominent role in this edition. Numerous comments from fellow teachers, college instructors, and economic educators are incorporated into the text. John Kessler, Kelly Markson, and Michelle Vachris were particularly helpful for the insights they gave us on how to improve this edition. Special thanks are extended to John Morton, Scott Niederjohn, Mark Schug, William Wood, Joe Connors, and Pam Cooper for their contributions to the development of new supplementary materials. And we want to express our appreciation to Kevin Reilly, Meryl Levavi, Gabriel Guma, Olya Kirilyuk, Diane Dilluvio, Lizz Blaise, Kiffin Steurer, and copy editor Kate Davis, and proofreaders Marinda Valenti and Sue McGrath of St. Martin's Press for their helpful comments and handling of the editorial responsibilities.

Through the years, the authors have had approximately fifty thousand students in our classes. Numerous discussions with students, both in and outside of class, have provided us with meaningful insights and presented us with challenging questions. Both have provided the foundation for this project. We cherish these interactions, and with this book we express our gratitude to these students, who have enriched our lives and continue to do so.

Digital Assets, Supplemental Units, and Website

For anyone who would like more readings and resources, a host of items are available at CommonSenseEconomics.com.

For instructors officially adopting the *Common Sense Economics* textbook for their courses, an electronic package of assets is available. It includes a flexible course shell, learning objectives tied to national standards, PowerPoint slides, readings, audios, videos, discussion questions, and assessment items. The package is structured around the four parts of the book and is broken down into fifteen core modules, one for each week of a normal semester. Everything is ready to transfer to various course management systems, including Moodle. Visit commonsenseeconomics.com/adopt/ to begin the formal adoption process.

For instructors who would like more coverage and additional details on key topics, the *Common Sense Economics* team has developed a series of supplementary modules. The readings for these modules are available at commonsenseeconomics.com/supplementals/. An electronic package is also available for these supplements, which are listed on the next page.

Module A: Demand, Supply, and Adjustments to Dynamic Change

Module B: Macroeconomic Indicators

Module C: Fiscal and Monetary Policy

Module D: The Great Depression and the Great Recession

Module E: Economics, Work, and Happiness

Module F: Economics, Markets, and Morality

Module G: The Economics of Poverty

Module H: Economics of the Environment

Module I: Smart Choices for Earning More Income

Module J: Smart Choices for Managing Credit

Module K: Smart Choices for Saving and Investing

Module L: Smart Choices for Insurance

Suggested Additional Readings

Acemoglu, Daron, and James A. Robinson. *Why Nations Fail: The Origins of Power, Prosperity, and Poverty.* New York: Crown, 2012.

Bogle, John C. *The Little Book of Common Sense Investing: The Only Way to Guarantee Your Fair Share of Stock Market Returns.* Little Books, Big Profits. Hoboken, NJ: Wiley, 2017.

Brooks, Arthur. *Gross National Happiness: Why Happiness Matters for America—and How We Can Get More of It.* New York: Basic Books, 2008.

Council for Economic Education. *Learning, Earning, and Investing.* New York: 2004.

———. *Virtual Economics Version 5.0.* New York: 2018.

De Soto, Hernando. *The Mystery of Capital.* New York: Basic Books, 2000.

Folsom, Burton. *New Deal or Raw Deal?* New York: Simon & Schuster, 2008.

Friedman, Milton. *Capitalism and Freedom.* Chicago: University of Chicago Press, 2002.

Friedman, Milton, and Rose Friedman. *Free to Choose.* New York: Harcourt Brace Jovanovich, 1980.

Gwartney, James D., Robert Lawson, and Joshua Hall. *Economic Freedom of the World: 2022 Annual Report.* Vancouver: Fraser Institute, 2022.

Gwartney, James D., Richard L. Stroup, Russell S. Sobel, and David A. MacPherson. *Economics: Private and Public Choice.* 17th ed. Mason, OH: South-Western Cengage, 2022.

Hazlitt, Henry. *Economics in One Lesson.* New Rochelle, NY: Arlington House, 1979.

Henderson, David R., ed. *Concise Encyclopedia of Economics*. Indianapolis: Liberty Fund. Available online at http://www.econlib.org/library/CEE.html.

Hogan, Chris. *Everyday Millionaires: How Ordinary People Built Extraordinary Wealth—and How You Can Too*. Mahwah, NJ: Ramsey Press, 2019.

Lee, Dwight R., and Richard B. McKenzie. *Getting Rich in America*. New York: Harper Business, 1999.

Norberg, Johan. *Open: The Story of Human Progress*. Boston: Atlantic Books, 2020.

North, Douglass C. *Institutions, Institutional Change, and Economic Performance*. Cambridge: Cambridge University Press, 1990.

Rosenberg, Nathan, and L. E. Birdzell. *How the West Grew Rich*. New York: Basic Books, 1986.

Schug, Mark C., and William C. Wood. *Economic Episodes in American History*. Morristown, NJ: Wohl Publishing, 2011.

Smith, Adam. *An Inquiry into the Nature and Causes of the Wealth of Nations*. 1776. Library of Economics and Liberty. Available online at http://www.econlib.org/library/Smith/smWN.html.

———. *The Theory of Moral Sentiments*. 1759. Library of Economics and Liberty. Available online at http://www.econlib.org/library/Smith/smMS.html.

Sowell, Thomas. *Basic Economics: A Common Sense Guide to the Economy*. 5th ed. New York: Basic Books, 2014.

Tupy, Marian L., and Gale L. Pooley. *Superabundance: The Story of Population Growth, Innovation, and Human Flourishing on an Infinitely Bountiful Planet*. Washington, DC: Cato Institute, 2022.

Von Hayek, Friedrich. Nobel Prize Lecture: *The Pretence of Knowledge*. 1974. Available online at http://www.nobelprize.org/nobel_prizes/economic-sciences/laureates/1974/hayek-lecture.html.

Glossary

balanced budget: The state of government finances when current government revenue from taxes, fees, and other sources is just equal to current government expenditures.

bond: A promise to repay the principal (amount borrowed) plus interest at a specified time in the future. Organizations such as corporations and governments issue bonds as a method of borrowing from bondholders.

budget (household): Estimated income and itemized planned expenditures for a time period.

budget deficit: The amount by which total government spending exceeds total government revenue during a specific time period, usually one year.

budget surplus: The amount by which total government spending falls below total government revenue during a time period, usually one year.

capital formation: The production of buildings, machinery, tools, and other equipment that will enhance future productivity. The term can also be applied to efforts to upgrade the knowledge and skill of workers (human capital) and thereby increase their ability to produce in the future.

capital investment: Expenditures on the buildings, machinery, tools, and other equipment that will enhance future productivity.

capitalism: An economic system in which productive resources are owned privately and goods and resources are allocated through market prices.

capital market: The broad term for the various marketplaces where investments, such as stocks and bonds, are bought and sold.

certification: Confirms the education, training, and other qualifications of an individual. Unlike licensing, certification does not prohibit noncertified individuals from competing in the market.

competition: A dynamic process of rivalry among parties, such as producers or input suppliers, each of whom seeks to deliver a better deal to buyers when quality, price, and product information are all considered. Competition implies open entry into the market. Potential suppliers do not have to obtain permission from the government in order to enter the market.

compound interest: Interest that is earned not only on the principal but also on the interest previously earned.

consumer price index (CPI): An indicator of the general level of prices. This government-issued index attempts to compare the cost of purchasing a market basket of goods bought by a typical consumer during a specific period with the cost of purchasing the same market basket during an earlier period.

creative destruction: The replacement of old products and production methods by innovative new ones that consumers judge to be superior. The process generates economic growth and higher living standards.

crony capitalism: A situation in which the institutions of markets are maintained, but the allocation of resources, and the profit and loss of businesses, are substantially influenced by political decision-making rather than consumer purchases and market forces. To a large degree, the activities of business firms are directed and controlled by government subsidies, contracts, and regulations. In turn, many of the business firms will use contributions and other forms of political support to compete for government favors.

diversification: The strategy of investing in a number of diverse firms, industries, and instruments, such as stocks, bonds, and real estate, in order to minimize the risk accompanying investments.

economic efficiency: A situation that occurs when (1) all activities generating more benefit than cost are undertaken; and (2) no activities are undertaken for which the cost exceeds the benefit.

economic prosperity: Persistent increases in per capita income and improvements in the standard of living.

economies of scale: Reductions in the firm's per-unit costs that occur when large manufacturing plants are used to produce large volumes of output.

entrepreneur: A profit-seeking decision-maker who assumes the risk of trying innovative approaches and products and pursues projects in the expectation of realizing profits. A successful entrepreneur's actions will increase the value of resources.

equilibrium: A state in which the conflicting forces of supply and demand are in balance. When a market is in equilibrium, the decisions of consumers and producers are brought into harmony and quantity demanded will equal quantity supplied at the market-clearing price.

equities: Shares of stock in a company. They represent fractional ownership of the company.

equity mutual fund: An entity that pools the funds of investors and uses them to purchase a bundle of stocks. Mutual funds make it possible for even small investors to hold a diverse bundle of stocks.

exchange rate: The domestic price of one unit of a foreign currency. For example, if it takes $1.50 to purchase one English pound, the dollar-pound exchange rate is 1.50.

exchange traded funds (ETFs): An investment fund that holds financial assets, such as stocks, bonds, or foreign currency. They are traded through a broker, like a stock, at market prices during the trading day.

exports: Goods and services produced domestically but sold to foreign purchasers.

externalities: Spillover effects of an activity that influence the well-being of nonconsenting external parties. If the spillover effects are positive, they are also called external benefits. If the spillover effects adversely impact external parties, they are also called external costs.

extreme poverty rate: The percentage of the population with an income of less than $2.15 per day.

FICO score: A mathematically determined score measuring a borrower's likely ability to repay a loan, similar to a credit score. The FICO score takes into account a borrower's payment history, current level of indebtedness, types of credit used, length of credit history, and new credit. A person's FICO score will range between 300 and 850. A score of 700 or more indicates the borrower's credit standing is good and therefore the risk of providing them with credit would be low. FICO is an acronym for the Fair Isaac Corporation, the creators of the FICO score.

foreclosure rate: The percentage of home mortgages on which the lender has started the process of taking ownership of the property because the borrower has failed to make the monthly payments.

foreign exchange: The marketplaces in which the currencies of different countries are bought and sold.

government failure: A situation in which the structure of incentives is such that the political process, including democratic political decision-making, will encourage individuals to undertake actions that conflict with economic efficiency.

gross domestic product (GDP): The market value of all goods and services in their final (rather than intermediate) use that are produced within a country during a specific period. As such, it is a measure of income.

human capital: The abilities, skills, and health of human beings that contribute to the production of both current and future output. Investment in training and education can increase the supply of human capital.

import quota: A specific limit or maximum quantity or value of a good that is permitted to be imported into a country during a given period.

imports: Goods and services produced by foreigners but purchased by domestic buyers.

incentives: The expected payoffs from actions. They may be either positive (the action is rewarded) or negative (the action results in punishment).

incentive structure: The types of rewards offered to encourage a certain course of action, and the types of punishments to discourage alternative courses of action.

income transfers: Payments made by the government to individuals and businesses that do not reflect services provided by the recipients. They are funds taxed away from some and transferred to others.

indexed equity mutual fund: An equity mutual fund that holds a portfolio of stocks that matches their share (or weight) in a broad stock market index, such as the S&P 500. The overhead of these funds is usually quite low because their expenses on stock trading and research are low. The value of the mutual-fund shares will move up and down along with the index to which the fund is linked.

inflation: A continuing rise in the general level of prices of goods and services. During inflation, the purchasing power of the monetary unit, such as the dollar, declines.

institutions: The legal structure, rules, and procedures underlying action by the government. They include the number of legislative bodies (for example, single or bicameral); the selection process for legislative members and designation of their powers; the relationships among the legislative, executive, and judicial branches; and constitutional designation and constraints on the powers of governmental officials.

investment: The purchase, construction, and/or development of capital resources, including both nonhuman and human capital. Investments increase the supply of capital.

investment goods: Goods and/or facilities bought and/or constructed for the purpose of producing future economic benefits. Examples include rental houses, factories, ships, or roads. They are also often referred to as capital goods.

invisible hand: The tendency of market prices to direct individuals pursuing their own self-interests into activities that promote the economic well-being of the society.

"junk" bonds: High-risk bonds, usually issued by less-than-well-established firms, that pay high interest rates because of their risk.

law of comparative advantage: A principle that reveals how individuals, firms, regions, or nations can produce a larger output and achieve mutual gains from trade. Under this principle, each specializes in the production of goods that it can produce cheaply (that is, at a low opportunity cost) and exchanges these goods for others that are produced at a high opportunity cost.

law of demand: A principle that states that there is an inverse relationship between the price of an item and the quantity of it buyers are willing to purchase when other things are held constant. As the price of an item increases, consumers purchase less of it. As price decreases, they buy more.

law of supply: A principle that states that there is a positive relationship between the price of an item and the quantity of it producers are willing to supply when other things are held constant. As the price of an item increases, producers will supply more. As price decreases, they will supply less.

less-developed countries: Countries with low per capita incomes, low levels of education, widespread illiteracy, and widespread use of production methods that are largely obsolete in high-income countries. They are sometimes referred to as developing countries.

logrolling: The exchange between politicians of political support on one issue for political support on another.

loss: The amount by which sales revenue fails to cover the cost of supplying a good or service. Losses are a penalty imposed on those who use resources to produce less value than they could have otherwise produced.

managed equity mutual fund: An equity mutual fund that has a portfolio manager who decides what stocks will be held in the fund and when they will be bought or sold. A research staff generally provides support for the fund manager.

marginal: A term used to describe the effects of a change in the current situation. For example, the marginal cost is the cost of producing an additional unit of a product, given the producer's current facility and production rate.

marginal benefit: The change in total value or benefit derived from an action, such as consumption of an additional unit of a good or service. It reflects the maximum amount that the individual considering the action would be willing to pay for it.

marginal cost: The change in total cost resulting from an action, such as the production of an additional unit of output.

marginal tax rate: The percentage of an extra dollar of income that must be paid in taxes. It is the marginal tax rate that is relevant in personal decision-making.

market: An abstract concept that encompasses the trading arrangements of buyers and sellers that underlie the forces of supply and demand.

market failure: A situation in which the structure of incentives is such that markets will encourage individuals to undertake activities that are inconsistent with economic efficiency.

market forces: The information and incentives communicated through market prices; profits and losses that motivate buyers and sellers to coordinate their decisions.

middlemen: People who buy and sell goods or services or arrange trades. Middlemen reduce transaction costs.

minimum wage: Legislation requiring that workers be paid at least the stated minimum hourly rate of pay.

moderate poverty rate: The share of the population with an income of less than $3.65 per day.

monetary policy: The deliberate control of the national money supply and, in some cases, the credit conditions by the government. This policy establishes the environment for market exchange.

money: The asset that is commonly used to pay for things; the medium of exchange most commonly used by buyers and sellers.

money supply: The supply of currency, checking account funds, and traveler's checks in a country. These items are counted as money because they are used as the means of payment for purchases.

monopoly: A market characterized by (1) a single seller of a well-defined product for which there are no good substitutes; and (2) high barriers to the entry of any other firms into the market for that product.

moral hazard: A situation wherein providing protection against a risk increases the occurrence of the risky behavior because it reduces the potential adverse consequences of the action.

mortgage: An instrument used to borrow funds against an asset, such as a house.

The asset is used as security. If the borrowed funds are not repaid as promised, the lender can foreclose against the asset and use the sale proceeds to recover the unpaid balance of the loan.

mutual funds: An entity that pools the funds of investors and channels them into various categories of investments. There are a variety of mutual funds, including equity funds, bond funds, real estate funds, and money-market funds.

national debt: The sum of the indebtedness of a government in the form of outstanding interest-earning bonds. It reflects the cumulative impact of budget deficits and surpluses.

national income: The total income earned by the citizens of a country during a specific period.

nominal GDP growth: Growth in real GDP and inflation.

nominal return: The return on an asset in monetary terms. Unlike the real return, it makes no allowance for changes in the general level of prices (inflation).

occupational licensing: A requirement that a person obtain permission from the government in order to perform certain business activities or work in certain occupations.

open markets: Markets that suppliers can enter without obtaining permission from governmental authorities.

opportunity cost: The highest valued alternative good or activity that must be sacrificed as a result of choosing an option.

personal income: The total income received by domestic households and non-corporate businesses.

physical capital: Human-made resources (such as tools, equipment, and structures) used to produce other goods and services. They enhance our ability to produce in the future.

plunder: The act of acquiring things by taking them from others.

pork-barrel legislation: Government spending projects that benefit local areas but are paid for by taxpayers at large. The projects typically have costs that exceed benefits; the residents of the district getting the benefits want these projects because they don't have to pay much of the costs.

portfolio: The holdings of real and financial assets owned by an individual or financial institution.

price controls: Prices that are imposed by the government. The prices may be set either above or below the level that would be established by markets.

price floor: A government-established minimum price that buyers must pay for a good or resource.

principal: The amount of funds borrowed. The borrower will pay interest on this amount.

private investment: The flow of private-sector expenditures on durable assets (fixed investment), plus the addition to inventories (inventory investment) during a period. These expenditures enhance our ability to provide consumer benefits in the future.

private property rights: Property rights that are exclusively held by an owner, or group of owners, and can be transferred to others at the owner's discretion.

productive function: Government provision of (1) a legal and monetary environment for the smooth operation of markets; and (2) a few goods that are difficult to provide through markets.

productive resources: Resources such as capital equipment, structures, labor, land, and minerals that can be used to produce goods and services.

productivity: The average output produced per worker during a specific time period, usually measured as output per hour worked.

profit: Revenues that exceed the cost of production. The cost includes the opportunity cost of all resources involved in the production process, including those owned by the firm. Profit results only when the value of the good or service produced is greater than the cost of the resources required for its production.

protective function: A system of rules and laws that protect individuals and their property from damages associated with the use of force, fraud, or theft.

public choice: The study of decision-making as it affects the formation and operation of collective organizations such as governments. In general the principles and methodology of economics are applied to political-science topics.

public goods: Goods with the following two characteristics: (1) jointness in consumption—provision of the good to one party simultaneously makes it available to others; and (2) nonexcludability—it is difficult or virtually impossible to exclude nonpaying customers.

quartile: Data observations divided into four equal parts.

random-walk theory: The theory that current stock prices already reflect all known information about the future. Therefore the future movement of stock prices will be determined by surprise occurrences, which will cause prices to change in an unpredictable or random fashion.

rational ignorance effect: Voter ignorance resulting from the fact that people perceive their individual votes as unlikely to be decisive. Therefore they are rational in having little incentive to seek the information needed to cast an informed vote.

real GDP: Gross domestic product adjusted for changes in the price level.

recession: A downturn in economic activity characterized by declining real gross domestic product (GDP) and rising unemployment. As a rule of thumb, economists define a recession as two consecutive quarters in which there is a decline in real GDP.

rent-seeking: Actions by individuals and interest groups designed to restructure public policy in a manner that will either directly or indirectly redistribute more income to themselves.

resource: An input used to produce economic goods. Land, labor, skills, natural resources, and capital are examples. Human history is a record of our struggle to transform available, but limited, resources into things that we would like to have (economic goods).

rule of law: The effective understanding that everyone is subject to the same laws, preventing some from enacting laws that they will not have to abide by.

saving: The portion of after-tax income that is not spent on consumption.

scarcity: Condition in which people would like to have more of a good or resource than is freely available from nature. There is almost nothing we value that isn't also scarce.

secondary effects: Consequences of an economic change that are not immediately identifiable but are felt only with the passage of time.

shortsightedness effect: Misallocation of resources that results because public-sector action is biased (1) in favor of proposals yielding clearly defined current benefits in exchange for difficult-to-identify future costs; and (2) against proposals with clearly identified current costs but yielding less concrete and less obvious future benefits.

Smoot-Hawley trade bill: Legislation passed in June 1930 that increased tariff rates by approximately 50 percent. Other countries retaliated, and international trade fell sharply. The legislation was a major contributing factor to the Great Depression.

socialism: A system of economic organization in which (1) the ownership and control of the basic means of production rest with the state; and (2) resource allocation is determined by centralized planning rather than by market forces.

special-interest effect: The bias of the political process toward adoption of programs that provide substantial individual benefits to well-organized interest groups at the expense of small individual costs imposed on the bulk of voters. There is a tendency for such issues to be adopted even when they are inefficient.

special-interest issue: An issue that generates substantial individual benefits to a small organized minority while imposing a small individual cost on many other voters.

Standard & Poor's (S&P) 500 Index: A basket of five hundred stocks that are selected because they are thought to be collectively representative of the stock market as a whole. Over 70 percent of all U.S. stock value is contained in the S&P 500.

stock: Ownership shares of a corporation. Corporations raise funds by issuing stock ownership shares, which entitle the owners to a proportional share of the firm's profits. The stock owners are not liable for the debts of the corporation beyond their initial investment. However, there is no assurance that the owners will receive either their initial investment or any return in the future.

subsidy: A government payment or tax credit provided to either the producers or consumers of certain goods. The payments to producers of ethanol, which sum up to about $1.50 per gallon, provide an example.

substitutes: Products that serve similar purposes. An increase in the price of one will cause an increase in the demand for the other, and a decline in the price of one will cause a decline in the demand for the other (for example, hamburgers and tacos, butter and margarine, Chevrolets and Fords).

tariff: A tax levied on goods imported into a country.

TIPS (Treasury Inflation-Protected Securities): Inflation-indexed bonds issued by the U.S. Department of Treasury. These securities adjust both their principal and coupon interest payments upward with the rate of inflation so that their real return is not affected by the change in rate. TIPS have been issued in the United States since January 1997.

transaction costs: The time, effort, and other resources needed to search out, negotiate, and consummate an exchange of goods or services.

venture capitalist: A financial investor who specializes in making loans to entrepreneurs with promising business ideas. These ideas often have the potential for rapid growth but are usually also very risky and thus do not qualify for commercial bank loans.

Index

About the Authors

James D. Gwartney was a professor emeritus of the department of economics at Florida State University, where he taught for fifty-three years. He was the lead author of *Economics: Private and Public Choice* (Cengage Learning, 2020), a widely used economic principles text now in its seventeenth edition. Dr. Gwartney was also coauthor of the Fraser Institute's annual report Economic Freedom of the World, which provides information on the consistency of institutions and policies with economic freedom for one hundred sixty-five countries. His publications appeared in a variety of scholarly journals, including the *American Economic Review, Journal of Political Economy, Journal of Economic Education, Southern Economic Journal,* and *Journal of Institutional and Theoretical Economics.* From 1999–2000, he served as chief economist of the Joint Economic Committee of the U.S. Congress. He was a past president of the Southern Economic Association and the Association of Private Enterprise Education. Dr. Gwartney passed away in January 2024.

 Dwight R. Lee received his PhD from the University of California, San Diego, in 1972. He has served on the faculty at the University of Colorado, Virginia Tech University, George Mason University, and the University of Georgia, where he was the Ramsey professor of

Economics and Private Enterprise from 1985–2008. He was the William J. O'Neil Professor of Global Markets and Freedom at Southern Methodist University in Dallas from 2008–2014. He is currently an affiliated visiting faculty fellow in the Institute for the Study of Political Economy in the Miller College of Business at Ball State University. Professor Lee's research has covered a variety of areas, including the economics of the environment and natural resources; the economics of political decision-making; public finance; law and economics; and labor economics. Lee has published over one hundred seventy articles in academic journals and nearly three hundred articles in magazines and newspapers; he has coauthored fourteen books and been the contributing editor of five others. Lee has lectured at universities and conferences throughout the United States, as well as in Europe, Central America, South America, Asia, and Africa. He was president of the Association of Private Enterprise Education from 1994–1995 and president of the Southern Economic Association from 1997–1998.

Tawni Hunt Ferrarini is a content consultant for the Gus A. Stavros Center for the Advancement of Free Enterprise and Economic Education at Florida State University. She is the former R. W. Plaster Professor of Economic Education at Lindenwood University and was recognized as the university's Scholar-Teacher of the Year for 2023–2024. Dr. Ferrarini is known nationally and internationally for her economic education work and her dynamic presentations. She specializes in informing diverse audiences about economic fundamentals, integrating economic reasoning into various disciplines, and using technology to increase audience engagement. Her reputation as an accomplished researcher, textbook author, presenter, and workshop leader contributed to her selection as the 2015 president of the National Association of Economic Educators and her receipt of the National Association of Economic Educators' Technology Award and International Award. She serves on the advisory board of the Council on Economic Education–Japan and regularly consults with nonprofits, including Junior Achievement USA, Economic Fundamentals Initiative–Eastern Europe and Central

Asia, and the Korea Development Institute. Dr. Ferrarini publishes in journals of economic education, technology, and education. Her doctorate in economics is from Washington University in St. Louis, where she studied under the 1993 Nobel laureate Douglass C. North.

Joseph P. Calhoun is a teaching professor in the department of economics at Florida State University and director of the university's Gus A. Stavros Center for the Advancement of Free Enterprise and Economic Education. He currently teaches principles of economics and personal finance classes. He created and leads Unconquered by Debt, an innovative financial wellness program sponsored by the Stavros Center. At no charge, undergraduate students can take workshops or use online resources to develop financial literacy. Dr. Calhoun regularly gives presentations at national teaching conferences on the effective use of media and technology in the classroom. A strong supporter of study-abroad programs, he has taught in Florida State's international programs in England, Italy, and Spain. Dr. Calhoun has received numerous teaching awards at Florida State, including the university's Undergraduate Teaching Award. His doctoral degree is from the University of Georgia.

Jane Shaw Stroup (who also writes as Jane S. Shaw) is a writer and freelance editor. She is chairperson of the Raleigh-based James G. Martin Center for Academic Renewal, where she was previously president. Before that, Ms. Stroup was a senior fellow with the Property and Environment Research Center (PERC) in Bozeman, Montana. Among other books, she coauthored with Michael Sanera *Facts, Not Fear: Teaching Children About the Environment* (Regnery Publishing, 1996). Earlier, she was an associate economics editor of *Business Week*. She received her bachelor's degree in English literature from Wellesley College and, in 2020, a master's degree in history from North Carolina State University. She is a past president of the Association of Private Enterprise Education, an editorial adviser to *Econ Journal Watch* and CL Press, a member of the Editorial Advisory Panel of *Regulation*, and a member of the Editorial Advisory Council of the Institute of Economic Affairs (London). She is the widow of Richard L. Stroup, a previous coauthor of this book.